Alabama Real Estate License Exam Prep

All-in-One Review and Testing to Pass Alabama's Pearson Vue Real Estate Exam

Fourth Edition

Stephen Mettling
David Cusic
Ryan Mettling
Jane Somers

Performance Programs Company
6810 190th Street East
Bradenton, FL, 34211
www.performanceprogramscompany.com

Material in this book is not intended to represent legal advice and should not be so construed. Readers should consult legal counsel for advice regarding points of law.

ISBN 978-1965482339

Contents

Introduction

Welcome licensee candidates and future real estate professionals!

We know you have worked hard just to get here – you've completed or nearly completed your pre-license curricula, and now all you have to do is pass the state license exam. But easier said than done – and that's where we come in. We know the exam can be tough, and very nerve-wracking to prepare for. That's why we created Alabama Real Estate License Exam Prep (AL-RELEP) the way we did. Since we have been managing real estate schools and developing curriculum for forty years, we know how all this works – or fails to work. Let us assure you – you made the right decision buying this publication to prepare for your Alabama exam. Here's why.

First, AL-RELEP is comprehensive in that it contains both key content review and testing practice. And the text review is Alabama-specific – not just simplistic national content, but terse, relevant and accurate state laws and regulations presented as a well-organized set of state 'key point reviews' ideal for pre-test memorization. But let's not dismiss the importance of the national content either. AL-RELEP's national key point reviews are a succinct compression of tested national principles and practices that comprise the national portion of state license exams from coast to coast. Our content is drawn from our own national textbook, Principles of Real Estate Practice – one of the most widely used principles textbooks in the country. Finally, our national content, as well as our question selection, is further tailored to the state testing outline promulgated by Pearson Vue for Alabama. Thus the breadth and depth of the law reviews and test questions reflect the topic emphasis of your Alabama license exam.

A word about the test questions… AL-RELEP's testing practice section consists of ten national practice tests, five state practice tests, and one state exam sample test. The test questions are designed to cover the content covered by the law reviews – which reinforces your learning of the total body of information tested by your state exam. The questions are direct, to the point, and designed to test your understanding. When you have completed a given test, you can check your answers against the answer key in the appendix. You may also note that each question's answer is accompanied by a brief explanation, or "rationale" to further reinforce your understanding.

Your particular study and testing practice strategy using AL-RELEP is up to you. But to fully exploit its comprehensive content coverage, you should try to review and memorize the key point reviews as much as possible. Then you should make every effort to take each exam, review your mistakes, and re-read the key point reviews that cover your weaker areas.

In the end, as you know, it's all up to you. Unlike other publications, we are not going to tell you that using this book will guarantee that you pass your state exam. It still takes hard work and study to pass. But we have done our best here to get you ready. Following that, the most we can do is wish you the best of success in taking and passing your state exam. So good luck!!

About the authors

For nearly fifty years, Stephen Mettling has been actively engaged in real estate education. Beginning with Dearborn in 1972, then called Real Estate Education Company, Mr. Mettling managed the company's textbook division and author acquisitions. Subsequently he built up the company's real estate school division which eventually became the country's largest real estate, insurance and securities school network in the country. In 1978, Mr. Mettling founded Performance Programs Company, a custom training program publishing and development company specializing in commercial, industrial, and corporate real estate. Over time, Performance Programs Company narrowed its focus to real estate textbook and exam prep publishing. Currently the Company's texts and prelicense resources are used in hundreds of schools in over 48 states. Mr. Mettling has authored over 100 textbooks, real estate programs and exam prep manuals.

David Cusic, Ph.D., has been a training consultant, author, and Performance Programs Company partner for over forty years. As an educator with international real estate training experience, Dr. Cusic has been engaged in vocation-oriented education since 1966. Specializing in real estate training since 1983, he has developed numerous real estate training programs for corporate and institutional clients nationwide. Dr. Cusic is co-author of the Company's flagship title, Principles of Real Estate Practice by Mettling and Cusic, now complemented by over 18 state supplements and 20 exam prep texts.

Ryan Mettling, partner and currently publisher of Performance Programs, is an accomplished online curriculum designer, author and course developer. His other principal publication is Real Estate Math Express. Mr. Mettling graduated Valedictorian from the University of Central Florida's College of Business Administration.

Jane Somers has been a writer and educator for more than 30 years. She has directed the academic programs for a multi-campus college and has in recent years become an accomplished developer of online and classroom real estate curricula for a national real estate licensing organization, specializing in state licensing laws. Ms. Somers is also active in condominium association management and has served as president of a condominium owners association for ten years.

All of us at Performance Programs Company want to thank Bo Evans for his help reviewing the Alabama-specific portions of Alabama Real Estate License Exam Prep.

Section I: National Principles & Law
Key Point Review

Rights

Land / Real Estate / Real Property

Land:	surface, all ***natural things*** attached to it, subsurface, and air above the surface.
Real estate:	land + **manmade** permanent attachments
Real property:	real estate + bundle of rights

Constitution guarantees private ownership of real property.

Physical Characteristics of Real Estate

Immobility

- land cannot be moved from one site to another; its location is forever fixed

Indestructibility

- land is permanent and cannot be destroyed since by definition it extends below ground and into the sky
- since land is permanent, it does not depreciate
- only improvements depreciate and are insurable

Non-homogeneity

- land is non-homogeneous; no two parcels of land are exactly the same since they have a different location

Land versus Real Estate

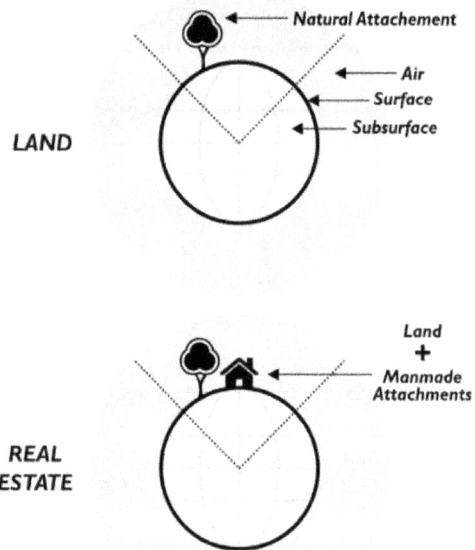

Real Estate as Property

    The bundle of rights

        "PUTEE":

        P ossession

        U se

        T ransfer

        E xclusion

        E ncumberable

Legal Title v. Equitable title

Legal title

- full legal ownership of property and the bundle of rights as they apply to it
- contrasts with equitable title

Equitable title

- an interest that gives a lienholder or buyer the right to acquire legal title to a property if certain contractual conditions occur

Property characteristics:

- **property is** either real or personal
- property is either tangible or intangible

Real Property Rights

Airspace = air rights

Surface (of the earth) = surface rights

Subsurface = subsurface or mineral rights

Water rights:

- **Doctrine of Prior Appropriation**

  - state controls water usage
  - state grants usage permits

- **riparian rights (rivers and streams)**

  - applies to rivers and streams
  - if waterway is navigable: owners own land to water's edge
  - if waterway is not navigable: owners own land to midpoint of waterway

- **littoral rights (lakes and seas)**

  - applies to **seas and lakes**
  - abutting property owners own to **high water mark**
  - state owns underlying land

  Memory Tip: R : River Riparian   L: Lake Littoral

Real Property vs. Personal Property

Real property

- land
- fixtures
- attachments

Personal property

- chattels
- trade fixtures
- emblements

Differentiation criteria: item is real or personal property depending on why, how item is attached to the real estate. Depends on the owners'

- intention; adaptation; functionality; relationship of parties; contract provisions

Trade fixtures

- personal property items temporarily attached to real estate in order to conduct business

Emblements

- plants or crops that are considered personal property despite being attached to land

Conversion

- real to personal property referred to as severance
- personal to real property referred to as affixing

Factory-built housing – mobile homes and manufactured homes

- units are real or personal property: real if permanently affixed to ground; otherwise personal

Regulation Of Real Property Interests

Federal regulation
- grants rights of ownership
- controls broad land usage standards
- regulates anti-discrimination laws
    - examples: land grants; federal flood zones; fair housing laws; FHA; EPA

State regulation
- governs real estate business
- sets regional usage standards
    - examples: license laws; water rights; development regulation

Local regulation
- levies real estate taxes
- controls specific usage
    - examples: property assessing; zoning; building permits; tax levies

Judicial regulation
- applies case law and common law to disputes
- **contrasts with statutory law**

Interests & Estates

Interests and Estates in Land

Interests

Possession / Possessory

- estate in land

Non-possession / Non-possessory:

- private: encumbrance
- public: public interest

Estates In Land

- include right of possession
- leasehold = limited duration
- freehold: duration is not limited

Freehold (own)

- fee simple
  - absolute
  - defeasible
- life estates
  - conventional
  - legal

Leasehold (lease)

- estate for years
- periodic
- estate at will
- estate at sufferance

Freeholds

Fee simple

- *not limited* by one's lifetime
- absolute: *highest* form of ownership interest
- defeasible: *reverts* to previous owner per conditions

Life estate

- passes *to another* on death of named party
- remainder: *named party* to receive estate
- reversion: *previous owner* to receive estate

Conventional life estate

- *limited* to lifetime of life tenant/ named party
- **ordinary**: estate passes to remainderman or previous owner when life tenant dies
- **pur autre vie**: limited to lifetime of another, passes to remainderman or previous owner

Legal life estate	• created by operation of state law as opposed to a property owner's agreement
	• designed to protect family survivors
	• **Homestead:** rights to one's *principal residence*
	- laws protect homestead from creditors
	- family must occupy the homestead
	- cannot be conveyed by one spouse
	- endures over life of head of household
	- interests extinguished if property destroyed

Leaseholds

Estate for years	• specific, *stated duration*, per lease; expires at end of term; if tenant fails to vacate at lease expiration, tenancy becomes a **holdover tenancy** which is a periodic tenancy
Periodic	• lease term *renews automatically* upon acceptance of rent; renews indefinitely if landlord accepts rent
Estate at will	• for *indefinite period* subject to rent payment; cancelable with notice
Estate at sufferance	• tenancy *against landlord's will* and without an agreement

Ownership

Forms of Ownership

Tenancy in severalty	• *sole* ownership of a freehold estate; passes to heirs
Tenancy in common	• co-tenants individually own undivided interests
	• *any ownership share possible*
	• no survivorship
	• can convey to outside parties
Joint tenancy	• equal undivided interest jointly owned
	• survivorship (may require express provision)
	• requires *four unities* to create: time, title, interest, possession
Tenancy by the entireties	• *husband and wife* own equal undivided interest
	• Now applies to same-sex couples in some states
Community property	• *joint property ownership* by spouses as opposed to separate property

Joint Tenancy & Four Unities

Unity of ownership	• owners hold single title jointly
Equal ownership	• owners always hold equal shares
Transfer	• may transfer to new owner as a tenancy in common interest with remaining joint tenants
Survivorship	• on death, interests and rights pass to other joint tenants
Creation	• requires "four unities," *PITT*: 1. *P*ossession: acquire same possessory rights 2. *I*nterest: acquire equal, undivided interests 3. *T*ime: acquire interests at same time 4. *T*itle: acquire interests with same deed

Community Property

Separate	**Community**
• acquired *before marriage*	• all other property earned or acquired during the marriage
• acquired by *gift or inheritance*	
• acquired with *separate-property funds*	
• *income* derived from *separate property*	

Estates in Trust

- *trustor* gives title, deed, trust agreement to trustee
- *trustee* renders fiduciary duties to trustor and beneficiary
- *beneficiary* receives ownership benefits
- **living / testamentary trust** – conveyance of real, personal property during one's lifetime
- **land trust** – grantor and beneficiary are same party; beneficiary uses, controls property but does not appear on public records

Condominiums

- ownership of a *unit of airspace* plus an *undivided interest* in the *common elements* as tenant in common with other owners
- may be sold, encumbered or foreclosed *without affecting other unit owners*
- creation: by developer's declaration
- individually taxed
- managed by condo association
- owners share common area expenses

Cooperatives

- ownership of
  - *shares in owning corporation*
  - *proprietary lease* in a unit
- corporation has sole, undivided ownership
- owners potentially liable for expenses of entire co-op; creditors may foreclose on entire property

Time Shares

- lease or ownership interest in property for periodic use on a scheduled basis
- **lease**: tenant leases property per the lease's schedule
- **freehold**: tenants in common own undivided interests, pay expenses per separate agreement

Encumbrances & Liens

Encumbrances

- non-possessory interests limiting legal owner's rights
- do not include possession
- two types:
  - encumbrances that affect use
  - encumbrances that affect ownership, value, transfer

Encumbrances affecting use: easements, encroachments, licenses, deed restrictions

Encumbrances affecting ownership, value, transfer: liens, deed conditions

Easements

Characteristics	• rights to use portions of another's property • affirmative easement: allows a use • negative easement: prohibits a use
Appurtenant	• *attaches* to the estate • *dominant* tenement's *right to use* or restrict adjacent *servient* tenement • *by necessity*, to *landlocked* owners • party wall easement in a shared structure: to not damage or destroy
In gross	• *does not attach* to the estate • **personal**-- not transferrable, ends upon death of easement holder • **commercial**-- transferrable, granted to a business

14

By prescription	• property used without permission; can come to exist regardless of owner's consent
	• obtainable through ***continuous, open, adverse use*** over a period of time which varies by state
License	• ***personal*** right to use a property
	• does not attach
	• non-transferrable
	• revocable
	• ceases upon death of owner

Encroachments

- unauthorized intrusions of one owner's real property onto another's
- may require survey to detect
- may become prescriptive easements if not remedied over prescription period

Deed restrictions

- conditions, covenants imposed on property by deed or subdivision plat
- goes with the property upon transfer
- established to control quality, standards of a subdivision
- apply to land use, type of structure, setbacks, minimum house size, etc.

Deed conditions

- created upon property transfer
- if violated, ownership may revert to previous owner

Deed covenants

- created by mutual agreement
- enforceable by injunction

Liens

- claims attaching to real and personal property as security for debt
- recorded on title effectively reducing equity in the amount of the lien
- does not convey ownership unless a mortgage in a title theory state
- lien attaches to the property
- property can be encumbered by multiple liens
- lien terminates upon payment, recording satisfaction

Lien types and characteristics

Voluntary / involuntary	• mortgage lien / tax lien
General / specific	• against any & all assets / against car or house
Superior / junior	• paid before juniors / paid after superiors by date of recording

Lien Priority

- order in which liens against a property are satisfied
- determined by superior v junior class and by date of recordation
- the highest priority lien is paid by foreclosure proceeds before any other lien

Superior Liens by rank (not by date of recordation; paid before junior liens)

- real estate tax liens
- special assessment liens
- federal estate tax liens
- state inheritance tax liens

Junior Liens (by date of recording)

- federal income tax liens
- judgment liens
- mortgage liens
- vendors' liens
- mechanics' liens (by date work performed)
- broker's liens (to pay commission owed)

Foreclosure

- Liquidation or transfer of collateral property by judicial, non-judicial, or strict foreclosure

Mortgage lien foreclosure
- liquidation of collateral property by *judicial, non-judicial,* or *strict* foreclosure

Judicial foreclosure
- lawsuit by creditor followed by court-ordered public sale to enforce lien; may entail *deficiency judgments*, *redemption rights*
- **deficiency judgment** -- judgment by court on borrower to forfeit other property to pay off any shortfalls from foreclosure
- **redemption right** -- borrower's right to reclaim property before or after foreclosure sale

Non-judicial foreclosure
- *"power of sale"* granted to lender; no suit; *no deficiency*

Strict foreclosure
- court orders *legal transfer of title directly to lender* without public sale

Deed in lieu of foreclosure
- *"power of sale"* granted to lender; no suit; *no deficiency* judgment; *no redemption* period after sale

Short sale
- side skirts foreclosure; lender agrees to loan concessions in the conveyance so that seller can afford to sell, since s/he owes more than property is worth
- lender must approve selling terms and may take actions to recover deficiency from borrower

Lien vs. Title Theory State

- **lien theory state** -- lender of mortgaged property holds equitable title rather than legal title; **borrower holds legal title.**

- **title theory state** – **lender holds legal title** to the mortgaged property until the mortgagor satisfies the terms and obligations of the loan.

Legal vs. Equitable Title

- **Legal title:** owner enjoys full bundle of rights
- **Equitable title:** party can obtain legal title subject to agreements with creditors

Notice

Notice:	• how ownership is evidenced to the public
Actual notice:	• *knowledge acquired directly* through demonstrable evidence, e.g., presenting or inspecting a deed, visiting a party in possession
Constructive notice:	• *knowledge one could have obtained*, as presumed by law; imparted by recording in public records "for all to see"

Voluntary / Involuntary Title Transfer

Voluntary transfer	**Involuntary transfer**
• deed	• descent (without will, with heirs)
• will	• escheat (without will nor heirs)
• public grant	• foreclosure (loan default)
	• eminent domain (public good)
	• adverse possession (hostile, open use)

Deeds of Conveyance

Key characteristics:

- grantor grants deed to grantee
- legal title transfers upon intentional delivery and grantee's acceptance

Deed Validity

Requirements:

1. grantor
2. grantee
3. in writing
4. legal description
5. granting clause
6. consideration
7. grantor's signature
8. acknowledgement
9. delivery and acceptance

Deed Clauses

Premises	• granting
Habendum	• type of estate
Reddendum	• restrictions
Tenendum	• other property included

Deed Types

Bargain and sale	"I own but won't defend"
General warranty	"I own and will defend"
Special warranty	"I own and warrant myself only"
Quitclaim	"I may or may not own, and won't defend"
Special purpose deeds	used for different purposes, interests conveyed, or by different parties

Transfer Tax

- **Documentary stamp tax:** tax on conveyance of real property based on price of property conveyed
- Facilitates ad valorem assessment
- Payment evidenced on deed

Wills

Key characteristics

- will transfers estate to heirs upon death
- maker = owner; devisor or testator
- heir = beneficiary or devisee

Types of wills

- witnessed: in writing and two witnesses
- holographic: will in testator's handwriting
- nuncupative: oral will written by witnesses; generally not valid for property transfer

Validity of will

- legal age; mentally competent; entitled "last will & testament;" signed, witnessed, voluntary

Testate / Intestate

Order of Title Transfer

Dies testate with heirs:	• first to creditors
	• then to homestead
	• then **to heirs by will**

18

Dies intestate with heirs:	• first to creditors
	• then to homestead
	• then *to heirs by laws of descent*
Dies intestate, no heirs:	• first to creditors
	• then **to state by escheat**

Involuntary Title Transfer

Adverse possession

- "unwanted owner" may claim ownership to a property
- must show "claim of right" as reason
- must be notorious possession (unconcealed)
- must be hostile (possessor claims ownership)
- must be continuous for a statutory period of time

Title Records

Features

- Instruments affecting title must be recorded
- Gives public notice of ownership, condition of title
- Determines property marketability
- Protects lienholders; establishes chronology for lien priority

Key terms
- chain of title – successive property owners from original grant to present
- cloud on title – unrecorded claims
- suit to quiet title – lawsuit to settle claims
- abstract of title: written chronology of recorded owners, transfers, encumbrances

Forms of Title Evidence

- title insurance (best form of evidence)
- attorney's opinion of abstract (also called "opinion of title")
- title certificates
- Torrens registration
- Marketable title – must be delivered by seller; title must be free of claims, encumbrances; best assured by title insurance policy

Leases

Key characteristics

- lease is both an instrument of conveyance and contract of covenants between tenant and landlord
- lease conveys **temporary, exclusive** use of premises in exchange for rent and right of reversion

Tenant rights and obligations

- rights: use, possession, quiet enjoyment, profits
- tenant obligations: pay rent; maintain premises; follow rules

Landlord rights and obligations

- rights: receive rent; repossess upon expiration; monitor tenant compliance
- obligations: property condition, habitability, support services

Estate Types

Gross lease	• landlord pays expenses; tenant pays higher rent than net
Net lease	• tenant pays some or all expenses; rent is less than gross
Percentage lease	• landlord receives rent minimum plus percentage of retailer's sales
Residential lease	• gross lease hybrid; short term; uniform terms reflect landlord-tenant standards
Ground lease	• landlord owns and leases ground but does not own improvements
Proprietary lease	• for cooperative unit owners; indefinite term; assigned to new unit owner on sale
Leasing of rights	• leasehold transfer of rights for limited use; examples: air, mineral, water rights

Lease Termination

Causes	- default	- term expiration
	- notice	- voluntary agreement
	- property destruction	- condemnation
	- death	- abandonment under certain conditions

Uniform Residential Landlord and Tenant Act

Purposes	• balance landlord and tenant rights • standardize leases • have uniform eviction procedures • protect tenants • serve as model for state legislation
Leases	• clear lease terms • fair market rent • cannot waive rights
Deposits	• limits on amounts • tenant's right to interest • rules and deadlines for returning
Landlord Obligations	• bargain in good faith • provide maintenance and repairs • comply with building codes • provide safety and access • procedure for delivery of notices
Tenant Obligations	• maintain condition • abide by rules and regulations • no damage or abuse • abide by approved uses • no disturbance of other tenants

Land Use

Planning and Zoning Definitions

Building code:	A standard of construction of an improved property established by local government officials
Certificate of occupancy:	A document confirming that a newly constructed or renovated property has fully complied with all building codes and is ready for occupancy
Concurrency:	A planning policy that requires developers to correct foreseen negative impacts of a development during the construction period of the project itself rather than afterward
Condemnation:	1. A decree that a parcel of private property is to be taken for public use under the power of eminent domain. 2. A government order that a property is no longer fit for use and must be demolished.
Deed restriction:	A provision in a deed that limits or places rules on how the deeded property may be used or improved
Eminent domain:	A power of a government entity to force the sale of private property for subsequent public use
Land use control:	Regulation of how individual owners use property in a municipality or planning district. Control patterns are in accordance with a master plan

21

Master plan:	An amalgamated land use plan for a municipality, county, or region which incorporates community opinion, the results of intensive research, and the various land use guidelines and regulations of the state. Acts as a blueprint for subsequent zoning ordinances and rulings
Non-conforming use :	A legal or illegal land use that is not consistent with the current zoning ordinance
Police power:	A government's legal authority to create, regulate, tax, and condemn real property in the interest of the public's health, safety, and welfare
Restriction:	A limitation on the use of a property imposed by deed, zoning, state statute, or public regulation
Special exception:	A land use in conflict with current zoning that is authorized because of its perceived benefit to the public welfare
Variance:	A land use that conflicts with current zoning but is authorized for certain reasons, including undue hardship to comply and minimal negative impact to leave it alone
Zoning ordinance:	A municipal land use regulation

Land Use Planning

Goals of land use control

- preserve property values; promote highest and best use; safeguard public health, safety and welfare; control growth; incorporate community consensus
- process: develop plan; create administration; authorize controls

The master plan

- long term growth and usage strategies; often required by state law
- local plans fuse municipal goals and needs with state and regional laws

Planning objectives

- control growth rates: how much growth will occur and at what rate
- control growth patterns: type of growth desired, where it should be located
- accommodate demand for services and infrastructure

Plan development

- research trends and conditions; blend local and state objectives into master plan

Planning management

- commission makes rules, approves permits, codes, and development plans

Public Land Use Controls

Zoning

- "police power" granted by state-level enabling acts; zoning ordinance: creates zones, usage restrictions, regulations, requirements
- enables urban land managers to create separate land uses that do not conflict with one another nor create incompatible adjacencies

Types of zone

- residential, commercial, industrial, agricultural, public, PUD
- residential zoning regulates *density*, or number of dwellings in an area
- commercial zoning regulates *intensity*, or how much commercial activity is permitted in relation to size of the site

Zoning administration

- Zoning Board of Adjustment oversees rule administration and appeals

Zoning Appeals

- **Nonconforming use:** legal if use existed prior to zone creation, illegal otherwise
- **Variance:** use exception granted based on hardship
- **Special exception:** based on public interest
- **Amendment:** change of zones; rezoning

Eminent Domain

- allows a government entity to purchase a fee or easement interest in privately owned real property for the **public good** and for **public use** in exchange for "just compensation"

Planned Unit Development (PUD)

- PUD zoning designed to regulate use of whole tracts of land with a singular design
- Design purposes are to achieve optimum space efficiency and open space

Subdivision Regulation

- plat of subdivision and relevant requirements must be met and approved; must meet FHA requirements for insured financing
- location, grading, alignment, surfacing, street width, highways
- sewers and water mains
- lot and block dimensions
- building and setback lines
- public use dedications
- utility easements
- ground percolation

Building Codes

- comprehensive onsite and offsite construction and materials standards; must be met to receive certificate of occupancy

Environmental Restrictions

- flood control; solid waste disposal; air quality; water quality; marine protection; noise control; toxic substances controls; lead paint; CERCLA; Superfund

---

Private Land Use Controls

Deed Restriction

- also "covenants; conditions and restrictions", or "CC & Rs"
- limits in deed on how property can be used; cannot be discriminatory or anti-fair trade
- Eg: minimum area of residence; limits on commercial activity

Declaration restriction

- attaches to property; cannot extinguish by agreement or quit claim deed
- similar to deed restriction; purpose is to optimize, preserve value
- can enforce by injunction

Deed condition

- similar to deed restriction
- violation gives grantor right to re-possess property and sue for legal title

HOA regulation

- HOA determines rules and regs for the development via CCRs and by-laws
- Egs: fees, pet rules, rent payments; maintenance standards; occupancy limits; parking; noise; insurance requirements
- disputes settled by civil courts

Zoning Appeals

Zoning Board of Adjustment:	oversees rule administration and appeals
Nonconforming use:	legal if use existed prior to zone creation, illegal otherwise
Variance:	use exception granted based on hardship
Special exception:	based on public interest
Amendment:	change of zones; rezoning

Environmental Laws

Legislation	Date	Regulated
Solid Waste Disposal Act (later part of RCRA)	1965 (1976, 1999, 2002)	landfills
Air Quality Act, Clean Air Act	1967 (1970)	air quality standards
National Environmental Policy Act (NEPA)	1969 (1970)	created EPA
Flood Control Act	amended 1969	building in flood zones; flood insurance
Resource Recovery Act	1970	solid waste disposal
Water Quality Improvement Act	1970	dumping in navigable waters; wetlands
Water Pollution Control Act amendment	1972	dumping in navigable waters; wetlands
Clean Water Act	1972 (1977)	dumping in navigable waters; wetlands
Lead-based paint ban (US Consumer Product Safety Commission rule)	1978	lead-based paint in residences
PCB ban (EPA rule)	1979	polychlorinated biphenyls
RCRA amendment	1984	underground storage tanks

Comprehensive Environmental Response, Compensation and Liability Act (CERCLA)	1980	hazardous waste disposal
Superfund Amendment and Reauthorization Act	1986	hazardous waste cleanup costs
Asbestos ban (EPA rule)	1989	asbestos in building materials
Residential Lead-based Paint Hazard Reduction Act (EPA and HUD rule)	1992 (1996)	lead-based paint disclosure and treatment
Flood Insurance Reform Act	1994	flood insurance in flood zones
Brownfields legislation	2002	industrial site cleanup

Legal Descriptions

Purpose

- to accurately locate and identify the boundaries of a parcel of real property to a degree acceptable by courts of law in the state where the property is located
- general criterion is that it alone provides sufficient data for a surveyor to locate the parcel

Metes and Bounds Method

- describes perimeter by landmarks, monuments, distances, angles
- usable within rectangular survey system
- starting at point of beginning (POB), follow perimeter, **return to POB**

Lot and Block System (Recorded Plat Method)

- used to describe properties in residential, commercial, industrial subdivisions
- tracts of land divided into lots, then grouped into blocks

Rectangular Survey System

Key points:
- simplify and standardize property descriptions
- all land in system surveyed using longitude and latitude lines
- lines created uniform grids of squares called townships

Meridians:
- north-south lines six miles apart

Parallels:
- east-west lines six miles apart

Range:
- north-south strip between meridians

Tier:	• east-west strip of area between parallels; also called township strip
Township:	• the six-mile by six-mile square at the intersection of a range and a tier
Section of a township:	• a 1 mile x 1 mile square; 1 section = 640 acres; 36 sections per township
Fractions of a section:	• going from the smallest to largest unit, indicate size and location within successively larger quarters or halves of the section: E 1/2 of the NE 1/4 of the NE 1/4 of Section 8

Contract Law

Contract Defined

- An agreement between two or more parties who have a "meeting of the minds," and have pledged to perform (or refrain from performing) some act
- A *valid* contract is *legally enforceable* by meeting certain requirements of contract law.
- If a contract does not meet requirements, it is not valid and the parties to it cannot resort to a court of law to enforce its provisions

Contract Status

Valid

- meets all requirements

Valid but unenforceable

- certain oral contracts; if performed, cannot change outcome

Void

- not valid; unenforceable

Voidable

- may be rescinded due to subsequent discoveries: if performed, cannot change outcome

Contract Validity

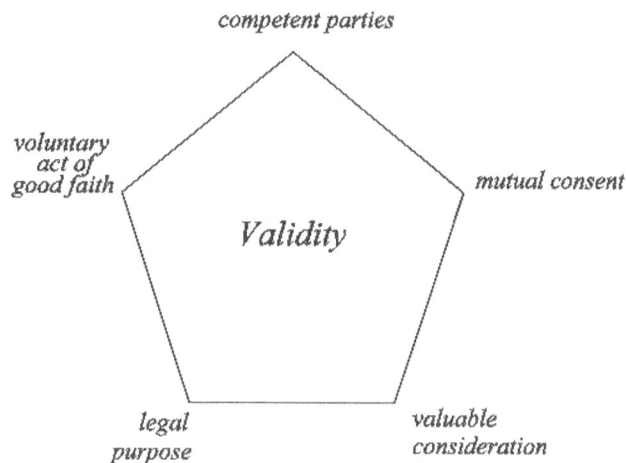

```
                    competent parties
                           ╱╲
                         ╱    ╲
   voluntary           ╱        ╲
   act of            ╱            ╲    mutual consent
   good faith      │    Validity    │
                   │                │
                    ╲              ╱
                     ╲            ╱
              legal    ╲        ╱    valuable
              purpose              consideration
```

Competent parties

- legal age
- mental competency
- legitimate authority

Mutual consent

- clear and unequivocal **offer and acceptance** with an underlying **meeting of the minds**

Valuable consideration

- exchange of valuable consideration for performance by the other party; not "love and affe

Legal purpose

- promise, intent and content must be lawful; if illegal, contract is void – cannot contract to the law

Voluntary, good faith

- no duress, coercion, fraud or misrepresentation

Conveyance Contract Requirements

- must be in writing
- must contain legal description
- must be signed by one or more parties
- **exception: per Statute of Frauds,** leases for one year or less may be verbal and still be enforceable

Offer / Counteroffer / Acceptance

Offer

- intention to enter into contract
- must contain all intended terms
- must be in writing
- expires in "reasonable time" or date and time specified

Acceptance

- unequivocal and manifest agreement to offer
- no changes to offer whatsoever
- signed, preferably dated

Completed contract

- communication of acceptance to offeror
- if by mail, offer is communicated upon mailing

Counteroffer

- new or amended terms of a received offer
- original offer is void

Revoking an offer

- may be done at any time prior to offeree's communication of acceptance

Termination of an offer

- acceptance; rejection; revocation; expiration; counteroffer; death or insanity of either party

---

Contract Assignment

- assignable unless expressly prohibited or contract is a personal service contract (listings)

Contract Preparation

- restricted unless licensed as attorney or a party to the contract
- licensees must be aware of contract preparation restrictions in the states where they operate

---

Contract Classifications

Oral vs. written

- oral, or parol, contract may not be enforceable

Express vs. implied

- express: all terms expressly agreed to
- implied: unintentional agreement deemed to exist due to terms implied by actions

Bilateral vs. unilateral

- bilateral: both parties promise to perform
- unilateral: one party performs only if other party performs

Executed vs. executory

- executed: fully performed
- executory: performance yet to be completed

Termination

Causes

- performance
- infeasibility
- mutual agreement
- cooling-period rescission
- revocation
- abandonment
- lapse of time
- invalidity of contract
- breach of contract

Breach & Remedies

Rescission	• cancel contract; return deposits
Forfeiture	• defaulting party gives up something according to contract terms
Liquidated damages	• damages due a damaged party as stated in contract
Suit for damages	• civil suit for money damages not covered by contract
Specific performance	• suit to force party to fulfill contract promises

Agency

The Agency Relationship In Real Estate

- principal (client) hires agent (broker) to find ready, willing, and able customer (buyer, seller, tenant, landlord)
- client – agent relationship governed by fiduciary duties of trust, confidence, good faith

Universal / General / Special

Universal	• represent in all matters • can contract for principal
General	• represent in business matters • agent can contract for principal
Special	• represent in single business transaction • normally agent cannot contract for principal • characterizes the brokerage relationship

Agency Creation

- Express written **or oral** agreement (listing)

  - established for a specified transaction
  - contains an express expiration

- **Implied** agreement by actions of either party

  - can be intentional or unintentional
  - can obligate the agent to fiduciary duties and professional standards of care
  - not allowed to exist in some states

Termination

- **Voluntary**

  - fulfillment
  - expiration
  - mutual agreement

- **Involuntary**

  - incapacity
  - abandonment or destruction of property
  - renunciation
  - breach
  - bankruptcy
  - revocation of license

Duties & Obligations

Agent's Fiduciary Duties to Client

- **Skill, care and diligence:**   proactive; competent; act within bounds of expertise

- **Loyalty:**   place client interest above customer and self

- **Obedience:**   provided actions, instructions are legal

- **Confidentiality:**   extends beyond listing term indefinitely

- **Full disclosure;**   property condition; customers; material facts

- **Accounting;**   proper handling of monies and documents

Obligations Owed Customers

- honesty and fair dealing
- reasonable care and skill
- proper disclosure

Breach of duty: potential consequences

- loss of listing; compensation; license suspension, suit for damages

Misrepresentation and Fraud

Puffing – licensee boasting about property's benefits

Fraud

- misstatement or failure to disclose material fact
- knowledge that statement was false or fact should have been disclosed
- party relied on misstatement
- party was damaged by misstatement

Misrepresentation – misstatement or concealment of fact

- intentional misrepresentation: **purposeful misstatement** of material fact
- intentional omission: **purposeful concealment** of material fact
- negligent misrepresentation: **unintended misstatement** that agent should have known
- negligent omission: **unintended concealment** that agent should have known

Single / Dual / Sub / No Agency

Single agency	• seller or buyer agency • tenant or landlord representation
Subagency	• outside brokers and agents who help listing agent • listing broker's own agents • (disallowed in some states)
Dual agency	• representing both sides • potentially illegal or conflict of interest • must disclose & obtain written consent

- **Types of dual agency**
    - voluntary by consent
    - involuntary by actions of parties (implied agency)
    - duties: all but full disclosure and loyalty

- **Dual agency duties**
    - disclose to both parties; obtain written consent
    - owes duties of skill, care, diligence, obedience, confidentiality accounting
    - does not owe duties of full disclosure and loyalty; exclusive representation of client's interest

Designated agency	• broker selects one subordinate to represent buyer and another to represent the seller in a given transaction under provisions of a designated agency agreement • cannot disclose confidential information except to broker • designated agents are not dual agents; brokers are considered disclosed consensual dual agents for that transaction

No agency	• "facilitator" or "transaction broker"
	• representing neither party in the transaction
	• duties to both parties: accounting; skill, care and diligence; honesty and fair dealing; disclosures affecting property value

---

Disclosure Rules

(Note: Agency disclosure rules vary by state – see State section for laws in your state.)

Objectives of disclosure

- declare
- explain
- offer choice
- obtain documented consent

Seller agent disclosures to client

- in writing
- on or before listing is executed

Seller agent disclosures to customer

- in writing
- upon first face-to-face contact, or upon substantive communication, depending on state law
- oral disclosure permitted but must have written follow-up

Buyer agent disclosures to seller

- in writing
- upon first contact with listing agent or seller
- substantive contact is assumed

Dual agent disclosures

- "informed, written consent"
- may not disclose price or financing positions or motivations unless authorized

Facilitator disclosures

- on becoming transaction broker or on substantive contact, whichever is first

---

Listing Agreements

Key characteristics	• broker's **enforceable contract** of employment
	• establishes **special agency** relationship
	• defines **roles** of parties
	• creates **fiduciary duties** for the agent
	• describes agent's **scope of authority**
	• establishes compensation to be paid to the licensee
Parties	• listing broker-- fiduciary of buyer client or seller client
	• subagent-- fiduciary of listing broker's client
	• customer-- non-fiduciary principal in transaction

Fiduciary duties	• to client: loyalty; obedience; disclosure; skill; care; diligence; accounting; confidentiality • to customer: honesty, care and disclosure
Authority	• limited agency agreement • broker may not contract for client unless specifically authorized • clients liable only for broker's acts within scope of authority
Contract law	• unilateral contract • oral listing is valid and enforceable • exclusive listing in some states must be written to be enforceable • personal service contract-- not assignable

---

Types

Exclusive right-to-sell

- given to one broker
- usually must be written
- must expire
- broker gets commission if property transfers during period

Exclusive agency

- exclusive excepting owner
- oral or written
- must expire
- broker gets commission unless owner sells

Open listing

- non-exclusive
- oral or written
- no stated expiration
- procuring cause gets commission
- no commission if client procures customer

Net listing

- all sale proceeds above a seller's minimum price go to the broker
- discouraged, if not illegal

Multiple listing

- listing placed in MLS
- owners consent to rules and provisions of MLS

Limited services agreement

- licensee and agreement must disclose that licensee is acting as a limited service representative
- licensee provides services expressly listed in agreement as well as conventional brokerage services that will not be rendered
- agreement must be in writing
- may need to comply with minimum services requirements imposed by state regs

Buyer agency agreements

- create a fiduciary relationship with the buyer
- if exclusive, buyer agrees to only work with the buyer representative in procuring a property
- must have an expiration date along with other requirements of a valid listing

---

Compensation / Termination

Compensation	<ul><li>negotiated between agent and principal</li><li>put in writing in contract between parties</li><li>where disputed among agents, agent with procuring cause is owed commission</li><li>based on results: find ready willing and able customer</li></ul>
Causes for termination	<ul><li>performance</li><li>infeasibility</li><li>mutual agreement</li><li>revocation</li><li>abandonment</li><li>breach</li><li>expiration</li><li>invalidity</li><li>incapacitation or death</li><li>involuntary transfer</li><li>destruction of property</li></ul>
Agent's performance	<ul><li>may perform only authorized tasks</li><li>must verify owner and property data</li><li>may delegate duties to salespeople and other brokers</li></ul>
Revoking a listing	<ul><li>clients always have power to revoke during period</li><li>may incur liability for commission or damages</li></ul>

Brokerage

Who May Broker

(Varies from state to state)

Yes

1. sole proprietorship
2. for-profit corporation
3. general or limited partnership
4. joint venture

No

1. non-profit corporation
2. business trust
3. cooperative association

Broker-Agent Relationship

Legal relationship

- salesperson
  - is agent & fiduciary of broker
  - acts in broker's name
  - is subagent of client

- salesperson may not
  - have two employers
  - be paid by other parties
  - bind clients contractually

Salesperson's employment status

- employee or independent contractor
- defined by agreement

Obligations and responsibilities

- agent to broker:
  - obtain & sell listings
  - follow policies and employment provisions
  - promote ethics and broker's reputation
- broker to agent:
  - provide data, office support, compensation, training
  - uphold ethics, policies, and employment agreement

Agent compensation

- commissions per schedule after any previously negotiated splits with cooperating brokers

Commingling & Conversion

Not allowed !!

Commingling
- mixing broker's personal or business funds with trust funds
- includes failure to deposit funds in a timely manner

Conversion
- using trust funds for personal or business purposes

Advertising Requirements

- no misleading ads
- ads must contain broker's ID
- broker is responsible for content
- no blind ads (concealed identity)
- must disclose if agent owns property

Telephone Consumer Protection Act

- regulates unsolicited telemarketing calls
- solicitors must identify themselves, how they can be contacted
- must comply with any do-not-call request
- consumers can place phone numbers on Do-Not-Call list

CAN-SPAM Act

- bans sending unwanted email 'commercial messages' to wireless devices
- requires express prior authorization
- requires an 'opt out' choice to terminate the sender's messages

---

Anti-Trust Laws

Sherman, Clayton anti-trust laws	• NO restraint of trade; monopolies; • predatory pricing; exclusive dealing
no collusion:	• two or more businesses conspiring to disadvantage a competitor
no price fixing:	• two or more brokers agreeing to fix prices
no market allocation:	• colluding to restrict competition in a market segment in exchange for a competitor's reciprocal agreement
no group boycotting	• cannot "gang up" on a competitor in a given market in any way that limits the competitor's business

---

Sale Contracts

Key characteristics

- binding, bilateral contract for purchase and sale
- the enforceable "blueprint" for closing
- contract is executory, or to be fulfilled
- expires upon closing
- must be in writing
- for validity, must
  - contain valuable consideration
  - identify property
  - be signed by all

Creation / Deposit / Contingencies

Creation	• created by unqualified acceptance of an offer • gives buyer equitable title, and power to force specific performance
Deposit, or earnest money escrow	• secures contract validity and buyer's equitable interest

	• varies in amount
	• deposit controlled by disinterested party who must act according to escrow instructions
Contingencies	• conditions that must be met for the contract to be enforceable
	• must be clear
	• have expiration date
	• require diligence to satisfy
Buyer default	• seller can cancel, claim liquidated damages or sue for specific performance (i.e., buyer's deposit)
Seller default	• buyer can cancel or sue for damages or specific performance

Primary Clauses

- parties
- consideration
- legal description
- price and terms
- loan approval provisions
- earnest money
- escrow
- closing and possession dates
- conveyed interest

- type of deed
- title evidence
- property condition warranty/disclosures
- closing costs
- damage and destruction
- default
- broker's agency disclosure and who pays commission
- seller's representations: property condition, marketable title

Options

Essentials	• optionor gives option to optionee to buy at a given time and price; optionee must pay for option right
	• unilateral contract: seller must perform, buyer need not
	• if option is exercised, option becomes bilateral sale contract
	• options are assignable
Contract requirements	• non-refundable consideration for the option right
	• price and terms of the sale
	• option period expiration date
	• legal description
	• must be in writing
	• must meet contract validity requirements
	• option should be recorded
Common clause provisions	• how to exercise option
	• terms of option money forfeiture
	• how option money will be applied to purchase price

Contract for Deed

Essentials	• purchase price is paid over time in installments • seller retains title, buyer takes possession, equitable title • at end of period, buyer pays balance, gets legal title
Interests and rights	• seller may encumber or assign interest • seller remains liable for underlying mortgage • buyer may use, possess, or profit • buyer must make periodic payments, maintain the property, and purchase at the end of the term
Default and recourse	• buyer may sue for cancellation and damages or specific performance • seller may sue for specific performance or damages, or may need to foreclose

Economics

Supply

• the quantity of a product or service available for sale, lease, or trade at any given time

Demand

• the quantity of a product or service that is desired for purchase, lease, or trade at any given time

Supply / Demand / Price

Real Estate Supply	• property available for sale or lease; measured in dwelling units, square feet, acres
Real Estate Demand	• property buyers and tenants wishing to acquire; measured in households, square feet, acres
Interaction	• if supply increases relative to demand, price decreases • if demand increases relative to supply, price increases

Supply-Demand Cycle

unmet demand →
    construction adds supply →
        market equilibrium →
            construction adds more supply →
                oversupply →
                    construction stops →
                        market equilibrium →
                            demand absorbs supply →
                                unmet demand →
                                    cycle repeats

Real Estate Supply-Demand Cycle

Factors Influencing Supply and Demand
- cost, availability of financing
- availability of developable land
- construction costs
- capacity of infrastructure
- governmental regulation and police powers
- changes in the economic base
- in- and out-migrations of major employers
- labor availability
- land availability

Government Influences on the Real Estate Market
- local zoning power
- local control and permitting of new development
- local taxing power
- federal influence on interest rates
- environmental legislation and regulations

Market Indicators

- **vacancy rates**
  - increases indicate buyer / tenant market & falling prices / rents
  - decreases indicate seller / landlord market & rising prices / rents

- building **permits** – increases indicate declining vacancy; increasing prices & construction
- prices
  - increases indicate rising demand or declining supply or both
  - decreases indicate falling demand or rising supply or both

Appraisal

Concepts and Principles of Value

Supply and demand	• When demand exceeds supply, scarcity exists, values rise. • When supply exceeds demand, surplus exists, values decline. • When supply and demand are equal, the market is in balance, values stabilize.
Utility	• A property's use in the marketplace contributes to the demand for it.
Transferability	• How readily or easily title or rights to real estate can be transferred affects the property's value.
Anticipation	• The benefits a buyer expects to derive from a property over a holding period influence what the buyer is willing to pay for it.
Substitution	• A buyer will pay no more for a property than the buyer would have to pay for an equally desirable and available substitute property.
Contribution	• The contribution to value of an improvement is equal to the change in market value that the addition of the improvement causes.
Change	• Market conditions affect the benefits that can arise from the property.
Highest and best use	• A property achieves its maximum value when it is put to whichever use generates the greatest income and return. The highest and best use must be legally permissible, physically possible, financially feasible, and maximally productive.
Conformity	• A property's maximal value is attained when its form and use are consonant with surrounding properties and uses

Progression and regression	• The value of a property is influenced by the values of neighboring properties.
Assemblage	• Conjoining adjacent properties can create a combined value in excess of the values of the unassembled properties. This excess value is called **plottage value.**
Subdivision	• The division of a single property into smaller properties can result in a higher total value.

Types of Value

Market value	• an estimate of the price at which a property will sell at a particular time; this type of value is the one generally sought in appraisals and used in brokers' estimates of value
Insured value	• the face amount a casualty or hazard insurance policy will pay in case a property is rendered unusable
Reproduction value	• the value based on the cost of constructing a precise duplicate of the subject property's improvements, assuming current construction costs
Replacement value	• the value based on the cost of constructing a functional equivalent of the subject property's improvements, assuming current construction costs
Salvage value	• the nominal value of a property that has reached the end of its economic life; also an estimate of the price at which a structure will sell if it is dismantled and moved
Assessed value	• the value of a property as estimated by a taxing authority as the basis for ad valorem taxation
Depreciated value	• a value established by subtracting accumulated depreciation from the purchase price of a property
Book value	• the value of the property as carried on the accounts of the owner; the value is generally equal to the acquisition price plus capital improvements minus accumulated depreciation
Investment value	• the value of an income property as indicated by the capitalized value of the cash flow the property generates

Market Value Requirements

The price willing buyer and seller would agree on given:

- a cash transaction
- reasonable market exposure
- parties have market and property use information
- there is no pressure to complete the transaction
- transaction is arm's length: parties are not related
- marketable title
- no hidden influences

Measuring Living Area

Essential standards:

- Generated by American National Standards Institute and Fannie Mae
- Gross living area (GLA) = area of all rooms "above grade" measured from the exterior walls including stairwells, excluding "open areas."
- Above grade = above the surface of the ground.
- Living area below-grade must be counted as basement area
- Minimum ceiling height 7 feet.
- Two-story properties (or more) with sloped ceilings, at least 50% of the ceiling area must have a height of 7 feet or more.
- Finished space: To be counted in GLA footage, space must be finished, i.e., have a floor covering and a ceiling.
- can count entry areas but not seasonal porches
- living area must be under heat and attached
- must be attached to the main house itself; cannot count unattached outbuildings
- Attics and basements: Cannot count partially finished heated areas.
- Cannot count garage areas; may meet a local standard if fully heated, finished and improved for other household uses.
- Stairs and closets generally fully countable in GLA.

Sales Comparison Approach

1. Identify comparable sales
2. Compare comps to the subject and make adjustments to the comparables
3. Weight values indicated by adjusted comparables for the final value estimate of the subject

Adjusting Comparables

Rules for selecting comparables
- must be physically similar
- in subject's vicinity
- recently sold in arm's length sale

Rules for adjusting comparables
- never adjust the subject!
- deduct from comparable if better than subject
- add to comp if worse than subject
- Remember: ("Subtract if Superior !")

Weighting adjustments
- best indicator has fewest and smallest adjustments and smallest net adjustment from the sale price

Cost Approach

Types of cost appraised

- reproduction – cost of making a precise replica
- replacement – cost of making a functional equivalent

Steps in the approach

1. Estimate land value
2. Estimate replacement cost of improvements
3. Estimate total depreciation
4. Subtract: (cost of improvements - depreciation) = depreciated improvements cost
5. Add land back in: (land value + depreciated improvements) = value estimate of property

Key Aspects of Depreciation

Depreciation	• **loss of value** from deterioration, functional obsolescence, or economic obsolescence
Deterioration	• **wear and tear** from use and aging
Functional Obsolescence	• **outmoded** physical or design **features**: curable or incurable
Economic Obsolescence	• loss of value due to adverse **changes in surroundings**: incurable
Curability	• curable: cost to cure is less than resulting contribution to value • incurable: cost to cure exceeds contribution to value

Income Approach

- Based on the principle of anticipation: the expected future income stream of a property underlies what an investor will pay for the property
- Also based on the principle of substitution: that an investor will pay no more for a subject property with a certain income stream than the investor would have to pay for another property with a similar income stream.

Steps in the Income Approach

1. Estimate potential gross income
2. Estimate effective gross income (total potential income - vacancy)
3. Estimate net operating income (NOI) (effective income - expenses)
4. Select and apply capitalization rate (NOI ÷ cap rate)

Gross rent multipliers (GRMs)

- Simplified income-based methods to estimate value
- Method consists of applying a multiplier to the estimated gross rent of the subject
- Multiplier is derived from market data on sale prices and gross rent
- Does not necessarily produce accurate value estimates

GRM Formula

- GRM = price divided by monthly rent
- Value = GRM times monthly rent

Preparing a Comparative Market Analysis

Steps

1. Identify comparables sold, for sale properties, and expired listings
2. Compile comparison data for each comparable: price, sale date, location, age, lot size, site aspects, living area, bedrooms, etc.
3. Complete adjustments for differences; rules:
   a. Never adjust the subject
   b. Add value to the comparable if a feature is inferior to the subject
   c. Subtract value from the comp if a feature is superior to the subject
4. Derive total adjustments for each comparable
5. Reconcile all value-adjusted comps to the subject to identify a value estimate

Regulation of Appraisal Practice

FIRREA

- Financial Institutions Reform, Recovery and Enforcement Act (**FIRREA**) enacted in 1989 to regulate appraisal practices
- requires that competent individuals whose professional conduct is properly supervised perform all appraisals used in federally-related transactions
- As of January 1, 1993, federally-related appraisals must be performed only by state-certified appraisers
- **USPAP** - Uniform Standards of Professional Appraisal Practice – competency standards established by the **Appraiser Qualifications Board** of the Appraisal Foundation

USPAP

- Uniform Standards of Professional Appraisal Practice
- requires recognized appraisal methods
- must exercise a defined level of due diligence
- must properly report results
- must make proper disclosures and assumptions

Finance

Mortgage Transaction

Elements
- promissory note: promise to repay loan
- mortgage: pledge of property as collateral for loan

Mechanics
- borrower gives lender promissory note and mortgage
- lender gives borrower funds and records a lien

Hypothecation
- use of real property as collateral for a mortgage loan

Financial components
- original principal: capital amount borrowed on which interest payments are calculated
- loan balance: remaining unpaid principal at any point in the life of the loan
- interest: charge for the use of money; rate fixed or variable
- Annual Percentage Rate (APR) includes interest and all other finance charges; lender must disclose on residential properties
- point: one percent of the loan amount
- loan origination fee: charged by lender at origination to obtain required return
- term: period of time for repayment of interest and principal
- payment: the periodic payment of interest and/or principal
- down payment: borrower's cash payment applied to the purchase price
- loan-to-value ratio: the loan's share of the total value of the property
- equity: at closing, the borrower's cash invested in the property; thereafter, the difference between the market value and the loan balance

Trust Deed Transaction

Elements
- promissory note: trustor's promise to repay loan
- deed of trust: title to property as collateral for loan

Mechanics
- trust deed conveys title from the borrower/trustor to a third-party trustee
- trustee holds title on behalf of the lender/beneficiary until the debt is repaid

Promissory note
- legal instrument executed by borrower stating debt amount, loan term, method and timing of repayment, interest rate, promise to pay; may repeat other provisions from mortgage document or deed of trust; negotiable instrument assignable to a third party

Mortgage Clauses

Payment of principal and interest: prepayment and late charges
- borrower must make timely payments according to the terms of the note
- late payments or early payoffs may trigger penalties

Funds for taxes and insurance
- borrower must make monthly payments to cover taxes and hazard insurance
- borrower may also have to pay flood insurance and mortgage insurance premiums
- **escrow account:** reserve account for periodic payments of taxes and insurance.
- Real Estate Settlement Procedures Act (RESPA) limits funds the lender can require for this purpose.

PITI
- borrower's monthly payment for principal and interest is called the p&i payment (principal and interest)
- the amount which includes the escrow payment is called PITI (principal, interest, taxes, insurance).

Charges and liens
- borrower is liable for paying any charges, liens, or other expenses that may have priority over the mortgage or trust instrument.

Hazard or property insurance
- borrower must keep property insured as the lender requires.

Occupancy, preservation, maintenance and protection of the property
- borrower must take and maintain occupancy as the borrower's principal residence according to requirements
- borrower must not abuse or neglect the including use for illegal purposes, creating hazardous waste on the property, or destroying the improvements

Protection of lender's rights in the property
- lender may take actions to protect its rights in the property if the borrower jeopardizes the property's value. The costs of these actions would be charged to the borrower

Mortgage insurance
- Lender may require private mortgage insurance, or PMI which protects the lender against loss from borrower default
- applies to loans that are not backed by the Federal Housing Administration (FHA) or Veterans Administration (VA) and that have a down payment of less than 20% of the property value

Inspection
- lender may inspect the property with reasonable cause to fear damage to the collateral

Condemnation
- if the property is condemned or taken by eminent domain, lender reserves a claim on any resulting proceeds

Transfer of the property or a beneficial interest in borrower
- if borrower sells the property without the lender's approval, the lender may demand immediate repayment of the loan balance. this alienation clause, aka a due-on-sale clause, allows lender to prevent unapproved loan assumptions
- the requirement to repay the loan before the scheduled due date is called **acceleration**.

Borrower's right to reinstate
- if lender holds borrower in default, borrower has the right to reinstatement by performing certain actions, usually paying overdue payments plus expenses the lender
- clause is called a redemption clause
- gives the borrower time to satisfy obligations and prevent a forced sale

Release
- agreement to release the lien obligation when borrower has paid off the loan
- release clause, aka **defeasance** clause, may require lender to execute a **satisfaction of mortgage,** aka **release of mortgage**
- if deed of trust, lender directs trustee to execute a **release deed** or **deed of reconveyance** to the borrower as trustor.
- release deed or satisfaction should be recorded as necessary

Escalation clause
- allows lender to increase the loan's interest rate

Loan Qualification

Equal Credit Opportunity Act
- lender must evaluate applicant according to applicant's own income and credit information
- lender cannot deny credit based on
  - discounted income from part-time work
  - future plans to have family
  - locational factors
  - protected classes

Income qualification
- income ratio and debt ratio qualify borrower's income; income ratio applied to gross income determines housing expense maximum; debt ratio takes revolving debt into account
- income ratios: 25-28% conventional; 31% FHA-insured
- debt ratios: 36% conventional; 43% FHA and 41% VA

Cash qualification
- lender verifies applicant's sources of cash for down payment; extra cash enhances income qualification evaluation

Net worth
- extent to which applicant's assets exceed liabilities as a further source of reserves

Credit evaluation
- lender obtains credit reports to evaluate applicant's payment behavior

Loan commitment
- written pledge by lender to grant loan under specific terms; firm, lock-in, conditional, take-out

Loan-to-value ratio (LTV)
- relationship of loan amount to property value
- expressed as a percentage
- 80% LTV = loan is 80% of property value

Private mortgage insurance (PMI)
- must insure portions of purchase price to adjust LTVs that are too risky for conventional lenders, e.g., decreasing a 90% LTV to 80% with PMI insurance
- may be removable via increasing property value and decreasing loan balance

Laws Affecting Mortgage Lending

Truth-in-Lending and Regulation Z
- **Reg Z** implements **Truth-in-Lending Simplification and Reform Act** and **Consumer Credit Protection Act**
  - Lender must **disclose finance charges** and APR prior to closing;
  - Borrower has limited right of rescission, but excludes primary residence
  - Lender must follow **advertising requirements** for full disclosure of costs, loan mechanics

Equal Credit Opportunity Act (ECOA)
- prohibits discrimination in lending based on
  - race or color
  - religion
  - national origin
  - sex
  - marital status
  - age
  - dependency upon public assistance
- licensees assisting in qualifying must also comply
- denied applicants must get notice within 30 days

Real Estate Settlement Procedures Act (RESPA)
- standardizes settlement practices & ensures buyers understand settlement costs
- lender must:
  - provide CFPB booklet explaining loans, settlement costs and procedures
  - provide CFPB Loan Estimate of settlement costs within three days of application
  - provide CFPB Closing Disclosure three days before loan consummation

National Flood Insurance Act
- borrowers of "federally-related loans" must obtain flood insurance if property is in designated flood-hazard area
- flood-zone maps indicate where homeowners must obtain insurance

---

The Mortgage Market

Supply and demand for money
- relationship between supply and demand for money affects interest rates, consumer prices, availability of mortgage money; regulated by Federal Reserve

Federal Reserve control of money supply among banks
- sells T-bills to reduce money supply and increase interest rates; buys T-bills to increase supply and decrease rates
- sets the reserve requirement for member banks
- increase reserves to tighten money and raise interest rates
- decrease reserves to loosen money and lower interest rates
- sets the discount rate for member banks
- increase rate to tighten money
- decrease rate to increase money supply

Federal Home Loan Bank System (FHLBS)
- counterpart to the Fed for savings and loan associations

Federal Deposit Insurance Corporation (FDIC)
- insures deposits up to $250,000 per depositor, per insured bank, for each account ownership category

The primary mortgage market
- originates mortgage loans directly to borrowers;
- includes savings and loans, commercial banks, mutual savings banks, life insurance companies, mortgage bankers, credit unions

The secondary mortgage market
- buys existing loans to provide liquidity to primary lenders; Fannie Mae, Ginnie Mae, Freddie Mac, investment firms, life insurance companies, pension funds

Role of FNMA, GNMA, FHLMC and FAMC
- FNMA buys conventional, FHA- and VA-backed loans and pooled mortgages; guarantees payment on mortgage-backed securities
- GNMA guarantees payment on certain types of loans
- FHLMC buys and pools mortgages; sells mortgage-backed securities
- FAMC, or Farmer Mac operates in the agricultural financing markets by stimulating and expanding ag credit availability for agribusinesses

Mortgage loan originator v. lender/banker v. broker
- mortgage loan originator: solicits, negotiates mortgage loans; requires MLO license
- mortgage broker: an intermediary who brings mortgage borrowers and mortgage lenders together, but does not use its own funds to originate mortgages
- mortgage banker: person or entity who funds or services loans for others and/or who sells mortgages to the secondary market

Types of Mortgages

Conventional mortgages
- Originated by banks and private financial institutions
- No government-related insurance or guarantees as with FHA or VA
- Typically require 20% down payments; smaller down payments may require PMI
- Assumptions require approval

Government loan programs
- **FHA** – federally insured loan programs (see following page)
- **VA** – federally guaranteed loan programs (see following page)

Amortized fixed-rate v adjustable loans
- **Amortized:** payments include increasing increments of principal which retire loan balance over loan term
- Fixed rate: interest rate does not change – can have for amortized or interest-only loans
- Adjustable loans: interest rate fluctuates up or down with an index; payments may also vary

Adjustable Loan Characteristics

- **mechanics**: rate adjusts up or down with index; payments may or may not change;
- negative amortization: loan balance increases if payments are less than what is owed given the balance and rate, i.e., unpaid monthly amounts are added to the principal balance
- rate and payment caps: maximum amounts the interest rate or payments can increase in a given adjustment period or over the life of the loan; protects borrower from unaffordable increases
- index and margin: interest rate tied to any number of financial indices; margin equals a fixed point spread between the index and the interest rate
- **teaser rates:** to attract borrowers, adjustable loans may have low initial rates which increase over subsequent adjustment periods to a more permanent market level.

Custom Mortgages

- **partially amortized with a balloon:** payments will not retire principal balance over life of the loan, thus requiring a lump-sum payment, or "balloon" payment at end of term
- **interest-only loans:** loans where payments are interest only, and the principal balance is retired in full at maturity using a balloon payment
- **biweekly mortgage:** loan payments are every-two weeks, a device that reduces total interest paid, but also shortens risk period for the lender
- **package mortgage:** mortgage loans which also finance articles of personal property as part of the purchase transaction
- **home equity loans:** funds borrowed using the homeowners equity for collateral; funds can be used for any purpose
- **purchase money mortgage:** a seller-financed loan to the buyer of portions of the purchase price using the property as collateral; usually accompanied by a senior underlying first mortgage
- **reverse annuity mortgage:** a financial arrangement where the homeowner pledges equity to a lender in exchange for periodic payments of the pledged equity; in essence it is the periodic receipt of equity liquidation in exchange for an increase of debt owed on the property.

FHA Loans

Insured loans granted by approved lenders to qualified borrowers.

Loan term:	• 15, 30 years
Qualifying ratios:	• income: 31% • debt: 43%
Minimum downpayment:	• 3.5%
Mortgage insurance:	• required at 78% LTV or above • premium = one-time 1.75-2.25% of loan amount, plus annual premium
Points:	• None
Maximum loan amount:	• varies by Metropolitan Statistical Area

VA Loans

Guaranteed loans:	• granted by approved lenders to qualified veterans
Qualifying ratios:	• depends on lender
Minimum downpayment:	• None
Points:	• 1.25 - 3.3, depending on downpayment, type of loan, type of veteran

Investment

Investment Terminology

Appreciation:	an increase in the value of a property owing to economic forces beyond the control of the investor
Asset:	a tangible or intangible item of **value**
Basis;	a measurement of how much is invested in the property for tax purposes; adjusted basis is the **original** cost of the asset plus capital improvements minus depreciation
Capital gain (or loss):	the difference between the net **sales** proceeds of an asset and its adjusted basis
Cash flow:	the remaining positive or negative amount of income an investment produces after subtracting all operating expenses and debt service from gross income
Equity:	that portion of a property's value owned by the legal owner, expressed as the difference between the property's market value and all loan balances outstanding **on** the property
Leverage;	the relationship between the yield rate of an investment and the interest rate of funds borrowed to finance the investment; if the yield rate is greater than the loan rate, positive leverage results; if the yield rate is less than the **loan** rate, negative leverage results
Liquidity;	the degree to which an investment is readily marketable, or convertible to another form of asset; if immediately salable, an investment is liquid; the longer it takes to sell, the more illiquid the investment; real property is relatively illiquid in comparison with other types of investment
Tax shelter:	an investment that produces depreciation or other non-cash losses that a taxpayer can deduct **from** other income to reduce tax liability

Investment Characteristics

Ownership benefits	• income • appreciation • tax shelter: depreciation and interest deductions
Ownership risks	• relatively illiquid • management intensive • negative leverage and price movements

Investment Entities

Direct	• investor buys directly and manages personally
Syndicate	• group of investors who combine funds to buy, develop, and/or operate a property
General partnership	• all members own and manage
Limited partnership	• general partner manages; limited partners own but do not manage
Real Estate Investment Trust	• investors buy trust certificates; trust invests in real estate assets • investors share returns per ownership percent

Taxation of Real Estate Investments

Income-producing investments are taxed on
- the annual income they make, plus
- on any gain realized when sold

Taxable income
- gross income minus allowed expenses and deductions
- net income from the investment is added to the investor's other ordinary taxable income

Cost recovery, or depreciation
- deduction of a portion of property's value from gross income each year over the depreciable life of asset
- depreciable life defined by tax laws

Depreciable basis
- the non-land, or improvement portion of an income-producing property
- cannot depreciate land value

Depreciation schedules / terms
- 27.5 years to 39 years

Capital gain and loss
- the taxable gain (profit) or loss incurred when the income property is sold
- if sales proceeds exceed the current adjusted basis there is a gain; if less, then it is a loss

Adjusted basis
- the **cost** of the investment plus **capital improvements** less **depreciation**

Interest
- deductible from income for tax purposes
- cannot deduct principal

Tax liability On Sale Of Residence

- seller of a principal residence owes tax on capital gain that results from sale unless excluded
- capital gain is the amount realized minus the adjusted basis
- gains tax exclusion: up to $250,000 for a single seller and $500,000 for a married couple can be excluded from gains tax every two years

Gain on Sale

selling price of old home	$350,000
- selling costs	35,000
= amount realized	315,000
beginning basis of old home	200,000
+ capital improvements	10,000
= adjusted basis of old home	210,000
amount realized	315,000
- adjusted basis	210,000
= gain on sale	105,000

Investment Analysis of an Income Property (See also Math Section, "Investment")

Pre-tax Cash Flow

potential rental income	$70,000
- vacancy and collection loss	4,200
= effective rental income	65,800
+ other income	2,000
= gross operating income	67,800
- operating expenses	35,000
- reserves	3,500
= net operating income (NOI)	29,300
- debt service	20,000
= pre-tax cash flow	$9,300

After-tax cash flow

pre-tax cash flow
- tax liability
= after tax cash flow

Taxable Income	**Tax Liability**
NOI	taxable income
+ reserves	x tax bracket
– interest	= tax liability
– depreciation)	
= taxable income	

Taxation

Taxing Authorities

Taxing entities
- property tax, or ad valorem taxation -- not to be confused with an income-property's annual tax on taxable income
- no federal ad valorem taxation
  - can impose a tax lien, but not annual property tax
- states may levy property taxes
  - typically delegated to **county and local jurisdictions**
  - states may also impose tax liens

Tax districts which levy property tax
- counties
- cities
- municipalities
- townships
- special tax districts
- established to collect funds for schools, fire protection, parks, community colleges, libraries, road maintenance, other public services

Property Tax Calculation

Property tax
- **ad valorem** tax levied annually on the taxable value of a property in order to help fund government and public services
- taxable value is based on assessed value

Tax base and tax rate
- **tax base**
  - the total of all assessed values in a jurisdiction excluding exemptions
- **tax rate**
  - also, the **millage** rate
  - rate applied to taxable value of each property to determine its tax levy
- **assessed value**
  - the valuation of properties for tax purposes, completed by **assessors**
- **equalization factors**
  - value-adjusting factors applied to assessed value to increase fairness, evenness of tax levies

Homestead exemption
- a tax exemption of a portion of the assessed value of a principal residence
- granted to the homeowner, provided
  - he or she is the head of the family
  - has resided at the property for the required length of time

Other exemptions
- properties immune from ad valorem tax
  - government-owned properties
- exempt from taxes
  - properties owned by non-profit-organizations

Tax rate derivation
- (1) taxing entity determines **budget requirements** to be met by ad valorem tax
- (2) divide **tax requirement** by the **tax base**

Tax rate mills
- tax rate stated as mills ($.001), or
- dollars per $100 of assessed value, or
- dollars per $1,000 of assessed value, or
- as a percentage of assessed value

Tax billing and collection
- individual tax bill
  - (rate x taxable value)
- taxable value
  - (assessed value minus exemptions and adjustments)

Special assessments
- levied against specific properties that will benefit from the planned improvement
- assessment amount based on pro rata share of benefitting properties
- creates voluntary or involuntary tax lien

Tax Lien Enforcement

Tax lien enforcement process
- tax lien enforcement & collection occurs via
  - tax certificate issuance
  - certificate buyer pays taxes due
  - application for a tax deed
  - tax sale and foreclosure initiation

Sale of tax certificates
- tax certificate buyer pays taxes due
- after a period of time may apply for a tax deed

Tax deed conveyance
- conveys title in the tax sale

Tax sale
- buyer must pay taxes due
- defaulted taxpayer may be able to redeem property
- if not redeemed, state issues tax deed to convey title to buyer

Fair Housing Laws

Anti-discrimination
- federal and state laws prohibit discrimination in housing
- citizens entitled to live wherever they wish without discrimination
- **state fair housing laws** reflect national laws with certain differences
- **fair housing and local zoning**
  - fair housing does not preempt local zoning, but zoning cannot be discriminatory against protected classes

Civil Rights Act of 1866
- no discrimination in selling or leasing housing **based on race**
- **Executive Order 11063:** no **race discrimination** involving FHA- or VA-backed loans

Civil Rights Act of 1968
- Title VIII (Fair Housing Act)
- no housing discrimination based on **race, color, religion, national origin**
- certain exceptions permitted

Forms of illegal discrimination
- discriminatory misrepresentation
- advertising
- unequal services
- steering
- blockbusting
- restricting access to market
- redlining

Title VIII exemptions
- selling, leasing single family home without broker or discriminatory advertising, with conditions
- 1-4 unit rental building where owner is occupant
- leasing facilities owned by private clubs
- facilities owned by religious organizations and leased to members

Jones v. Mayer
- discrimination in selling/renting residential housing based on race is prohibited without exception or exemption

Equal Opportunity in Housing poster
- brokers must display
- affirms compliance with fair housing laws
- failure to display can be construed as discrimination
- see example on following slide

Fair Housing Amendments Act of 1988
- no discrimination based on
  - sex
  - against the handicapped
  - families with children
- **exemptions**
  - government-designated retirement housing

- o retirement community (62+ years of age)
- o retirement community if 80 % of dwellings have one person who is 55+
- o 1-4 unit dwellings where owners have no more than three houses

Discrimination by the client
- laws apply to owners as well as agents
- agent liable if goes along with client discrimination
- agent should withdraw from relationship with discriminatory client

Violations and enforcement
- file HUD complaint
- file suit in court
- may obtain injunction, damages
- violators subject to prosecution

Fair financing laws (See also Finance Section)
- Equal Credit Opportunity Act (ECOA)
    - o lenders must be fair, impartial in loan qualifying
    - o may not discriminate based on race, color, religion, national origin, sex, marital status, age
    - o must state reasons for credit denial
- Home Mortgage Disclosure Act
    - o prohibits redlining
    - o lenders must report location of loans

Americans with Disabilities Act (ADA)
- purpose is to prohibit discrimination against persons with disabilities
- applies to accessing public, employment, education, transportation facilities
- applies to private employers with 15+ employees and public employees
- **Title I: Employment**
    - o must have equal opportunity, enforced by ECOA
- **Title II: State, local government**
    - o cannot discriminate in state and local services
- **Title III:** Public **accommodations**
    - o cannot discriminate in public accommodations, commercial facilities
- **Title IV:** Telecommunication
    - o concerns accommodations in telecommunications, public service messaging
- **Title V:** miscellaneous
    - o general provisions as to how ADA affects other laws, insurance, lawyers
- licensees should clearly understand provisions of Title I and III
- ADA requirements
    - o landlords must modify housing to be accessible without hindrance
    - o access must be equivalent to that provided for non-disabled persons
- penalties
    - o violations can result in citations, license restrictions, fines, injunctions

Property Disclosures

Residential property condition
- Seller's Disclosure Form
    - o sellers (not agents) must complete form in many states for prospective buyers
    - o describes property condition at time of sale on state-approved forms
- owner's role
    - o seller must affirm whether or not problems exist with property or its systems
    - o if unknown, seller must so state; if a defect is known, seller must disclose

- o if seller is unaware of a problem, s/he can state "no representation" which removes liability for not disclosing
- o seller must sign, deliver to buyer and buyer must acknowledge receipt
- licensee's role
  - o must disclose any material facts that are known or reasonably should have known
- right of rescission
  - o if seller does not complete and deliver form, buyer receives a right to rescind contract and reclaim deposit
  - o right to cancel continues until closing or occupancy
- property condition and material facts
  - o material fact = a fact affecting the property's value or the prospect's decision to contract
  - o property stigmas are not material facts (previous crime, suicide, disease, etc.)
  - o no requirement to disclose non-material facts
  - o material facts can include the surrounding area in addition to the immediate premises

Environmental issues

- licensees and principals are responsible for disclosing, remediating hazards
  - o lead-based paint
    - ▪ if property built before 1978, must disclose possible lead hazard
    - ▪ use form "Protect Your Family from Lead in Your Home"
  - o mold
    - ▪ must be disclosed if present in home
  - o asbestos
    - ▪ can cause lung cancer; must be removed by experts to prevent contamination
  - o air quality
    - ▪ can/should test for carbon monoxide, radon, formaldehyde, other toxic chemicals prior to sale
  - o carbon monoxide
    - ▪ emitted by gas space heaters, chimneys, furnaces, stoves, etc.
    - ▪ detectors should be in every home
  - o septic systems
    - ▪ can release contaminants into soil
    - ▪ should inspect periodically and prior to any conveyance
  - o radon
    - ▪ detectable radioactive ground gas that can cause cancer;
  - o urea formaldehyde
    - ▪ hazard in foam insulation and pressed wood products, eg, particle board
  - o underground storage tanks (UST)
    - ▪ commercial hazard if leaking; should disclose presence of any UST
- Clean Air Act
  - o controls air pollution, air quality on national scale
  - o creates pollutant- emission standards
- Clean Water Act
  - o governs, sets standards for controlling water pollution
  - o applies to all waters connected to navigable waterways
- Safe Drinking Water Act
  - o regulates, protects public supply of drinking water
  - o sets protection standards, requires water suppliers to report discovered health risks
  - o sellers must disclose property's source of drinking water, proximity to septic systems
  - o should test any well system
- Brownfields Law
  - o brownfields = abandoned commercial sites likely to contain toxic material
  - o law provides funds, liability protections and tax exemptions for reclamation
- Environmental Protection Agency (EPA)
  - o integrates federal environmental research, funding, monitoring, standard-setting, and enforcement into one agency
- licensee disclosure obligations, liabilities

- licensees should have general awareness and know where to get expert help
- not expected to have expert knowledge of law or physical condition
- critical role is to
  - be aware of potential hazards
  - disclose material facts, have attorney draft disclosures
  - know where to find expert help

Warranties

- purpose and scope
  - aka, home service contracts, to cover service, repair of systems, appliances
  - typically annual contracts with costs depending on property size, location, type, degree of coverage
  - may be included in purchase price of a home
- limitations – warranties may exclude
  - pre-existing conditions, accidental breakages, poor installations, outdoor systems, certain appliances, etc.
  - homeowner must use warranty company to have services performed

Inspections

- process
  - inspections detect oversights or need for repairs
  - identify need for maintenance procedures
  - inspections uncover system, pest infestation, environmental issues
- termite inspections
  - not easily detectable by non-experts; should do annual inspections
- environmental inspections, audits
  - home inspections should include environmental issues / hazards
  - can also conduct site assessments which examine possible impairments
- environmental impact statements (EIS)
  - performed for federally, some privately funded development projects
  - addresses air, water quality, noise, health, safety, wildlife, traffic, sewer impacts of project
  - culminates in permit or permit denial
- licensee disclosure duties
  - in most states, licensees must disclose known, material facts on residential properties
  - must also disclose known results of any residential inspection
  - when not required, licensees should suggest professional inspections / audits

Homeowners' Associations

- property disclosures include homeowners' associations
  - must disclose if subject to common interest plan
  - must disclose association's membership obligation, dues, restrictions
  - association must provide required disclosure documents, forms, timing requirements
  - seller responsible for disclosures, agent must ensure seller complies

Codes Of Ethics

Sources of practitioner ethics

- federal, state legislation
- state license regulation
- industry self-regulation via trade associations, institutes
- predominant influence in practitioner ethics is the Code of Ethics of the National Association of Realtors®
  - covers all aspects of practice and transactions

Duties to clients
- most codes of ethics uphold commitment to fulfilling fiduciary duties, including
  - honesty in representing values, property condition
  - respecting other broker-client relationships
  - submitting all offers
  - avoiding commingling, conversion
  - maintaining transaction files
  - maintaining confidentialities
  - managing client property competently

Other Professional Practices

Duties to customers
- honesty and fair dealing
- disclosing sources of compensation
- conducting honest advertising that is not misleading

Disclosures
- comply with federal, state, and ethical disclosure requirements, including
  - disclosure in ads

Wholesaling
- the discouraged practice of simultaneously buying and selling property so that the wholesaler makes an immediate profit without actually taking possession of the property
- at closing, wholesaler assigns purchase contract to another buyer for a price that exceeds the price paid to acquire the contract
- wholesaler takes his profit as a fee
- some states require wholesaler to have a real estate license

Love letters
- the practice of buyers trying to enhance an offer's attractiveness by attaching personal letters to the seller that attempt to convince the seller that the buyer is the party the seller should sell to.
- offers can be construed as discriminatory

Professional relationships
- avoid disparagement of competitors
- do not exploit unfair advantages
- arbitrate differences, disputes rather than litigate
- respect agency relationships of others
- conform to accepted standards of co-brokerage practices

Closings

Settlement Process
- identify selling terms & costs
- determine non-prorated debits and credits
- complete prorated debits and credits
- complete closing statement
- disburse funds

Key Points On Closings	• seller must prove marketability of title (via title insurance)
	• must remove all encumbrances before title transfer
	• escrow officer disburses buyer's funds, loan monies once conditions are met
	• conditions include survey, inspections, title insurance, reserves, PMI

RESPA

Purpose	• clarify, disclose costs; eliminate kickbacks, undisclosed fees
Applicability	• for residential property
	• federally-related mortgage, including VA, FHA
	• Regulated by Consumer Financial Protection Bureau (CFPB)
Information booklet	• lender must provide CFPB booklet, "Your Home Loan Toolkit"
Loan estimate	• lender must provide CFPB's H-24 Loan Estimate of settlement costs within three days of application
Closing disclosure	• lender must use CFPB's H-25 Closing Disclosure
Referral fees and kickbacks	• RESPA prohibits payment of referral fees and kickbacks
	• business relationships between firms involved in the transaction must be disclosed

Truth-in-Lending Integrated Disclosures Rule (TRID)

Key points	• combines financial disclosure requirements of RESPA & Truth-in-Lending Act (TILA)
	• replaces "Good Faith Estimate" and HUD-1 forms
	• uses new "Loan Estimate" form" and "Closing Disclosure" form
Forms and procedures	• lender must provide mandatory: "Your Home Loan Toolkit" booklet at loan application
	• Loan Estimate form: 3 business days after loan application
	• Closing Disclosure: 3 business days before consummation
	• Terms in both forms must generally be the same
Good faith	• Loan Estimate costs based on best information available
	• Closing Disclosure costs equal estimate costs within certain tolerances
Types of charges	• no limitation on increase over estimate
	• 10% tolerance charges
	• 0 tolerance charges

Applicable transactions	• most closed-end consumer mortgages, including: construction loans, loans secured by vacant land, loans to trusts
	• not covered: home equity loans, reverse mortgages, loans on mobile homes, loans by small lenders (no more than 5 loans per year)
The H-25 form	• 5 pages, variable by loan type

Debits & Credits

Amount buyer must produce:	excess of *buyer's debits* over credits
Amount seller must receive:	excess of *seller's credits* over debits
Buyer's credits	• earnest money
	• loan amount
	• seller's share of prorations buyer will pay
Buyer's debits	• purchase price
	• expenses (per agreement or custom)
	• buyer's share of prorations prepaid by seller
	•
Seller's credits	• purchase price
	• buyer's share of prorated items prepaid by seller
Seller's debits	• expenses (per agreement or custom)
	• seller's share of prorated items the buyer will pay
	• loan balance and other liens to be paid off

30-Day 12-Month Proration

Formula:	Monthly Amount = (Annual amount ÷ 12)
	Daily Amount = (Monthly amount ÷ 30)
	Proration = (Monthly amount x no. of months) + (Daily amount x no. of days)
Example:	An annual tax bill is $1,800. Closing is on April 10. What is the seller's share of the taxes?
	1. ($1,800 ÷ 12) = $150 monthly amount
	2. ($150 ÷ 30) = $5.00 daily amount
	3. ($150 x 3 months) = $450 Jan - Mar; ($5 x 10) = $50 Apr 1 - Apr 10; ($450 + 50) = $500 seller's share

365-Day Method

Formula:	Daily amount = Annual amount ÷ 365 days; or
	Daily amount = Monthly amount ÷ no. of days in month
	Proration = (Daily amount x no. of days)

Example: An annual tax bill is $1,800. Closing is on April 10. What is the seller's share of the taxes?

1. ($1,800 ÷ 365) = $4.93 daily amount
2. Jan 1 thru April 10 = (31 + 28 + 31 + 10) days, or 100 days
3. ($4.93 x 100 days) = $493 seller's share

Risk Management

Four Risk Management Strategies

1) **Avoidance**
   - refrain from risky activity
     - e. g., assuring buyers a property will appreciate
2) **Reduction**
   - reduce probability of loss
   - reduce severity of loss
   - share responsibility for a decision
3) **Transference**
   - pass risk to another party
   - get E & O insurance
   - by contract; insurance
4) **Retention**
   - accept risk
   - take responsibility for consequences
   - eg, pricing strategy on a listing

Risk Management Procedures

- **education**
  - knowledge and skill reduce risk
  - understand forms and contracts
- **disclosure**
  - provide information to reduce misunderstanding & lawsuits
- **disclosure areas**
  - agency
  - property condition
  - fiduciary / statutory duties
  - personal interest in selling a property
  - documentation and record keeping
  - maintain evidence of compliance, transaction recordkeeping

Insurance Types–To Manage Risk

- general liability
- errors and omissions (E & O, to cover negligence in discharging service duties)
- fire and hazard
- flood
- casualty
- workers'
- personal property
- consequential loss
- surety bond

Primary Areas of Risk

Agency

- fulfill agency disclosure requirements
- discharge fiduciary duties and duties to customers
- avoid conflicts of interest
- uphold legal confidentialities

Property disclosures

- seller's property condition disclosure
- material facts disclosure
- lead paint, infestations, mold, radon

Listing and selling

- listing agreement accuracy
- comparative market analysis results
- closing cost estimates
- advertising
- authorizations and permissions
- exceeding expertise

Contracting process

- contracts for real estate must be in writing
- inaccuracy endangers contract
- avoid unauthorized practice of law
  - may fill in blanks on standard contract forms
  - do not give legal advice to public

Fair housing

- advertising may not state preference, limitation or discrimination based on race, color, religion, national origin, sex, handicap, familial status
- licensee must not be involved with discriminatory actions of a client or customer
- make sure listing and purchase contracts are in compliance

Antitrust

- cannot collude on prices; fix prices
- cannot conspire with other companies to restrict trade or unjustly impair a competitor
- cannot create monopolies
- cannot allocate markets among competitors

Rules and regulations	• prime causes of discipline
	o commission of prohibited acts
	o practicing with an expired license
	o disclosure failures
	o earnest money mishandling

Misrepresentation	• **unintentional**
	o inaccurate information conveyed unknowingly
	o occurs most often in measurements, property characterizations
	• **intentional**
	o fraud
	o knowingly conveying false information
	• ways to reduce risks in misrepresentation
	o measure and calculate areas accurately
	o do not over-rely on measurements by others
	o refrain from exaggeration
	o avoid stating opinions a consumer might take for expertise

Recommending providers	• risks include
	o consumer dissatisfaction
	o possible liability for undisclosed business relationship
	• best practices
	o do not recommend vendors
	o provide a list of trusted vendors with a disclaimer and no recommendation

Trust fund handling	• mishandling of earnest money deposits
	• commingling trust funds
	• conversion of trust funds
	• errors in use of trust accounts

Property Management

Management Functions

Types of manager	• individual, managing properties for multiple owners; building manager, employed to manage a single property; resident, employed to live and manage on site.
	• may specialize in a property type
	• manager is a fiduciary of the principal
	• specific functions determined by management agreement

| **Reporting** | • monthly, quarterly, annually |
| | • annual operating budget, cash flow reports, profit and loss statements, budget comparison statements |

Budgeting	<ul><li>operating budget: rental rates, capital expenditures, reserves, salaries and wages; projects income based on past performance and current market</li><li>expenses, variable and fixed; capital expenditures: outlays for major renovations and construction; cash reserves set aside for variable expenses</li></ul>
Renting	<ul><li>keep property rented and tenanted;</li><li>select compatible tenants and collect scheduled rents</li><li>legal issues: compliance with fair housing laws, Americans with Disabilities Act, and ECOA</li></ul>
Property maintenance	<ul><li>balance costs of services, owner financial objectives, and tenant needs</li><li>routine, preventive, or corrective; staffed in-house or contracted out</li></ul>
Construction	<ul><li>tenant alterations, renovations, expansion, environmental remediation</li><li>legal concerns: Americans with Disabilities Act</li></ul>

The Management Agreement

Components	<ul><li>names; description; lease term; owner's purpose; responsibilities; authority; budget; allocation of costs; reporting; compensation; Equal Opportunity statement</li></ul>
Rights, duties and liabilities	<ul><li>landlord: receive rent; receive premises in specified condition; enter and inspect; examine books; contract, hire vendors, set rents; pay management fee; comply with laws</li><li>manager: hire and fire; contract; perform management tasks without interference; maintain financial records, make reports, budget, collect rent, find tenants, maintain property, meet owner goals; liability for trust funds; comply with laws</li></ul>

Leasing Considerations

Landlord rights and responsibilities	<ul><li>rights: enter premises, receive payment, retake on termination, pursue remedies</li><li>responsibilities: provide habitable conditions; maintain heating, cooling, electrical, plumbing; keep clean and in repair</li></ul>
Tenant rights and responsibilities	<ul><li>rights: quiet enjoyment, habitable conditions, right to sue for default</li><li>responsibilities: pay rent, obey rules, give proper notice, return property in prescribed condition, use only for intended purpose</li></ul>

Evictions	• actual: legal procedure; notice, suit, judgment, taking • constructive: tenant vacates on account of landlord failure to maintain premises
Termination of a lease	• expiration, performance, agreement, abandonment, breach, notice, destruction of premises, condemnation, foreclosure, death of either party (tenancy at will), death of landlord (life estate)
Security deposit procedures	determined by law, rules, and agreement

Section II: Real Estate Math Review

Basic Math

Fractions

Adding and subtracting same denominator:

       Formula: $a/c + b/c = (a + b) \div c$

       Example: $1/2 + 1/2 = (1 + 1)/2 = 2/2 = 1$

Adding and subtracting different denominators:

       Formula: $a/c + b/d = (ad + bc)/cd$

       Example: $1/2 + 1/3 = (3 + 2)/6 = 5/6$

Multiplying:

       Formula: $(a/c) \times (b/d) = ab/cd$

       Example: $(2/5) \times (4/6) = 8/30 = 4/15$

Decimals and Percents

Converting decimals to percentages

       Formula: *Decimal number x 100 = Percentage number*

       Example: $.022 \times 100 = 2.2\%$

Converting percentages to decimals

       Formula: *Percent number $\div$ 100 = Decimal number*

       Example: $2.2 \div 100 = .022$

Multiplying percents

       Formula: *1. Percent number $\div$ 100 = Decimal number*

                        2. Beginning number x Decimal number = Product

       Example: 75% of 256 (75% x 256) = ?

                        1. $75 \div 100 = .75$

                        2. $256 \times .75 = 192$

Dividing by percents

Formula: 1. *Percent number ÷ 100 = Decimal number*

                2. *Beginning number ÷ Decimal = Dividend*

Example: 240 ÷ 75% = ?

                1. 75% ÷ 100 = .75

                2. 240 ÷ .75 = 320

Decimals, Fractions, and Percentages

Converting fractions to percents

Formula: (1)   a / b or a ÷ b = a divided by b = decimal number

             (2)   decimal number x 100 = percent number

Example: (1)   2 / 5 = 2 divided by 5 = 0.4

             (2)   .4 x 100 = 40%

Converting a percent to fraction and reducing it

Formula: (1)   X% = X ÷ 100 or X / 100

             (2) $\dfrac{X \div a}{100 \div a}$ where a is the largest number that divides evenly into both numerator and denominator

Example: (1)   40% = 40 ÷ 100, or 40 / 100

             (2) $\dfrac{40 \div 20}{100 \div 20} = \dfrac{2}{5}$

Converting fractions to decimals and percentages

Formula: *Decimal x 100 = Percent number*

Example: .75 x 100 = 75%

Equations

Additions and Subtractions

Formula: *if*   *a = b + c*

             then   *b = a - c (subtracting c from both sides)*

             and   *c = a - b (subtracting b from both sides)*

Example: 10   = 6 + 4

6	= 10 - 4
4	= 10 - 6

Multiplications and Divisions

Formula: *if*   *a = b x c*

then   *b = a / c*   *(dividing both sides by c)*

and   *c = a / b*   *(dividing both sides by b)*

Example: 10 = 2 x 5

2 = 10 ÷ 5

5 = 10 ÷ 2

Linear and Perimeter Measurement

Linear measure of rectangles

Formula: *Side A = Area ÷ Side B*

Example: A rectangular house has one side 40' side long and area of 1,200 SF. What is the length of the other side?

Side A = (1,200' ÷ 40') = 30'

Perimeter measurement

Formula: *Perimeter = Sum of all sides of an object*

Example: A five-sided lot has the following dimensions:

Side A = 50' Side B = 60'
Side C= 70' Side D = 100'
Side E = 30'

What is the perimeter of the lot?

P = 50' + 60' + 70' + 100' + 30' = 310'

Area Measurement

Square and rectangle

Formula: *Area = Width x Depth (Horizontal) or Width x Height (Vertical)*

Width= Area ÷ Depth (Height)

Depth (Height)= Area ÷ Width

Example: A house is 40' deep and 30' wide. What is its area?

70

Area = 40' x 30' = 1,200 SF

Triangle

Formula: *Area = (Height x Base) ÷ 2*

Note: Base is also sometimes referred to as "width"

Example: An A-frame house has a front facade measuring 30' across and 20' in height. What is the area of the facade?

Area = (30' x 20') ÷ 2 = 300 Square feet (SF)

Square foot-to-acre conversion

Formula: *Acres = Area SF ÷ 43,560 SF*

Example: How many acres is 196,020 SF?

196,020 SF ÷ 43,560 SF = 4.5 acres

Acre-to-square foot conversion

Formula: *SF = Number of acres x 43,560 SF*

Example: How many square feet is .75 acres?

.75 acres x 43,560 SF = 32,670 SF

Linear and Area Conversion Chart

Linear measures

(cm = centimeter; m = meter; km = kilometer)

1 inch	=	1/12 foot	=	1/36 yard		
1 foot	=	12 inches	=	1/3 yard		
1 yard	=	36 inches	=	3 feet		
1 rod	=	16.5 feet	=	1/320 mile		
1 mile	=	5280 feet	=	1760 yards	=	320 rods
1 centimeter	=	1/100 m				
1 meter	=	100 cm	=	1/1000 km		
1 kilometer	=	1,000 m				

Area measures

1 square inch	=	1/144 sq. foot				
1 square foot	=	1/9 sq. yard	=	144 sq. inches		
1 square yard	=	9 sq. feet	=	1,296 sq. inches		
1 acre	=	1/640 sq. mi	=	43,560 SF	=	208.71 ft x 208.71 ft
1 square mile	=	640 acres	=	1 section	=	1/36 township
1 section	=	1 mi x 1 mi	=	640 acres	=	1/36 township
1 township	=	6 mi x 6 mi	=	36 sq. mi	=	36 sections

Metric conversions

(cm = centimeter; m = meter; km = kilometer)

1 inch	=	2.54 cm				
1 foot	=	30.48 cm	=	.3048 m		
1 yard	=	91.44 cm	=	.9144 m		
1 mile	=	1609.3 m	=	1.60 km		
1 centimeter	=	.3937 inch				
1 meter	=	39.37 inches	=	3.28 feet	=	1.094 yards
1 kilometer	=	3,281.5 feet	=	.621 mile		

Fractions of sections, acres, and linear dimensions

Fraction		# Acres
1 section	=	640 acres
1/2 section	=	320 acres
1/4 section	=	160 acres
1/8 section	=	80 acres
1/16 section	=	40 acres
1/32 section	=	20 acres
1/64 section	=	10 acres

Calculating Area from the Legal Description

Formula:

(1) *First multiply all the denominators of the fractions in the legal description together.*

(2) *Then divide 640 by the resulting product.*

Examples:

How many acres are in the Northern 1/2 of the Southwestern 1/4 of Section 6?

640 / (2 x 4) = 640 / 8 = 80 acres

How many acres are in the Western 1/2 of the Northwestern 1/4 of the Northeastern 1/4 of Section 8?

640 / (2 x 4 x 4) = 640 / 32 = 20 acres

Volume Measurement

Formula:

Volume = Width x Height x Depth   (assume objects with 90 degree angles)

Base = Volume ÷ (Height x Depth)

Height = Volume ÷ (Base x Depth)

Depth = Volume ÷ (Base x Height)

Example:

What is the volume of a 40' x 30' x 20' house?

40' x 30' x 20' = 24,000 cubic feet

Leases

Percentage Lease Rent Calculation

Formula: *Monthly percentage rent = Sales × percent of sales charged*

Example: A store generates $50,000 per month. The lease calls for 1.5% percentage rent. Monthly rent amount?

                ($50,000 × .015) = $750 / month

Contracts for the Sale of Real Estate

Percentage of Listing Price Calculation

Formula: *Percentage of listing price = Offer ÷ Listing price*

Example: A property listed for $300,000 receives an offer for $240,000. The offer's percentage of listing price is:

                $240,000 ÷ $300,000 = 80%

Earnest Money Deposit Calculation

Formula: *Deposit = Offering price × required or market-accepted percentage*

Example: A seller requires a 2% deposit on a property listed for $320,000. The required deposit (assuming a full price offer) is:

                $320,000 × 2% = $6,400

Appraisal & Value

Adjusting Comparables

Rules:
1. Never adjust the subject!

2. If the comparable is superior to the subject, subtract value from the comparable.

3. If the comparable is inferior to the subject, add value to the comparable.

Example: The subject has a $10,000 pool and no porch. A comparable that sold for $250,000 has a porch ($5,000), an extra bathroom ($6,000), and no pool.

Adjustments to comp: $250,000 (+10,000 - 5,000 - 6,000) = $249,000 indicated value of subject

Gross Rent Multiplier

Formulas: *Sales price = Monthly rental income x GRM*

Monthly rental income = Sales price / Gross Rent Multiplier

Note: Gross rent multiplier is often abbreviated as GRM.

Examples:
1. What is the value of a fourplex with monthly rent of $2,800 and a GRM of 112?

   $2,800 rent x 112 GRM = $313,600

2. What is the GRM of a fourplex with monthly rent of $2,800 and a value of $313,600?

   313,600 price ÷ $2,800 rent = 112 GRM

Gross Income Multiplier

Formulas: *Gross Income Multiplier = Sales price ÷ Annual income*

Sales price = Annual income x Gross Income Multiplier

Annual income = Sales price ÷ Gross Income Multiplier

Note: Gross income multiplier is often abbreviated as GIM.

Examples:
1. What is the value of a commercial property with an annual income of $33,600 and a GIM of 9.3?

   $33,600 income x 9.3 GIM = $312,480

2. What is the GIM of a commercial property with annual income of $33,600 and a value of $312,480?

   $312,480 price ÷ $33,600 = 9.3 GIM

Cost Approach Formula

Formula: *Value = Land value + (Improvements + Capital additions - Depreciation)*

Example: Land value = $150,000; home replacement cost = $450,000; new garage added @ $60,000; total depreciation = $30,000

Value = $150,000 + (450,000 + 60,000 - 30,000) = $630,000

Depreciation

Formulas: *Annual depreciation = Beginning depreciable basis ÷ Depreciation term*

Depreciable basis = (Initial property value + Any capital improvements - Land value)

Note: The depreciation term is in number of years.

Example: Property value = $500,000; land value = $110,000; depreciation term = 39 years

Step 1: ($500,000 - $110,000) = $390,000 depreciable basis

Step 2: ($390,000 ÷ 39 years) = $10,000 annual depreciation

Income Capitalization Formula

Formulas: *Value = Annual Net Operating Income ÷ Capitalization rate*

Capitalization rate = Annual Net Operating Income ÷ Value

Annual Net Operating Income = Value x Capitalization rate

Examples:
1. A property generates $490,000 net income and sells at a 7% cap rate. What is its value?

   $490,000 ÷ 7% = $7,000,000 value

2. A property has a net income of $490,000 and sells for $7,000,000. What is its cap rate?

   $490,000 ÷ 7,000,000 = .07, or 7%

3. A property's value is $7,000,000 and the cap rate is 7%. What is the property's net operating income?

   $7,000,000 x .07 = $490,000

Net Operating Income (NOI, Net Income)

Formula: *NOI = Potential rent - Vacancy loss + Other income - Operating expenses*

Note: NOI does not include debt payments!

Example: A building has 10 office suites generating annual potential rent of $10,000 each. Vacancy = 10% and annual expenses are $35,000. Vending machines yield $5,000. What is the NOI?

$100,000 rent - 10,000 vacancy + 5,000 other income - 35,000 expenses = $60,000 NOI

Finance

Points

Definition: 1 point = 1% of the loan amount or .01 x loan amount

Formulas: *Points = Fee paid ÷ Loan amount*

                    Fee paid = Loan amount x Points

                    Loan amount = Fee paid ÷ Points

Examples:
1. A borrower pays $25,000 for a $500,000 loan. How many points are paid?

   $25,000 ÷ 500,000 = .05 = 5 points

2. A borrower pays 5 points on a $500,000 loan. What is the fee paid?

   $500,000 x .05 = $25,000

3. A borrower pays $25,000 as 5 points on a loan. What is the loan amount?

   $25,000 ÷ .05 = $500,000

Rules of Thumb: 1 point charged raises lender's yield by .125%

                    8 points charged raises lender's yield by 1%

Example: A lender wants to yield 7% on a 6.5% loan. How many points must he or she charge?

                    (7% - 6.5%) = .5%

                    .5% ÷ .125% = 4 points

Interest Rate, Principal and Payment

Caveat!   Interest rates in mortgage financing apply to the <u>annual</u> interest payment and <u>exclude</u> principal payment. Remember to convert annual payments to monthly or vice versa as the question requires, and to exclude principal payments from your calculations!

Formulas: *Payment = Principal x Rate*

                    Principal = Payment ÷ Rate

                    Rate = Payment ÷ Principal

Examples:
1. A borrower has a $1,000,000 loan @ 6% interest. What are the annual and monthly payments?

   Annual payment = $1,000,000 x .06 = $60,000
   Monthly payment = $60,000 ÷ 12 = $5,000

2. A borrower has a $5,000 monthly payment on a 6% loan. What is the loan principal?

Principal = ($5,000 x 12) ÷ 6% = ($60,000 ÷ .06) = $1,000,000

3. A borrower has a $5,000 monthly payment on a $1,000,000 loan. What is the loan rate?

Rate = ($5,000 x 12) ÷ $1,000,000 = ($60,000 ÷ 1,000,000) = .06 = 6%

Total Interest, Interest Rate, and Loan Term

Formulas:

Interest-only loan: *Total interest = Loan amount x Rate x Term in years*

Amortized loan: *Total interest = (Monthly PI payment x 12 x term) - Loan amount*

Examples:

1. A borrower obtains a 10-year interest only loan of $500,000 @ 6%. How much interest will he or she pay?

($500,000 x .06 x 10) = $300,000

2. A borrower obtains a 10-year amortized loan of $500,000 @ 6% with monthly payments of $5,551. How much interest will he or she pay?

($5,551 x 12 x 10) - $500,000 = $166,120

Amortization Calculation

Formulas:

Month 1:   *Principal paid = Monthly payment - (Loan amount x Rate ÷ 12)*

Month 2:   *New loan amount = (Previous month principal - Principal paid)*

Principal paid = Monthly payment - (New loan amount x Rate ÷ 12)

Example:

A borrower obtains a 30-year $100,000 amortized loan @ 7% with a $665.31 monthly payment. What is the principal paid in the second month?

Month 1:   Principal paid = $665.31 - ($100,000 x 7% ÷ 12) = $665.31 - (583.33 interest paid) = $81.98

Month 2:   New loan amount = $100,000 previous month beginning loan amount - $81.98 principal paid = $99,918.02

Principal paid = $665.31 - ($99,918.02 x 7% ÷ 12) = $665.31 - (582.86 interest paid) = $82.45

Loan Constants

Formulas:

Monthly payment = (Loan amount x Loan constant) / 1000

Loan amount = (Monthly payment ÷ Loan constant) x 1000

Loan constant = (Monthly payment ÷ Loan amount) x 1000

Examples:

1. A borrower obtains a loan for $1,000,000 with a 6.3207 constant. What is the monthly payment?

   Monthly payment = ($1,000,000 ÷ 1,000) x 6.3207 = $6,320.70

2. A borrower has a monthly payment of $6,320.70 on a loan with a monthly constant of 6.3207. What is the loan amount?

   Loan amount = ($6,320.70 ÷ 6.3207) x 1,000 = $1,000,000

3. A borrower obtains a loan for $1,000,000 with a monthly payment of $6,320.70. What is the loan constant?

   Loan constant = ($6,320.70 ÷ $1,000,000) x 1,000 = 6.3207

Loan - to - Value Ratio (LTV)

Formulas: *LTV ratio = Loan ÷ Price (Value)*

             Loan = LTV ratio x Price (Value)

             Price (Value) = Loan ÷ LTV ratio

Examples:

1. A borrower can get a $265,600 loan on a $332,000 home. What is her LTV ratio?

   LTV Ratio = $265,600 ÷ 332,000 = 80%

2. A borrower can get an 80% loan on a $332,000 home. What is the loan amount?

   Loan = $332,000 x .80 = $265,600

3. A borrower obtained an 80% loan for $265,600. What was the price of the home?

   Price (value) = $265,600 ÷ .80 = $332,000

Financial Qualification

Income ratio qualification

Formula: *Monthly Principal & Interest (PI) payment = Income ratio x Monthly gross income*

Example: A lender uses a 28% income ratio for the PI payment. A borrower grosses $90,000 per year. What monthly PI payment can the borrower afford?

             Monthly PI payment = ($90,000 ÷ 12) x .28 = $2,100

How much can the borrower borrow if the loan constant is 6.3207? (See also- loan constants)

Loan amount = ($2,100 ÷ 6.3207) x 1,000 = $332,241.68

Debt ratio qualification

Formulas:

Debt ratio = (Housing expense + Other debt payments) ÷ Monthly gross income

Housing expense = (Monthly gross income x Debt ratio) - Other debt payments

Example:

A lender uses a 36% debt ratio. A borrower earns $90,000 / year and has monthly non-housing debt payments of $500. What housing payment can she afford?

Housing expense = ($90,000 ÷ 12 x .36) - 500 = ($2,700 - 500) = $2,200

Investment

Appreciation Calculations

Simple appreciation

Formulas:

Total appreciation = Current value - Original price

Total appreciation rate = Total appreciation ÷ Original price

Average annual appreciation rate = Total appreciation rate ÷ number of years

One year appreciation rate = (Annual appreciation amount) ÷ (Value at beginning of year)

Examples:

1. A home purchased for $200,000 five years ago is now worth $300,000. What are the total appreciation amount, total appreciation rate, and average appreciation rate?

   Total appreciation = ($300,000 - 200,000), or $100,000

   Total appreciation rate = ($100,000 ÷ 200,000), or 50%

   Average annual appreciation rate = 50% ÷ 5 years = 10%

2. A home costing $250,000 is worth $268,000 one year later. What is the one-year appreciation rate?

   One-year appreciation rate = ($18,000 ÷ 250,000) = 7.2%

Compounded appreciation

Formula:

Appreciated value = Beginning value x (1+ annual rate) x (1+ annual rate) ...... for the number of years in question

Example:

A $1,000,000 property is expected to appreciate 5% each year for the next 3 years. What will be its appreciated value at the end of this period?

Appreciated value = $1,000,000 x 1.05 x 1.05 x 1.05 = $1,157,625

Rate of Return, Investment Value, Income

Formulas:

Where Income = net operating income (NOI); Rate = rate of return, cap rate, or percent yield; and Value = value, price or investment amount:

Rate = Income ÷ Value

Value = Income ÷ Rate

Income = Value x Rate

Examples:

1. An office building has $200,000 net income and sold for $3,200,000. What was the rate of return?

   Rate = ($200,000 NOI ÷ 3,200,000 price) = 6.25%

2. An office building has $200,000 net income and a cap rate of 6.25%. What is its value?

   Value = ($200,000 ÷ 6.25%) = $3,200,000

3. An office building sells for $3,200,000 at a cap rate of 6.25%. What is its NOI?

   Income = $3,200,000 x 6.25% = $200,000

Basis, Adjusted Basis, and Capital Gain

Formulas:

Capital gain = Amount realized - Adjusted basis, where

Amount realized = Sale price - Selling costs

Adjusted basis = Beginning basis + Capital improvements - Total depreciation

Total depreciation = (Beginning depreciable basis ÷ Depreciation term in years) x Years depreciated

Depreciable basis = Initial property value + Capital improvements - Land value

Example:

Tip: work example backwards from last formula to first formula.

An apartment building was purchased for $500,000, with the land value estimated to be $100,000. The owner added a $100,000 parking lot. The property was depreciated on a 40-year schedule (for present purposes!). Three years later the property sold for $700,000, and selling costs were $50,000. What was the capital gain?

1. depreciable basis = $500,000 purchase price + 100,000 parking lot - 100,000 land = $500,000

2. total depreciation = ($500,000 ÷ 40 years) x 3 years = $37,500

80

3. adjusted basis = $500,000 purchase price + 100,000 parking lot - 37,500 total depreciation = $562,500

4. amount realized = $700,000 sale price - 50,000 selling costs = $650,000

5. capital gain = $650,000 amount realized - 562,500 adjusted basis = $87,500

Depreciation

Formulas: *Annual depreciation = (Beginning depreciable basis) ÷ (Depreciation term in number of years)*

Depreciable basis = (Initial property value + Capital improvements - Land value)

Example: Property value = $500,000; land value = $110,000; depreciation term = 39 years

1. ($500,000 - 110,000) = $390,000 depreciable basis

2. ($390,000 ÷ 39 years) = $10,000 annual depreciation

Equity

Formula: *Equity = Current market value - Current loan balance(s)*

Example: A home that was purchased for $150,000 with a $100,000 loan is now worth $300,000. The current loan balance is $80,000. What is the homeowner's equity?

Equity = $300,000 value - $80,000 debt = $220,000

Net Income

Formula: *NOI = Potential rent - Vacancy loss + Other income - Operating expenses*

Note: NOI does not include debt payments!

Example: A building has 10 office suites generating annual potential rent of $10,000 each. Vacancy = 10% and annual expenses are $35,000. Vending machines yield $5,000. What is the NOI?

$100,000 rent - 10,000 vacancy + 5,000 other income - 35,000 expenses = $60,000 NOI

Cash Flow

Formula: *Cash flow = (Net Operating Income - Debt service) where debt service is PI payment*

Example: A building generates $100,000 NOI after expenses and has a debt payment of $40,000. What is its cash flow?

Cash flow = $100,000 - 40,000 = $60,000

Investment Property Income Tax Liability

Formula: *Tax liability = (NOI + Reserves - Interest expense - Depreciation) x Tax bracket*

Example: An office building has NOI of $200,000, an annual reserve expense of $20,000, interest expense of $130,000 and annual depreciation of $50,000. Assuming a 28% tax bracket, what is its income tax liability?

Tax liability = ($200,000 + 20,000 - 130,000 - 50,000) x 28% = $11,200

Return on Investment

Formula: *ROI = NOI ÷ Price*

Example: An investment property generates a cash flow of $100,000 and appraises for $1,500,000. What is the owner's return on investment?

ROI = $100,000 ÷ 1,500,000 = 6.67%

Return on Equity

Formula: *ROE = Cash flow ÷ Equity*

Example: An investment property generates a cash flow of $100,000. The owner has $500,000 equity in the property. What is the owner's return on equity?

ROE = $100,000 ÷ 500,000 = 20%

Real Estate Taxation

Converting Mill Rates

Definition: 1 mill = $.001; a mill rate of 1 mill per $1,000 = .1%; a 1% tax rate = 10 mills

Formula: *Tax = (Taxable value ÷ 1000) x Mill rate*

Example: A tax rate on a house with a $200,000 taxable value is 7 mills per thousand dollars of assessed valuation. What is the tax?

Tax = ($200,000 ÷ 1,000) x 7 mills = $1,400

Tax Base

    Formula: *Tax base = Assessed valuations – Exemptions*

    Example: A town has a total assessed valuation of $20,000,000 and exemptions of $4,000,000. What is the tax base?

                       $20,000,000 - 4,000,000 = $16,000,000

Tax Rate, Base, and Requirement

    Formulas: *Tax rate = Tax requirement ÷ Tax base*

                    Tax base = Tax requirement ÷ Tax rate

                    Tax requirement = Tax base x Rate

    Example: A town has a tax base of $160,000,000 and a budget of $8,000,000. What is the tax rate?

                    Tax rate = ($8,000,000 ÷ 160,000,000) = .05, or 5%, or 50 mills

Special Assessments

    Formula: *Special assessment = Total special assessment cost x Homeowner's share*

    Example: A homeowner owns 100' of an 800' seawall that must be repaired. The total assessment will be $80,000. What is the homeowner's assessment?

         1.   Homeowner's share = 100' ÷ 800' = .125, or 12.5%

         2.   Special assessment = $80,000 x 12.5% = $10,000

Commissions

Commission Splits

    Formulas: *Total commission = Sale price x Commission rate*

                    Co-brokerage split = Total commission x Co-brokerage percent

                    Agent split = Co-brokerage split x Agent percent

                    Broker split = Co-brokerage split - Agent split

    Example: A $300,000 property sells at a 7% commission with a 50-50 co-brokerage split and a 60% agent split with her broker. What are total, co-brokerage, agent's, and broker's commissions?

Total commission = $300,000 x .07 = $21,000

Co-brokerage splits = $300,000 x .07 x .50 = $10,500

Agent split = $10,500 x .60 = $6,300

Agent's broker's split = $10.500 - 6,300 = $4,200

Seller's Net

Formula: *Seller's net = Sale Price - (sale price x commission) - Other closing costs - Loan balance*

Example: A home sells for $260,000 and has a loan balance of $200,000 at closing. The commission is 7% and other closing costs are $2,000. What is the seller's net?

Seller's net = ($260,000 - (260,000 x .07) - 2,000 - 200,000) = $39,800

Price to Net an Amount

Formula: *Sale Price = (Desired net + Closing costs + Loan payoff)) (1 - Commission rate)*

Example: A homeseller wants to net $50,000. The commission is 7%, the loan payoff is $150,000, and closing costs are $4,000. What must the price be?

Sale price = ($50,000 + 4,000 + 150,000) ÷ .93 = $219,355

Closing Costs, Prorations

30-Day 12-Month Method

Formulas: *Monthly amount = Annual amount / 12*

Daily amount = Monthly amount / 30

Proration = (Monthly amount multiplied by the # months) + (Daily amount multiplied by the # days)

Example: An annual tax bill is $1,800. Closing is on April 10. What is the seller's share of the taxes?

1.   Monthly amount = ($1,800 ÷ 12) = $150; no. of months = 3

2.   Daily amount = ($150 ÷ 30) = $5.00; no. of days = 10

3.   Proration = ($150 x 3) + ($5 x 10) = ($450 + 50) = $500 seller's share

365-Day Method

Formula: *Daily amount = (Annual amount ÷ 365) or (Monthly amount ÷ Length of month)*

Proration = Daily amount multiplied by the # days

Example: An annual tax bill is $1,800. Closing is on April 10. What is the seller's share of the taxes?

1. Daily amount = ($1,800 ÷ 365) = $4.93

2. Jan 1 thru April 10 = (31 + 28 + 31 + 10) days, or 100 days

3. Proration = $4.93 x 100 days = $493 seller's share

Income Received in Advance (Rent)

Logic: *Credit buyer and debit seller for buyer's share*

Example: Seller receives $1,000 rent. The month is ¾ over.

1. Buyer's share is ($1,000 x 25%) = $250

2. Credit buyer / debit seller $250.

Expenses paid in Arrears (Tax)

Logic: *Credit buyer and debit seller for seller's share*

Example: Buyer will pay $1,000 taxes. The year is ¾ over.

1. Buyer's share is ($1,000 x 25%) = $250

2. Credit buyer / debit seller $750.

Insurance Coverage

Recovery with Co-Insurance Clauses

Formula: Recovery = (Damage claim) x (Percent replacement cost covered ÷ Minimum coverage requirement)

Example: An owner insures a home for $500,000. Replacement cost is $750,000. A co-insurance clause requires coverage of 80% of replacement cost to avoid penalty. Fire destroys the house. What can the owner recover from the insurer?

Claim recovery = $750,000 x (67% cost covered ÷ 80% required) = $628,125

Section III: Alabama Laws & Rules

The following key point reviews are a condensation of Alabama statutes and rules impacting or relevant to real estate licensure. The primary sources are Section 34-27 of Articles 1, 2, 4, and 5 of the Alabama Real Estate Law of 1951 and Chapter 790-X-1, 2, and 3 of the Alabama Real Estate Commission Rules.

Table of Contents

Part I: The Alabama Regulatory Environment

The Real Estate Commission

Commission Key Characteristics

- created in 1927 by Legislative Act 1927
- purpose is to serve and protect public via licensing and regulation
- enforces license laws
- creates and enforces its own rules to regulate real estate professionals
- nine commissioners appointed by governor with consent of Senate
- one commissioner cannot be member of real estate industry or trade association

Commission Structure

- 9 members
- 7 members

  - 10 years Alabama residents and citizens
  - 10 years licensed real estate broker or salesperson
  - each from different US Congressional District

- 1 African-American member
  - 10 years Alabama resident and citizen
  - resident of any congressional district in state
  - 10 years licensed real estate broker or salesperson
  - subsequent African-American members to be from different congressional districts

- 1 consumer member
  - serving no more than 2 consecutive terms
  - from any congressional district in state
  - subsequent consumer members to be from different congressional districts
  - at least 21 years old
  - 10 years Alabama resident and citizen
  - registered Alabama voter
  - no felony convictions
  - real property owner
  - not licensed real estate broker or salesperson for past 10 years
  - not related by blood or marriage or employed by real estate licensee
  - cannot have any federal or state license law violation convictions
  - serve 5-year staggered terms
  - serve no more than 2 consecutive terms
  - remain in office until successor appointed and confirmed
  - terms expire September 30 of 5th year of term
  - new chairperson selected with each new member appointment
  - quorum to conduct business is 5 members

Commission Functions

- license and regulate practice of real estate
- prescribe rules
- enforce laws
- investigate and prosecute complaints
- establish Recovery Fund
- administer internal operations

- may employ executive director, assistant executive director, and other staff
- may use advisory committees, working groups, and task forces
- must adopt seal for authenticating records and documents
- no liability for damages resulting from duties as commissioner

Definitions

- **broker** – person licensed as broker under Articles 1 and 2 of Alabama Real Estate License Law
- **qualifying (principal) broker** – licensed broker responsible for supervising real estate acts of all entities and licensees associated with a company or proprietorship
- **salesperson** – person licensed as salesperson under Articles 1 and 2 of Alabama Real Estate License Law
- **company** – sole proprietorship, corporation, partnership, branch office, or lawful business organization licensed under Articles 1 and 2 of Alabama Real Estate License Law to conduct real estate transactions
- **commission** –fee paid to broker or salesperson in relation to real estate transactions
- **engagement** – contractual relationship between qualifying broker and associate broker or salesperson licensed under that qualifying broker
- **license period** – October 1 of an even-numbered year to September 30 two years later
- **expired license** – license not renewed by license period deadline or one placed on inactive status; may still be renewed within prescribed time frame
- **lapsed license** – no longer valid license; may not be renewed so individual must meet all licensure requirements of first-time applicant
- **place of business** – designated office for conducting business; not to be used as living space; must have separate business phone; must be identified as real estate office; must be space for keeping business records and files
- **team** – two or more licensees at a real estate company who work together to provide services requiring a license and are a distinct entity

Exemptions

- no real estate license required for

  - property owner selling or leasing own property or owned by spouse, child, or parent
  - attorney performing legal work
  - unpaid power of attorney executing real estate transaction
  - trustee, receiver, administrator, executor, or guardian or acting under court order or trust
  - public officer performing official duties
  - broker's clerical assistant not showing properties
  - off-site condominium manager
  - apartment manager
  - licensed time-share seller
  - sale, lease, or transfer of cemetery lots

Revenue Fund

- money collected by Commission to be deposited into State Treasury and credited to Real Estate Commission Revenue Fund; not to include $30 recovery fund fee
- revenue funds disbursed by State Comptroller as directed by Commission Executive Director
- proportionate share of license fees and research and education fees to be reserved in Real Estate Commission Proportionate Fund to be disbursed quarterly for Real Estate Research and Education Center
- monies not allocated to Real Estate Research and Education Center are used for Commission expenses
- investment interest and income to be deposited into revenue fund for Commission expenses
- Commission expenses not to exceed total funds collected or amount appropriated by legislature
- withdrawn or disbursed funds must be budgeted and allotted in accordance with Alabama real estate law
- monies remaining in revenue fund at end of fiscal year transfer to following year

Disciplinary Actions and Process

Standards

- Alabama law sets forth actions and conduct which violate real estate laws and rules.
- Offended parties may file complaint with Commission against violator

Complaints

- Commission investigates complaints against licensees
- investigator works with Attorney General to determine probable cause
- probable cause determination results in filing of formal complaint
- formal complaints can be filed based on third party complaint or Commission's initiative
- formal complaint must include

  - name of accused
  - legal authority and jurisdiction
  - type and issuance date of accused's license
  - specific law and/or rule violated
  - brief description of accused's acts or omissions

- Commission

  - serves copy of complaint to accused by certified mail
  - notifies accused's qualifying broker in writing
  - schedules hearing and provides accused with 15-day notice
  - notifies complainant, licensee, and qualifying broker of complaint determination
  - notifies applicant of refusal to issue license
  - gives refused license applicant 15 days to request hearing

Hearings

- all accused have right to a hearing
- may be heard in person or by counsel, offer testimony, question witnesses
- accused may plead guilty and receive disciplinary action
- accuser may settle or withdraw complaint
- Commission may hold hearing regardless of settlement
- Commission may subpoena witnesses, records, and documents
- party subpoenaing witnesses to pay witness expenses
- Commission evaluates evidence and testimony to determine violation
- license law violations are Class A misdemeanors

Disciplinary Actions and Penalties

- Alabama Real Estate Commission (AREC) jurisdiction includes licensees and persons practicing without a license
- guilty determination results in

  - license revocation or suspension and/or
  - fine of $100 to $5,000
  - reprimand of licensee
  - possible required continuing education
  - possible restitution payments

- revocation or suspension may be stayed until education completed or restitution paid
- AREC may take action through attorney general
- Commission may issue cease and desist order to unlicensed violators after finding of probable cause
- order is final 15 days after service unless hearing requested
- if guilty verdict, violator can be fined for each violation
- unpaid fines enforceable in appropriate court

Rehearing

- accused may file application for rehearing if he or she disagrees with hearing finding
- must specify grounds for rehearing and file within 30 days of hearing finding
- AREC to schedule rehearing, enter order without hearing, or grant or deny application, all within 30 days of receiving application
- granted rehearing to be held as soon as practicable
- rehearing conducted by hearing officer appointed by AREC

Appeals

- AREC findings final unless appeal filed within 30 days of final order
- AREC to file case record within 30 days of service of appeal notice
- appellant to file complaint explaining appealed issues within 30 days of appeal being filed
- appeal conducted by court with no jury
- party losing the appeal pays cost of appeal

Recovery Fund

Purpose of the Fund

- to assist aggrieved party in recovering actual or compensatory damages not paid by licensee when ordered to do so
- damages to have been sustained in Alabama
- damages must be result of broker or salesperson's behavior in violation of license law or AREC rules
- no interest or court costs paid from Fund

Payment into the Fund

- funded by $30 fee from each license applicant in addition to any other fee
- fee refunded if no license issued
- only required to pay fee once at application for license unless Fund's balance is below required minimum
- monies deposited into state treasury and held in trust by AREC
- funds may be invested under Alabama law
- investment interest or income deposited into Revenue Fund with half of funds transferred to Real Estate Research and Education
- funds transferred not to reduce recovery fund's balance below $600,000

Payment from the Fund

- no payment for acts or omissions of

  - licensee working on the behalf of him/herself, a child, spouse, or parent; including when any of these has an interest in or wants to acquire subject property
  - inactive licensee

- - corporation, branch office, partnership except for its licensees as individuals
  - licensee while marketing or developing a time-share project

- total payments per licensee - $50,000
- total payments for multiple claims on same transaction - $25,000
- payments only to licensee or bonding company as principal party to transaction
- AREC may defend accused licensee or AREC itself, may settle claim, or may take action of review
- with court judgment against licensee

  - aggrieved may obtain court order for payment from Fund
  - only after all proceedings are done and
  - with 10-day written notice

- claimant must show

  - not spouse, child, or parent of debtor or personal representative
  - judgment has been obtained
  - balance due on judgment
  - joined any bonding companies who issued corporate surety bonds to debtor
  - amount recovered from debtor or others was applied to damages awarded by court

- if requirements met, court will issue court order for payment from Fund
- payments from Fund can result in termination of all licenses for debtor

Minimum Fund Balance

- AREC to collect $30 fee per license to restore balance that drops below $500,000
- fee is in addition to original Recovery Fund fee paid
- inactive licenses not required to pay additional fee until reactivated

Exemptions

- original license issued on inactive status – no fee until activated
- activation only valid after fees paid

Part II: Alabama Licensing Regulation

Licensing Requirements

Who Must Be Licensed

- Alabama license law specifies which activities require a license and how to obtain a license
- any person, sole proprietorship, partnership, corporation, branch office, or legal business organization practicing real estate for compensation must be licensed as broker or salesperson
- license must be on active status to practice

Activities Requiring a License

- in regard to any real estate located in Alabama

    o selling
    o buying
    o leasing or renting
    o exchanging or trading
    o optioning
    o negotiating
    o listing
    o locating
    o auctioning
    o procuring prospects

- presenting oneself as able to perform any of these acts

Qualifications for a Salesperson's License

- **personal requirements**

    o trustworthy and competent to safeguard public interest
    o at least 19 years old
    o US citizen or legally present in US or alien with permanent resident status
    o resident of any US state
    o no rejection or revocation of license or application in any state in past 2 years for grounds other than failing license exam
    o to obtain license, revoked licensees to meet all requirements for original license and be AREC approved

- **nonresident applicants**

    o no current license in other state
        ▪ with current license in other state, must apply for reciprocal license in Alabama
    o apply on AREC prescribed form
    o specify office where registered
    o show proof of
        ▪ high school graduation or equivalent
        ▪ 60-hour coursework completion
        ▪ other AREC requirements
    o nonresident for original license or reciprocal license to sign affidavit agreeing
        ▪ AREC jurisdiction over activities
        ▪ same investigations and discipline as Alabama licensees
        ▪ applicable civil actions against nonresident licensee

- AREC Executive Director or Assistant Executive Director to be served as nonresident's agent
- nonresident bound by all Alabama license laws

- **criminal background**

  - felony or moral turpitude crime conviction or guilty plea or nolo contendere may result in AREC rejection
  - Application of Determination of Licensing Eligibility used for guilty applicant
  - AREC to review conviction to determine licensure eligibility
  - state and national criminal history checks required for all applicants
  - AREC uses history to determine licensure qualifications and fitness
  - applicant to pay cost of history check

- **fingerprints**

  - submitted on approved card
  - taken by authorized official at law enforcement agency
  - card filled out and signed by applicant and official taking prints
  - card to contain quality prints following examples on back of card
  - criminal history review application to be submitted with fingerprints
  - fingerprint card examined by official taking prints to assure completion and adequacy of prints
  - criminal background and fingerprints requirements same for both salesperson and broker applicants

- **education requirements**

  - high school graduate or equivalent
  - completion of pre-license coursework

- **test requirements**

  - take and pass written examination
  - exam given by AREC or contracted testing agency (currently Pearson Vue)

Documentation Required for Application

- **proof of age**

  - valid driver's license
  - US passport
  - birth certificate
  - other documentation required by AREC

- **proof of US citizenship, permanent residency, legal presence status**

  - driver's license
  - non-driver identification
  - green card
  - US visa
  - other documentation required by AREC

- **proof of Alabama state residency**

  - driver's license
  - car tag receipt
  - property deed
  - residential lease agreement

- property tax bill
- voter's registration card
- other documentation required by AREC

- **proof of US high school completion**

  - high school diploma
  - high school transcript with graduation date
  - GED certificate
  - college diploma
  - college transcript with completion of 2 full terms
  - DD-214 showing high school completion
  - home schooled in US provide notarized transcript and letter of recommendation from home school group leader
  - no home school diplomas accepted

- **proof of high school completion outside US**

  - US college transcript showing high school education sufficient for college admittance
  - Document-by-Document Evaluation Report verifying foreign education equivalent to US education

- nonresidents with Alabama license who become residents to submit change of address to AREC within 10 days of residency
- nonresidents applying for reciprocal license to submit proof of licensure in resident state

Temporary Licensure

- to be obtained prior to original (permanent) license
- complete 60-hour pre-license course within 1 year of start date or start over
- pass state exam within 6 months of completing pre-license course or retake course
- find Alabama supervising qualifying broker within 90 days of passing exam
- qualifying broker to sign sworn statement of accepting responsibility for new licensee and of applicant's honesty, trustworthiness, and good reputation
- pay $30 Recovery Fund fee
- meet all other requirements
- license issued for 1 year
- temporary license required for enrollment into post-license course

Post-License Education

- complete 30-hour post-license course within 12 months of temporary licensure
- apply for original license
- pay all associated application fees
- course and application for license not completed within first 6 months of temporary licensure results in license placed on inactive status
- inactive status licenses have remaining 6 months of temporary licensure to complete course and application
- course and application not completed within 12 months results in license expiring and lapsing
- temporary licenses not renewable

Original Licensure

- complete post-license course and apply for original license on or before temporary license expiration date
- submit application, appropriate fees, and proof of post-license course completion to AREC on or before midnight on last day of month 1 year from temporary license issuance

- Recovery Fund fee paid with temporary license application, no need to pay again for original license

License Renewal

- must be renewed to remain current
- pay renewal fee
- complete continuing education
- renewal dates

    - license period 2 years, ending in even numbered years
    - license expires at midnight on September 30 of final year of license period
    - renewals due by August 31 of final year
    - renewals between September 1 and 30 charged late renewal penalty
    - not renewed by September 30 expires and placed on inactive status on October 1
    - renewed in even numbered year, regardless when issued
    - expired licenses can be renewed within 12 months of expiration
    - not renewed in 12 months results in license lapse
    - no correspondence from AREC after lapse
    - AREC may extend renewal date in cases of hardship with payment of renewal fees and penalties

- continuing education

    - complete 15 hours by September 30 of final year of license period
    - failure to complete continuing education results in license becoming inactive on October 1
        - inactive licensees required to follow reactivation procedures
        - inactive licensees not allowed to perform real estate activities
    - to include 3 hours of Risk Management: Initial Contact to Accepted Offer.
    - to include 12 hours of AREC-approved electives of core real estate courses, each at least 3 hours of instruction
    - courses taken in other states given elective credit when documentation submitted to AREC
    - more than 15 hours of course work, excess hours not carried over to subsequent license period
    - service as member of state legislature substitutes for 15 hours of continuing education
    - no continuing education required for first time renewal when licensed less than 1 year
    - post-license course work applied as continuing education for first license period
    - brokers and associate brokers must complete the required broker CE course and 9 hours of elective courses

- exemptions from continuing education

    - 65-year-old licensees with 10 years of licensure prior to September 30, 2000
    - inactive licensees while on inactive status; must complete to reactivate

Reciprocal License

- must hold license in qualifying state other than Alabama
- other state license must not be reciprocal or nonresident license
- other state license must be active or inactive
- qualifying state is where applicant completed pre-license course and passed national and state law exam
- must provide Certificate of Licensure issued within 120 days of application from state where licensed
- must complete 6 hours of course work in Alabama and pass state exam with 70% score
- must pass exam within 6 months of completing course work or retake course
- must then apply for reciprocal license and pay fees, including recovery fund fee
- reciprocal licensee to complete Alabama continuing education or prove other state license is active
- reciprocal license continuing education

- may complete 15 hours of Alabama course work or submit certification of licensure from state where licensed
- reciprocal licensees with Alabama license less than 1 year not required to complete continuing education

Co-brokering

- principal brokers licensed in other states to sign written co-brokerage agreement with Alabama qualifying broker to practice real estate in Alabama
- agreement to specify each parcel of property co-broker will handle, financial terms of agreement, and other material terms
- Alabama qualifying broker to confirm nonresident is a licensed principal broker prior to signing lease
- copy of agreement to be filed with AREC within 10 days of execution
- limited to three transactions per calendar year and to transactions totaling less than $50 million per year.
- Alabama qualifying broker to require listing or joint listing of involved property and a specification of all material terms, including financial terms
- Alabama qualifying broker to supervise property showings and negotiations
- earnest money to be held in escrow by Alabama broker unless seller and buyer agree in writing to other arrangement
- advertising to be in name of Alabama qualifying broker
- Alabama broker liable for co-broker's actions under agreement
- co-broker agrees to abide by Alabama laws and rules
- co-broker agrees civil action can be brought against him/her when applicable
- complaints against the licensed out-of-state principal broker will be forwarded to that licensee's state of licensure

License Status

Definition of a Licensee

- any real estate broker, salesperson, or company licensed as such under Alabama license law
- salespersons licensed under and work under supervision of qualifying broker
- brokers either associate brokers or qualifying brokers
- company is any sole proprietorship, corporation, partnership, branch office, or lawfully constituted business organization which is licensed as a company under Alabama license law
- broker or salesperson license registered to specific real estate office and issued to and held by person who meets requirements of Alabama license law

Transfer of License

- must give AREC notice in writing of intent to transfer and send copy to current qualifying broker
- must pay transfer fee
- new qualifying broker must file request for transfer with AREC with statement assuming liability for the transferred licensee
- licensee to mail license by certified or registered mail with return receipt requested to AREC with forms, certificates, and fees
- AREC issues new license certificate for remainder of term if transfer forms and fees submitted within 10 days after receipt of notice of transfer
- forms and fees not received within 10 days results in transfer being null and void and notice of incomplete transfer
- current qualifying broker to remain responsible for licensee's actions if transfer not complete

Evidence of Transfer

- mail receipt from sending transfer documents and fee to AREC used as evidence of transfer
- mailing date on receipt used as effective transfer date

Definition of Inactive License

- restricts licensee from performing real estate activities requiring license
- held at AREC office until activated to legally engage in real estate acts
- inactive when

  - held by AREC due to legal action, AREC order, or licensee request
  - issued to inactive at licensee's request
  - still renewable but not renewed by deadline
  - post-license education not completed and original license not applied for within first 6 months of temporary licensure; inactive for second 6 months of temporary licensure

Recovery Fund Fee Exemption

- no recovery fund fee required when license issued on inactive status
- fee to be paid prior to reactivating license
- any supplemental fee to be paid prior to reactivating license

Reactivation of Inactive License

- apply to AREC and pay fee
- complete continuing education for current license period prior to application
- complete continuing education for renewal for next license period by renewal deadline

Return of License

- to stop licensee from doing business in company's name

  - notify AREC
  - notify licensee
  - return license to AREC

Part III: Alabama Brokerage Regulation

Broker and Company Licenses

Broker Licenses

- must be registered to specific real estate office under qualifying broker
- personal requirements

  o US citizen, permanent resident alien, or legally present in US
  o at least 19 years old
  o high school graduate or equivalent
  o resident of any US state
  o no felony or moral turpitude crime conviction
  o no real estate license application rejection or license revocation in past 2 years

- provide same documentation as required for salesperson license
- criminal background

  o submit Application for Determination of Licensing Eligibility form to AREC if felony or moral turpitude conviction
  o both state and national criminal history checks required
  o submit fingerprints on approved card
  o AREC to determine fitness of applicant
  o applicant to pay cost of criminal history check

- must hold salesperson license in any state for 2 of previous 3 years prior to application for broker license
- submit proof of salesperson licensure to AREC with broker application
- complete 60-hour broker pre-license course
- pay and pass national and state licensure exam with 70% score within 6 months of course completion
- salesperson's license terminates when broker license issued
- salesperson's license certificate to be returned to AREC for broker license to be issued
- broker applicant to maintain place of business

Company and Branch Office Licenses

- any sole proprietorship, corporation, partnership, branch office, or lawfully constituted business organization
- corporations, LLCs, and sole proprietorships most common
- every qualifying broker and place of business to have company license
- qualifying broker to apply for license on approved form
- qualifying broker to be officer, partner, or employee of company
- applicant to maintain place of business
- multiple places of business require license for each location
- requirements

  o application to include location and qualifying broker name
  o each office under qualifying broker licensed at that address
  o qualifying broker serves only one location
  o branch and main company qualifying brokers share responsibility for actions at branch office
- activities to be performed under licensed company name and qualifying broker
- only qualifying broker approved activities allowed
- company license expires at midnight on September 30 of final year of license period
- individuals licensed under the company may work out of any company office

Responsibilities of Qualifying Broker

- qualifying broker to be Alabama-licensed broker with real estate as primary business
- responsible for all activities of company
- must supervise registered broker activities full time
- must assure all transactions comply with Alabama license law and AREC rules
- qualifying broker held responsible for violations and injuries to third parties in addition to the violating licensee's liability
- must display all current licenses publicly at place of business
- no employer-employee relationship established by these responsibilities

Termination of Qualifying Broker Status

- notify licensee and AREC in writing of desire to terminate status as qualifying broker for licensee
- notify company and AREC of desire to terminate status as qualifying broker for company
- return licensee's license certificate to AREC
- AREC to issue new certificate registered to new qualifying broker
- no licensed-required acts to be performed until new qualifying broker licensed

Qualifying Broker for More Than One Company

- serve only one company unless

  - all companies agree in writing
  - written consent filed with AREC
  - all businesses share the same company address

Temporary Qualifying Broker

- company officer, member, or salesperson to apply for temporary qualifying broker license within 30 days of death or disability of previous qualifying broker
- must be broker or have been salesperson for at least 1 year
- company to operate under temporary qualifying broker no longer than 6 months from the date the commission issues the temporary qualifying broker license
- must designate fully licensed broker as qualifying broker within same 6 months
- no designation results in company license and all licenses under the company being placed on inactive status

Place of Business

- licensees must maintain place of business identified with name of company on exterior sign, if allowed, or inside office if exterior sign not allowed
- licensees located within city limits are to operate from office also located in city limits
- office to be separate space with business phone and sign
- business records to be kept in place of business
- licensees located in rural areas may operate from home office used specifically for real estate business and not living purposes
- home office to be used by only one broker
- home office to have separate business phone, separate entrance, and sign

Teams

- defined as two or more licensees in the same company who work together to provide services and are a distinct group
- the qualifying broker designates the team leader but cannot delegate any qualifying broker duties to that person

- a team does not need to be licensed or registered as a separate business organization with the commission
- the team leader must provide a list of team members to the qualifying broker
- licensees may only be a member of one team

Trust Funds

Purpose

- escrow account to hold funds belonging to others
- set up by qualifying broker at federally insured bank in Alabama
- each client's funds insured up to $250,000
- keeps clients' money separate from broker's money
- account accessible only by client or broker for use in real estate transaction

Trust Funds Defined

- all funds belonging to or being held for others must be deposited into trust account
- include earnest money, security deposits, rent payments, etc. related to contract for sale, lease, or management of property
- include US currency, checks, notes, other forms of money, other items of value
- cash to be deposited immediately
- checks may be held before depositing if purchase offer designates length of time or event to occur before depositing
- if no time specified, check deposited when offer becomes contract
- salesperson or broker to submit all funds to qualifying broker for deposit

Qualifying Broker Trust Fund Responsibilities

- responsible for depositing and holding trust funds
- qualifying broker is trustee for account
- any of multiple qualifying brokers for one purchase contract to deposit and hold funds
- first broker to account for and transfer trust funds to be held by secondary qualifying broker
- qualifying broker providing trust fund services to client is responsible to public and AREC for funds
- at request of AREC, qualifying broker to account for any funds being held

Disbursement of Trust Funds

- qualifying broker to disburse funds within 7 days of transaction completion
- no transaction completion or if disagreement over who receives funds, qualifying broker to disburse funds only with court order or written agreement signed by all parties
- qualifying broker can deposit funds with appropriate court under rules of interpleader or other lawful procedure
- rules of interpleader remove qualifying broker as disburser and force disagreeing parties to litigate disbursement
- qualifying broker to then deposit disputed funds with court who decides who is entitled to funds
- qualifying broker thus released from disbursement liability

Trust Fund Management

- **proper accounting**

  - law defines handling of trust funds
  - penalties exist for mishandling funds

- law requires licensee to account for or remit money belonging to others
- law requires qualifying broker to deposit and account for funds held for others in trust account

- **commingling**

  - trust accounts to be separate from broker's personal or business accounts
  - trust accounts can hold funds belonging to multiple clients but no broker funds
  - no separation of broker and client funds is commingling; violation of law
  - some broker funds allowed in trust account to cover service fees
  - qualifying broker can lose license for using trust funds for personal or business expenses
  - qualifying broker responsible for any licensee's commingling, embezzling, and conversion of client's funds

- **violations and discipline**

  - reported trust fund violations investigated by AREC
  - AREC can issue subpoenas and hear testimony of witnesses
  - probable cause finding results in formal complaint and hearing
  - guilty determination results in imposition of
    - license suspension or revocation and/or fine
    - licensee reprimand
  - possible license suspension or revocation until approved continuing education completed and/or restitution paid
  - possible stay of license suspension or revocation until continuing education completed and/or restitution paid

Escrow Account Reconciliation

- qualifying broker to periodically reconcile broker's records with bank trust fund records
- all deposits and disbursements to be shown in broker's records and bank statements with discrepancies resolved
- trust fund records to be kept for 3 years
- records to show who funds belong to, date deposited, date withdrawn or disbursed, other pertinent information
- AREC reconciliation suggestions

  - tape canceled checks to check stub in checkbook
  - list pending contracts with amount of earnest money, cross off as transaction closes and funds are refunded
  - deduct bank services charges prior to paying commission to prevent overdrafts
  - separate pending and closed contracts
  - separate rental property accounts from property sales accounts

- keep written receipts for funds received
- monthly reconciliation recommended but not required by law
- balance bank statement with broker account records when statement received
- separate security deposit account and rent account recommended
- license to record deposits, tenants' names, property address, owner's name, deposit amount, and deposit date
- rent accounts to include record of payments to property owner, management company, and maintenance invoices

Estimated Closing Statement

Purposes of Estimated Costing

- real estate closing is transfer of property title from seller to buyer according to sales contract

- closing costs determined by sales contract, local tradition and custom, type of financing, and local, state, and federal laws
- closing statements detail final costs of transferring ownership
- estimated closing statement approximates closing costs and is to be provided to seller and buyer at offer or counteroffer
- estimated closing statements protect against mortgage fraud by eliminating unexpected costs charged by mortgage lender at closing
- to provide approximate transaction costs so each party informed and prepared
- statement provided to buyer at time of written offer
- statement provided to seller at time of offer presentation
- must contain accurate and complete estimates of buyer's and seller's costs
- buyer and seller acknowledge receipt of statements by signing both estimated and actual statements
- consumer protected by TILA (Truth in Lending Act), RESPA (Real Estate Settlement Procedures Act), and TRID (TILA-RESPA Integrated Disclosure)

    o TRID: loan estimate to be provided to borrower by lender within 3 business days of application for loan
    o TRID: closing disclosure to be provided to borrower 3 days prior to closing on mortgage loan

- differences in disclosures

    o estimated closing statement provided at time of offer by licensee to buyer and seller outlining transaction closing costs
    o loan estimate and closing disclosure provided by lender to borrower outlining loan costs; estimate provided within 3 business days of loan application; disclosure provided 3 days prior to closing
    o all mandated by Alabama law

Estimated Closing Expenditures

- estimated closing statement includes debits (charges) and credits for seller and buyer due at closing
- seller debits

    o real estate commission
    o applicable excise taxes
    o home repairs
    o prorated property taxes
    o title clearing
    o loans and liens against property

- seller credits

    o property purchase price
    o prorated prepaid utilities
    o prorated prepaid property taxes

- buyer debits

    o property purchase price
    o title insurance
    o mortgage loan origination fee
    o home inspection
    o property surveys
    o prorated prepaid utilities

- buyer credits

  - earnest money deposit
  - cash down payment
  - home repairs not paid by seller

Disclosure to Consumer

- per RESPA

  - buyer to be informed about closing costs
  - no inflation of closing costs for buyer
  - lender to disclose closing costs to borrower
  - lender prohibited from demanding excessive deposits for escrow accounts
  - seller and buyer to be given estimated closing statement at time of offer so no surprises at closing

- failure to disclose costs is violation of Alabama license law and RESPA
- law violation results in AREC investigation and possible license suspension or revocation, fine, or reprimand for each guilty verdict and possible continuing education and/or restitution

Advertising

Guidelines and Rules

- licensees must be honest
- licensees prohibited from false promises
- licensees prohibited from flagrant misrepresentation
- licensees prohibited from deceiving public
- licensees must advertise self as licensed broker or salesperson

Advertising with an Interest (Licensee Owns The Property)

- property owners managing, leasing, selling or advertising own property need not be licensed
- licensee advertising such property to disclose interest in property in writing to all involved parties
- licensee advertising such property to "timely" disclose real estate licensure; no definitive timeframe within law
- licensee intending to purchase property being sold by licensee's company to disclose intention and licensure to seller or seller's agent

Signage

- licensees have right to use signage on property to advertise sale, lease, or transfer
- no fee or tax on signage allowed by Alabama
- reasonable restrictions on size, height, and sign placement allowed by local, county, and city governments

Team Advertising

- include the name of at least one team member and the name of the company where the licensee is licensed
- include the term "team" or "group" in the team name
- receive the qualifying broker's written permission to include the team name

Recordkeeping

Retention Requirements

- estimated closing statements and actual closing statements to be retained in broker's files
- buyer, seller agents to retain statements signed by buyer & seller in qualifying broker's files
- cooperating brokers not required to maintain both buyer and seller's statements
- 3-year record retention recommended but not required

Part IV: Alabama Agency

Real Estate Consumer's Agency and Disclosure Act (RECAD)

Definitions

- **agency agreement** – written brokerage agreement between company and client creating fiduciary relationship
- **brokerage agreement** – written agreement between a company and consumer including terms, services provided, and any compensation to be paid to or through the company; includes agency and transaction facilitator agreements
- **brokerage service** – licensee services including activities requiring licensure; no rental or property management included
- **buyer's agreement** – agreement between a real estate company and a person buying real estate that the company will assist the person with the purchase as either a fiduciary or as a non-fiduciary
- **consumer** – person who gets information, advice, or services from licensee
- **client** – buyer or seller with agency agreement with broker
- **customer** – person getting brokerage services with no agency agreement
- **dual agency** –a licensee represents both buyer and seller after all of the parties have signed a consent agreement
- **fiduciary duties** – owed to client by agency agreement and performed under obligation and trust
- **informed consent** – consumer's agreement based on full disclosure needed to choose brokerage services
- **listing agreement** – agreement between a real estate company and a property owner selling real estate that the company will assist the property owner with the sale as either a fiduciary or as a non-fiduciary.
- **material fact** – fact of significance affecting a party's decision to enter into contract
- **single agent** – licensee representing only one party in transaction through a signed agency agreement
- **transaction facilitator** – licensee helping parties in transaction without being agent, fiduciary, or advocate for the parties' interests

Protection to the Consumer

- Real Estate Consumers Agency and Disclosure Act (RECAD) sets roles and duties of real estate brokers
- requires consumers to be informed of types of services available
- requires use of Real Estate Brokerage Services Disclosure form
- consumers not required to sign form but should acknowledge receiving it
- licensees to note on form consumer refusal to sign form
- form includes types of services and agency relationships available

Representing the Seller and/or the Buyer

- no agency relationship without signed brokerage arrangement
- a signed agency agreement must be in place prior to making an offer (buyer clients) or listing a property (seller clients)
- licensee may show a property without a signed agency agreement
- licensee may represent either buyer or seller depending on services offered by brokerage company
- licensee to act for or represent client in negotiations with other parties
- licensee to put client's best interests before other party's interests
- representing buyer – to negotiate best purchase price and terms
- representing seller – to negotiate best selling price and terms
- representing both – to represent both equally and fairly while avoiding conflict

Brokerage Services Disclosure and Agency Disclosure Office Policy

When to Disclose

- per RECAD, licensee to disclose non-agency relationship and available services as soon as reasonably possible before confidential information exchanged using a Real Estate Brokerage Services Disclosure form
- consumer then decides whether or not to sign agreement and decides what service arrangement to choose
- must be provided before providing any brokerage services

Offer to Purchase Required Language

- All offers to purchase must contain a prominent disclosure clause that lists the type of agency that the listing licensee and selling licensee are providing.
- The form must be completed and initialed by the licensee.

Agency Disclosure Office Policy

- RECAD requires qualifying brokers to adopt and maintain agency disclosure office policy to set types of services to offer and accept
- office disclosure policy includes a compensation disclosure explaining how the company and the licensee will be compensated
- qualifying brokers to explain policy to licensees at least yearly
- licensees required to sign acknowledgement form for receipt of policy statement
- licensees to provide office policy disclosure to consumers
- consumers not required to sign form but should acknowledge receiving it
- licensees to note on form consumer refusal to sign form
- office policy assures licensees know what services to engage in and what services to avoid
- engaging in services not included in office policy violates the law

Non-agency Disclosure

- no agency relationship is assumed, implied, or created until written agency agreement signed
- a transaction facilitatory relationship remains in effect until an agreement is signed
- licensee to use Brokerage Services Disclosure Form to explain available services
- services disclosure to be provided at initial contact with consumer or when reasonably possible prior to the licensee disclosing any confidential information and before providing any brokerage services

Customer or Client

- difference is whether or not an agency agreement has been signed
- client has signed agreement for specific services
- customer has no signed agreement but still obtaining brokerage services
- licensee obligated to both with additional obligations to client

Brokerage Relationships Allowed by RECAD

- **transaction facilitator**

    o licensee works with one or more parties in same transaction
    o non-agent to all parties
    o provides neutral third-party services to customers with or without written agreement
    o no fiduciary services
    o reduced liability for licensee
    o no written agreement means buyers or sellers are customers, not clients
    o services work best when marketing services and real estate expertise needed but no help with negotiations needed
    o licensee to be honest to all parties, show good faith, show no favoritism to either party
    o law requires licensee to exercise reasonable care and skill, answer questions, present written offers promptly and truthfully
    o law requires licensee to keep confidentialities unless disclosure required by law
    o transaction broker to honestly answer buyer's questions about property condition and disclose any hidden defects that could impact health or safety of occupants
    o transaction broker services with written agreement must have agreement form included in office policy

- **single agency**

    o licensee represents only one party in transaction
    o represented party is client with written agreement required
    o arrangement works best when advice and negotiating help needed from professional
    o buyers new to unfamiliar area benefit from single agency
    o agent required to be loyal and faithful to client
    o exists when two or more licensees under the same qualifying broker have separate agency agreements with different parties to the same transaction

- **dual agency**

    o written, informed consent required from both parties
    o dual agency illegal in many states but allowed in Alabama with parties' written consent
    o most often used when licensee represents both buyer and seller in same transaction
    o dual agency common in larger markets with company having many listed properties
    o seller agents can show properties to buyers also represented by same company
    o licensee's primary function is to help both parties reach mutually satisfactory terms and price
    o not to show favoritism or reveal either party's confidential information to other party
    o full range of services and loyalty of single agency not offered by dual agency
    o more assistance and guidance offered than transaction facilitator arrangement
    o dual agent to inform both clients about types of services provided and information to be shared with other party
    o dual agency form to be included in office policy

Consumer's Legal Rights

- per Alabama law, consumer has right to honest and fair representation by licensee
- consumer rights included in law as licensee's obligations to both customers and clients
- Alabama mandates consumers' rights to minimum level of services

    o helping consumer negotiate
    o presenting and receiving offers
    o answering questions

Licensee Duties to Customers

- provide customer with copy of agency disclosure office policy describing brokerage services available and how the licensee and real estate company are compensated
- allow customer to ask questions about services
- per AREC, licensee to sign, date, and provide copy of Brokerage Services Disclosure form and the agency disclosure office policy
- provide services honestly and in good faith
- exercise reasonable care and skill in providing services
- keep confidential information confidential unless

  - disclosure required by law,
  - information that becomes public knowledge,
  - disclosure authorized in writing

- account for all property belonging to others that comes into licensee's possession
- make timely disclosure of

  - licensee's personal / family interest in property
  - organization or business in which licensee has personal interest

- provide any party with requested information affecting transaction unless law prohibits disclosure
- accept and present all offers, counteroffers, and addenda in timely and truthful manner
- answer questions related to transaction accurately and completely
- may also

  - provide information about properties
  - show properties
  - assist in writing offer
  - provide financing information

Agent Duties to Clients

- includes all duties owed to customers
- put best interest of client ahead of interests of any other party to transaction unless that would violate legal duties to customer or violate law or rule
- disclose to client any material information that may not be discovered by client unless disclosure would violate duties to customer
- fulfill obligations required by agency agreement and any lawful instructions given by client within agreement unless instructions would violate duties to customers
- when representing multiple clients in same transaction, fulfill same duties to all clients unless duties to one or more clients would be violated
- obtain written and informed consent of all parties in dual agency

Services Provided by Licensees

- market property
- host open houses
- review contracts
- provide advice on pricing, home inspections, and other contractual terms
- negotiate with potential buyers or sellers
- find properties for buyers
- arrange property inspections
- provide information on property values, selling prices, taxes, etc.
- provide information on financing alternatives
- assist in writing and reviewing offers, counteroffers, and acceptances
- assist with transaction closing

Misrepresentation

Material Misrepresentation

- occurs when one party makes false statements about property or transaction that affects other party's decision to enter into contract
- generally applies only to statements of fact and not to opinions or predictions
- also occurs through omission or failure to disclose material facts
- misrepresentation most common lawsuit against licensees
- failure to disclose second most common lawsuit against licensees
- honest and timely disclosures best way to avoid misrepresentation
- misrepresentation classified as innocent, negligent, and fraudulent

Negligent Misrepresentation

- failure to correct false statements or omissions
- failure to disclose significant property defects without intent

Fraudulent Misrepresentation

- purposefully hiding property defect to make the sale

Caveat Emptor and Property Disclosures

- caveat emptor means "let the buyer beware"
- implies seller has no duty to disclose issues to buyer, putting responsibility for knowing property condition on buyer
- caveat emptor applies in Alabama for sale of used residential property
- exceptions to caveat emptor doctrine applicability

  - if fiduciary relationship exists between buyer and seller, legal responsibility exists to act in best interest of other party
  - if seller knows property may pose health or safety risk to buyer
  - if buyer asks directly about specific defects
  - failure of seller to disclose under these conditions results in seller being liable for damages

- buyer discovering defects later can sue seller for misrepresentation

  - buyer needs to prove seller knew the defect posed direct threat to buyer's health or safety

- new homes not included in rule of caveat emptor because new homes have implied warranty of habitability by builder
- requirements of implied warranty to be shown by buyer

  - buyer purchased new home from seller
  - seller built home
  - home was not inhabited before buyer's purchase
  - home built by seller for purpose of sale and was sold to buyer in defective condition, impairing home's intended use
  - buyer not aware of defective condition and had no knowledge or notice to reasonably discover defect
  - defective condition decreased fair market value of home, resulting in damage to buyer

- advisable for sellers to disclose material defects to buyer, regardless of caveat emptor or implied warranty of habitability
- seller's agent should insist defects be disclosed to avoid liability for misrepresentation
- seller should complete property disclosure form and provide to buyer prior to closing
- seller not required to complete disclosure but should do so to assure all legally required disclosures are made

Broker Liability

- client not liable for broker misrepresentations unless client knows or should have known about the misrepresentation
- client can be liable if broker is repeating facts or omissions client told broker
- broker not liable for false information provided by client, customer, or another licensee unless broker knows or should have known information was false
- buyer may sue broker for physical defects discovered after closing
- honest and thorough disclosure best way to avoid liability

Listings

Required Listing Services

- per Alabama license law

  - broker to deliver and present all offers, counteroffers, and addenda
  - assist in negotiating offers, counteroffers, and addenda
  - answer questions relating to transaction

- per AREC

  - take delivery and present offers, counteroffers, and addenda to seller so agent can assist in negotiations
  - listing agent to answer all seller's questions related to transaction; be available to answer questions

Seller Options

- negotiate listing agreements to meet needs, knowledge, and experience
- have seller contact information available to receive offers directly from selling agent, relieving listing agent from related duties
- control use of property for signage, either post on property or no signs at all
- licensee to consult with qualifying broker to ensure office policies are followed when negotiating with seller exercising negotiation rights

Part V: Alabama License Law Violations

General Issues

Procedures and Penalties

- failing to comply with Alabama license law and AREC administrative rules is violation punishable by loss of license, fines, reprimands, required coursework, restitution, or any combination of these
- AREC investigates licensee actions when written complaint received
- AREC determines if violation occurred

Violations

- **Pleading Guilty or Nolo Contendere**

  o entering guilty or nolo contendere plea, or being found guilty of felony or moral turpitude crime
  o pleading nolo contendere is not an admission of guilt but agreement to accept punishment
  o moral turpitude crimes involve conduct against community standards of justice, honesty, or good morals
  o moral turpitude crimes include forgery, robbery, rape, murder, kidnapping, and aggravated assault

- **Final Money Judgment**

  o final money judgments against licensee due to act or omission while pursuing real estate business
  o final money judgment against licensee due to act or omission involving goodwill of existing real estate business
  o often result of client or customer suing licensee over damages caused by licensee's action or omission

- **Not Fulfilling Obligations to Transaction Parties**

  o failure to meet obligations to customers or clients as outlined by license law
  o often result of licensee failing to make required disclosures, failing to present offers, failing to keep confidential information confidential

- **Failure to Report Legal Action Disposition**

  o failure to notify AREC of action taken against licensee in criminal or civil real estate matter
  o notification to AREC to be made within 10 days of receiving notice of action
  o notice to AREC to be in writing, sent certified mail, include copy of summons and complaint
  o notice of criminal charge to include charge and copy of indictment or allegations

Honesty and Good Faith Issues

Honesty and Good Faith

- personal qualifications for licensure include trustworthiness and competence
- first obligation of licensees to consumers is providing services honestly and in good faith

Violations

- **Dishonesty in procuring license**

  - using fraud, misrepresentation, deceit, or material misstatement of fact to obtain license or help another party obtain license
  - must meet licensure requirements as stipulated by law
  - violations include cheating on licensure exam, making false statements on application, allowing others to use licensee's name to obtain license, etc.

- **Dishonesty in personal real estate transactions**

  - dishonesty, fraud, or misrepresentation when selling, buying, trading, or renting licensee's or licensee's family's owned real property
  - violations include failure to disclose licensee's interest in the property, failure to disclose material facts about the property, failure to be honest and trustworthy, etc.

- **Failure to disclose defects**

  - failure to disclose structural or other defects to buyer
  - material misrepresentation regarding property defects
  - licensee must know about defects for violation to occur

- **False promises to influence or induce**

  - making false promises to influence, persuade, or induce another party to sign contract or agreement
  - failure to meet obligation of honesty to customer or client
  - law requires licensee to be honest in real estate transactions

- **Misrepresentation through other agents**

  - using another licensee to make false promises or misrepresentations to influence another party to sign a contract
  - making false promises, misrepresentations, or deceptions through any form of advertising
  - law requires licensee honesty and trustworthiness in real estate transactions

- **Deceitful advertising**

  - publishing or causing to be published deceptive advertising or advertising likely to be deceptive
  - law specifically prohibits deceptive advertising

- **Inducing a party to breach a contract**

  - licensee convincing party to breach contract in order to enter into another contract
  - licensee convincing contracted party to substitute new contract to benefit licensee more than original contract

- **Dishonest dealings, bad faith, untrustworthiness**

  - performing any act related to a real estate transaction that constitutes dishonest dealings, bad faith, or untrustworthiness
  - Alabama license laws and rules emphasize honesty and good faith; trustworthiness is licensure requirement

- **Unlicensed person acting on behalf of licensee**

  - unlicensed person performing real estate acts that require licensure
  - helping, employing, or establishing association with unlicensed person performing real estate acts without a license
  - requiring or expecting unlicensed person to perform real estate acts that require licensure
  - aiding, abetting, or conspiring with individual to circumvent licensing requirements

- law requires licensure for selling, buying, leasing, renting, exchanging, or negotiating any of these in regard to real property for compensation

- **Failure to disclose intention to purchase**

  - failure of licensee to disclose own interest in purchasing or selling property
  - licensee to disclose own interest to seller or buyer and to seller or buyer's agent
  - licensee to disclose own interest in purchasing property to seller agent who is licensee's associate
  - licensee to disclose own interest in purchasing property whether planning to buy directly or indirectly

- **Failure to disclose the true terms of a contract**

  - failure of licensee to disclose true terms of real estate sale to any lender, guaranteeing agency, or other interested party
  - licensee misrepresenting terms of sale to any lender, guaranteeing agency, or other interested party
  - any failure to disclose or acts of misrepresentation are violations of required honesty and trustworthiness

- **Acting negligently or incompetently**

  - acting negligently or incompetently in performing real estate acts which require licensure
  - law defines acts that require licensure and mandates licensees to be trustworthy and competent to perform those acts

Accountability and Reporting Issues

Accountability and Reporting

- law defines actions that constitute accountability and reporting violations

Violations

- **Mishandling trust funds**

  - failure to account for money belonging to others and received by licensee
  - failure of licensee to turn received funds over to qualifying broker for deposit into trust account
  - failure to immediately deposit cash received from others into trust account
  - failure to record amount of funds received, date received, name of client submitting funds
  - law mandates how trust funds are to be handled and what must be done with funds

- **Commingling**

  - mixing or commingling others' money with licensee's personal or business funds
  - law mandates funds belonging to others be turned over to qualifying broker and deposited into trust account designated for client funds with no licensee or company funds commingled in that account

- **Failure to keep funds in a separate, federally insured account**

  - failure to deposit funds belonging to others into separate federally insured account
  - failure to use trust accounts in financial institution located in Alabama
  - Alabama law requires security of federally insured accounts
  - federally insured accounts insure each deposit for $250,000

- **Failure to distribute & keep records**
  - failure of licensee to give copies of all documents to qualifying broker
  - failure of qualifying broker to keep records for 3 years
  - failure to include names and dates in records of funds belonging to others
  - law requires documents handled or created by licensees to be copied and given to qualifying broker to keep for at least 3 years
  - documents include contracts, leases, listings, received funds records, etc.

- **Paying commission to unlicensed person**
  - associating with unlicensed person performing acts that require licensure
  - paying unlicensed person compensation for performing acts that require licensure
  - no violation – owning unlicensed business whose sole purpose is receiving payments of profits, compensation, commissions, or fees
  - unlicensed business whose sole purpose is receiving payments of profits, compensation, commissions, or fees from performing real estate acts that require licensure
  - law requires individuals or companies to be licensed to perform certain activities related to real estate transactions if compensated for the activities

- **Undisclosed or post-closing rebates**
  - paying or receiving a rebate in a real estate transaction after closing
  - paying or receiving a rebate prior to or at closing without disclosing to all involved parties
    - rebate – unearned fee, kickback, or thing of value given in connection with real estate transaction
    - definition implies rebate is something given back after transaction has occurred
  - misrepresenting or failing to disclose true terms of sale to lender, guaranteeing agency, or other interested parties
  - to be disclosed to all parties including seller, buyer, lender, or guaranteeing agency (FHA, VA, HUD)
  - permissible incentives
    - cash to property owner for listing property with licensee
    - cash to customer as incentive to purchase property
    - an item of value to customer to influence purchase of property
    - 1 month's free rent to influence customer to rent apartment
    - repair expenses to influence buyer and seller to sign sales contract or close sale

- **Lottery inducements**
  - offering free lots or conducting lotteries to influence purchase or lease of property
  - violates not only license law but also other laws
  - offering free lots as incentive to purchase or lease property without disclosing gift and value
  - transferring ownership of lots after closing of property purchase or lease
  - offering lotteries of any kind violates Alabama criminal statutes and results in criminal charges

- **Accepting commission from anyone other than qualifying broker**
  - accepting commission payments or other compensation from anyone other than qualifying broker
  - owed commission and other compensation to be paid to qualifying broker who then pays licensee

- **Failure to provide estimated closing costs**
  - failure of licensee to provide estimated closing statement to seller and buyer
  - failure to provide estimated closing statement to buyer when offer written
  - failure to provide estimated closing statement to seller when offer received
  - failure to show all involved costs and approximate amount of costs on estimated closing statement

- **Failure to submit records**

  - failure to produce documents, books, or other records when AREC demands
  - omitting any document, regardless of reason, when AREC demands all records be produced for inspection
  - both licensees and qualifying brokers subject to law
  - hiding and/or not correcting errors on documents related to real estate transactions

- **Failure to provide AREC-requested information**

  - failure to provide information to AREC upon demand or in timely manner

- **Failure to return records**

  - failure, without legal cause, to return documents to rightful owner upon request

- **Failure to report address change**

  - failure of licensee to notify AREC in writing days after business address change
  - failure of qualifying broker to return company, broker, and salesperson licenses to AREC after business address change
  - failure to pay transfer fee for each returned license
  - failure to include both old and new business address with written notification to AREC
  - failure to perform all of above within 30 days after address change
  - licenses include business address so must be reissued with new address when address changes

Representation Issues

Duties

- licensee representing clients or customers in real estate transactions to fulfill duties and obligations to parties being represented

Violations

- **Unauthorized Dual Agency**

  - failure of licensee to obtain written consent from all parties to enter into dual agency agreement
  - dual agency – all parties to consent in writing to agent representing more than one party in same transaction

- **Failure to Provide Document Copies**

  - failure to provide copies of all transaction documents to involved party in timely fashion
  - each party has right to receive copies of each document related to transaction

- **Advertising without Prominently Displaying Brokerage Name**

  - failure to identify advertiser as licensed real estate broker or salesperson
  - failure to include name or trade name of qualifying broker or company prominently on advertising
  - qualifying broker allowing licensee to advertise without prominently displaying company name or trade name or name of qualifying broker
  - in this case, "prominently" means in a larger font than that used for terms such as "for sale" or "for lease," and it must appear in an area where it will be noticeable.

- **Improper Sign Placement**

  - placing sign on property without owner's consent
  - sign to meet all advertising requirements including owner's consent to place on property

- **Taking a Net Listing**
  - accepting net listing agreement for sale of property or interest in property
    - net listing stipulates net price owner to receive for property sale with any amount over net price going to broker as commission
  - net listings prohibited in Alabama

- **Omission of Expiration Date on Listing**
  - failure to include expiration date on listing agreement
  - allowing automatic extensions of listing agreement
  - failure to put listing agreement in writing
  - failure to provide copy of listing agreement to principal (seller)

- **Failure to Present All Offers**
  - failure to present all written purchase offers to client
  - under listing agreement, licensee's obligations to seller client includes presenting all written purchase offers received

Section IV: National Practice Tests

Test 1: Rights; Interests and Estates; Ownership

1.1 Which of the following would be defined as real estate as opposed to real property?

    a. Wells, driveways, and signs on a parcel of land.
    b. Mobile homes temporarily parked on a parcel of land.
    c. Timber that has been cut and is lying on a parcel of land.
    d. Business equipment an owner or tenant has placed on a parcel of land.

1.2 Which of the following would be considered a property improvement?

    a. An alteration to land to make it more useful.
    b. An increase in the value of a property.
    c. A chicken coop permanently attached to land.
    d. A parcel of land that has passed a percolation test.

1.3 Which of the following best describes the physical boundaries of land?

    a. The surface of the earth and infinite space above the surface.
    b. The center of the earth and infinite space above the earth.
    c. The surface of the earth and all water and minerals on or below the surface to the center of the earth.
    d. The surface of the earth and the air rights above the surface to the point defined by local zoning.

1.4 The "bundle of rights" refers to a set of rights

    a. enjoyed by the owner of a property.
    b. that is synonymous with the Bill of Rights.
    c. guaranteed to citizens by the Statute of Rights.
    d. specified in a deed or land contract.

1.5 Which of the following best describes the legal concept of personal property?

    a. Any item which is acquired in a fee simple sale transaction.
    b. Any item of property that is not definable as real property.
    c. Any movable property owned by an individual, partnership, or corporation.
    d. Any item that is not a natural item affixed to the earth.

1.6 The right to encumber a property means that the owner can

    a. sell the property to an encumbered party.
    b. pledge the property as collateral for debt.
    c. lease the property.
    d. assign the bundle of rights to another.

1.7 A property owner leases 60 acres of agricultural land for a renewable period of 5 years. In the context of real estate rights, this lease represents a(n)

    a. transfer of a portion of the bundle of rights.
    b. encroachment on the bundle of rights.
    c. conveyance of the complete bundle of rights.
    d. encumbrance of the tenant's rights.

1.8　A homeowner is very upset over a drone that a neighbor flies over his house. He takes his case to court to end this possible violation of rights. Does he have a case, and on what basis?

　　a. No. The neighbor is not physically on his property.
　　b. No. The drone is in the air, so he cannot exercise any surface rights.
　　c. Yes. The owner has the right to stop encroachments.
　　d. Yes. The drones infringe on his air rights.

1.9　Littoral rights apply to which of the following?

　　a. Boatable ponds entirely contained within the boundaries of an owner's property.
　　b. Streams and rivers.
　　c. Navigable lakes, seas, and oceans.
　　d. Navigable streams and rivers.

1.10　A retired couple has just bought a retirement home with a pier on a large lake. In this case the retirees' water rights extend to

　　a. the high water mark of the body of water at the shoreline.
　　b. the low water mark of the body of water at the shoreline.
　　c. the center of the lake.
　　d. the end of the pier.

1.11　A waterfront homeowner has just died. What will become of the water rights the owner enjoyed while living in the home?

　　a. They revert to the state when the property is sold.
　　b. They are extinguished.
　　c. They are a personal right belonging to an individual owner, not attaching to the real property.
　　d. They transfer with the property when the property is sold.

1.12　Riparian rights concern which of the following bodies of water?

　　a. Lakes.
　　b. Seas and oceans.
　　c. Streams and rivers.
　　d. Navigable lakes.

1.13　Which of the following best describes a "fixture?"

　　a. Any item of personal property positioned within the boundaries of a parcel of real estate.
　　b. An item of personal property that has been converted to real property.
　　c. An item of real property temporarily placed on land for the purpose of conducting a business.
　　d. An item of personal property that has been left in one location for a period of six months.

1.14　An item may be considered personal property as opposed to real property provided that

　　a. the owner intended to remove it after a period of time.
　　b. it can be removed without altering the appearance of the structure.
　　c. it is unnecessary to the physical integrity of the structure.
　　d. the owner installed it at some time after acquiring the real property.

1.15　Two people own a house, each having an undivided equal interest. Which of the following best describes what each party owns?

　　a. Fifty percent of the physical house and the land it rests on.
　　b　One hundred percent of the home and the land.
　　c. Fifty percent of the estate consisting of the indivisible whole of the real property.
　　d. Each owns one hundred percent of the estate represented by the real property and fifty percent of the physical house and the land it rests on.

1.16   A real property interest that includes the right to possess is considered

   a. an estate in land.
   b. a leasehold estate.
   c. a fee simple estate.
   d. the bundle of rights.

1.17   The right to control land usage by zoning and eminent domain is an example of

   a. a public interest.
   b. a police interest.
   c. an encumbrance.
   d. an estate in law.

1.18   If the duration of an owner's rights in an estate is not determinable, the owner has

   a. a tenancy at sufferance.
   b. a leased fee simple estate.
   c. a freehold estate.
   d. a leasehold estate.

1.19   The distinguishing feature of a leasehold estate is

   a. ownership of an interest by a tenant.
   b. temporary ownership of the full bundle of rights in a property.
   c. unlimited ownership of one right in the bundle of rights in a property.
   d. that the estate is limited by a lease term.

1.20   A landowner conveys a parcel of property with the provision that the land cannot be developed for
       retail purposes. The new owner immediately begins to develop a retail shopping outlet, the grantor
       finds out and takes the property back. What kind of estate did this landowner convey?

   a. Fee simple absolute.
   b. Life estate with reversion.
   c. Life estate with condition subsequent.
   d. Fee simple defeasible.

1.21   Ned grants his sister Alice an estate for as long as she lives. Her descendants, however, cannot
       inherit the estate. What kind of estate is it?

   a. An estate pur autre vie.
   b. An estate for years.
   c. An ordinary life estate.
   d. A legal life estate.

1.22   Homestead estates are examples of

   a. a conventional life estate.
   b. a legal life estate.
   c. an estate created by an owner's agreement.
   d. a fee simple absolute.

1.23   Louis owned a boat and a house before marrying Barbara. While she was single, Barbara owned a new car. The two got married and bought a second home. As a wedding present, Barbara's father bought Louis a motorcycle. Under the law of community property, what property can Louis sell without his wife's consent or signature?

   a. The boat and house.
   b. The boat, house, and motorcycle.
   c. The second home and the motorcycle.
   d. The boat and motorcycle.

1.24   Katelyn rents an apartment for one year. What rights has she acquired under the leasehold?

   a. The right to exclude everyone from the premises.
   b. The right to encumber the fee interest.
   c. The right to sell the premises.
   d. The right to possess and use the premises.

1.25   An estate from period-to-period will continue as long as

   a. the tenant makes, and landlord accepts, regular rent payments.
   b. the term specified in the lease.
   c. the period is less than a year.
   d. the landlord has not sold the property.

1.26   An estate at will

   a. cannot be terminated.
   b. is terminated only if so stated in the lessee's last will and testament.
   c. terminates on the death of lessor or lessee.
   d. terminates on the date specified in the lease agreement.

1.27   A tenant continues to occupy an apartment after lease expiration without the consent of the landlord. This type of estate is called

   a. an estate at sufferance.
   b. a holdover estate.
   c. a canceled leasehold.
   d. a hostile leasehold.

1.28   A tenant without a lease has been sending the landlord monthly rent checks, and the landlord continues to accept the payments. What kind of leasehold estate exists?

   a. Estate for years.
   b. Estate from period to period.
   c. Estate at will.
   d. Estate at sufferance.

1.29   A fee or life estate is held by an individual. This form of estate is referred to as a(an)

   a. tenancy in severalty.
   b. tenancy by the entireties.
   c. absolute fee simple.
   d. legal fee simple.

1.30 Six people have identical rights in a property and enjoy an indivisible interest. However any of the owners may sell or transfer his/her interest without consent of the others. This form of ownership is a

a. joint tenancy.
b. homestead ownership.
c. tenancy in common.
d. estate in severalty.

1.31 The "four unities" required to create a joint tenancy include which of the following conditions?

a. Parties must acquire respective interests at the same time.
b. Parties must be residents of the same state at the time of acquiring the interest.
c. Parties must be family members.
d. Parties must have joint financial responsibility.

1.32 Unlike tenants in common, joint tenants

a. own distinct portions of the physical property.
b. cannot will their interest to a party outside the tenancy.
c. may own unequal shares of the property.
d. cannot encumber their interest to outside parties.

1.33 Which of the following life estates is created by operation of law rather than by the owner?

a. Conventional life estate.
b. Ordinary life estate.
c. Legal life estate.
d. Community property life estate.

1.34 Which of the following is true of a homestead?

a. A homestead interest cannot be conveyed by one spouse.
b. A homestead interest cannot be passed to the children of the head of household.
c. A homestead interest is a form of conventional life estate.
d. A homestead is a primary or secondary residence occupied by a family.

1.35 A tenant in common can

a. sell or transfer his interest without the consent of the other tenants in common.
b. use his or her interest in the estate to encumber the entire estate.
c. sell, encumber or transfer his or her interest only to the other tenants in common.
d. sell, encumber or transfer his or her interest only with the consent of all the other tenants in common.

1.36 Which of the following would be considered community property?

a. Property acquired before marriage
b. A motorcycle bought after the marriage with separate property funds
c. Income derived from community property
d. A mother's heirloom wedding ring gifted to the wife after her wedding

1.37 When real property is held in a land trust, who controls the property?

a. The trustor
b. The trustee
c. The beneficiary
d. The mortgagee

1.38   In a community property state, John marries Patricia. Prior to the marriage John owned an SUV. During the marriage, John bought a Buick, John and Patricia bought a second property with money earned from Patricia's job, and each individual received a motorcycle from Patricia's uncle as a gift. What property is community property in this marriage?

a. The SUV, the Buick, and the second property.
b. The SUV, the Buick, the second property, and the motorcycles.
c. The Buick and the second property.
d. The Buick, the second property, and the motorcycles.

1.39   Which of the following is true of a cooperative?

a. A cooperative may hold an owner liable for the unpaid operating expenses of other tenants.
b. The owners have a fee simple interest in the airspace of their respective apartments.
c. Owners may sublease their apartments even if they sell their stock in the cooperative.
d. The proprietary lease is guaranteed to have a fixed rate of rent over the life of the lease term.

1.40   Which of the following is true of a tenancy in common?

a. The co-owners must be related.
b. The owners enjoy an indivisible interest.
c. The tenants must acquire their interests at the same time.
d. The tenants must pay equal amounts for their interest in the estate.

1.41   Carissa and Robert acquire a condominium as tenants in common. In this circumstance, Carissa can

a. sell her interest to a third party without the consent of Robert.
b. use her interest in the estate to mortgage the entire estate.
c. sell her interest only to Robert.
d. sell encumber or transfer her interest only with the consent of Robert.

1.42   When a tenant in common dies, what happens to the tenant's interest in the estate?

a. It is divided equally among the surviving tenants in common.
b. The surviving tenants must buy the interest from the deceased tenant's heirs or sell their interests to the heirs.
c. It becomes a joint tenancy.
d. It passes by probate to the deceased tenant's heirs.

1.43   Which of the following is true of a joint tenancy?

a. The tenants can determine the size of the share owned by each tenant.
b. The size of the tenant's shares is determined by the amount of equity each has invested in the property.
c. The tenants have an equal and indivisible ownership interest.
d. There can be no more than two co-owners, and each has a fifty percent interest.

1.44   In contrast to a tenancy in common, in a joint tenancy

a. there is a single title to the property.
b. there are as many titles to the property as there are co-owners.
c. title is held by a trustee.
d. co-owners who are married hold separate titles.

1.45   If a joint tenant sells his or her interest to an outside party,

a. the new owner becomes a tenant in common with the other owners, who continue to hold a joint tenancy with each other and a tenancy in common with the new owner.
b. the joint tenancy continues with the new owner as the third joint tenant.
c. the joint tenancy terminates and all owners become tenants in common.
d. the joint tenancy terminates and the owners must create a new joint tenancy to include the new owner.

1.46   When a joint tenant dies, what happens to the tenant's interest in the estate?

a. It passes to the decedent's heirs, who become joint tenants.
b. It passes as a tenancy in common to the decedent's heirs.
c. The joint tenancy terminates and becomes a tenancy in common with the decedent's heirs and the surviving tenants as co-owners.
d. It passes to the surviving joint tenants.

1.47   Under what conditions can two individuals own a property as tenants by the entireties?

a. If they so elect at the time of acquiring title.
b. If they are blood relatives.
c. If they are married.
d. If they incorporate.

1.48   When an estate is held in a trust, which party holds legal title?

a. The beneficiary.
b. The trustor.
c. The trustee.
d. The grantor.

1.49   Tanya buys a 4-bedroom condominium. As the new owner, she has the right to

a. sell or mortgage the unit without impediment from individual owners of neighboring units.
b. sell the interest in the physical unit separately from the interest in the common elements.
c. prevent non-owners from using the unit owner's portion of the common elements.
d. exclusively possess and use those portions of the common areas structurally or functionally necessary for the operation of the unit.

1.50   A condominium owner's share of maintenance and operations expenses are based on

a. the unit's pro rata share of floor space.
b. the unit's pro rata share of the property value as defined in the declaration.
c. the number of shares the owner purchased in the condominium association.
d. the assessed value of the condominium unit.

1.51   By contrast to a condominium, the owner of a cooperative owns

a. shares in a corporation or association and a proprietary lease in a physical unit.
b. a fee simple interest in a physical unit plus a tenancy in common in common elements.
c. a tenancy in common in a physical unit and the common areas.
d. a ground lease in the physical unit's pro rata share of land and a proprietary lease in the unit.

1.52   In a cooperative, real property is owned only by

a. the individual unit owners.
b. the individual unit owners and the cooperative association.
c. the cooperative developer.
d. the corporate entity of the cooperative association.

1.53 In a time-share freehold, owners acquire

   a. undivided interests in the property as tenants in common.
   b. a renewable periodic tenancy from for a portion of a year.
   c. a pro rata share of a leased fee.
   d. a tenancy in severalty for a portion of a year.

1.54 A party has just purchased a manufactured housing unit. When is this property considered real property?

   a. As soon as it is purchased
   b. As soon as it is constructed
   c. As soon as it is affixed to the ground.
   d. This form of property is considered personal property at all times.

1.55 Kiki's annual lease expires on December 31st. On January 7th, Kiki has still not vacated the premises. In this case, what happens to this person's tenancy and what is the resulting leasehold estate called, if anything?

   a. The tenancy becomes a leasehold by prescription.
   b. The estate becomes a holdover tenancy, a periodic leasehold estate.
   c. The estate becomes a delinquent estate for years tenancy subject to immediate eviction.
   d. There is no subsequent tenancy; the tenant must vacate immediately.

2.1   Which of the following describes an encumbrance?

   a. A third party's right to encroach upon a property without the permission of the property owner.
   b. A third party's right to claim the sale proceeds of a property that has been mortgaged as collateral for a loan.
   c. A third party's interest in a real property that limits the interests of the freehold property owner.
   d. Another's right to acquire a freehold interest in a property against the property owner's wishes.

2.2   Which of the following is true of easements in general?

   a. They involve the property that contains the easement and a non-owning party.
   b. They apply to a whole property, not to any specific portion of the property.
   c. They only involve the legal owner of the property.
   d. They may require a specific use, but cannot prohibit one.

2.3   Mr. King wants to offer 100 acres of his property for sale. Since the property is landlocked, he will have to put in a driveway to the road that will run across his remaining property. What kind of easement will he have to grant?

   a. An easement in gross.
   b. A commercial easement.
   c. A personal easement.
   d. An easement appurtenant.

2.4   If property Alpha has a court-ordered easement across property Beta in order for Alpha to have access to a public road, the easement is a(n)

   a. easement by prescription.
   b. personal easement.
   c. easement by necessity.
   d. easement in gross.

2.5   An encroachment is

   a. an easement that has not been recorded on the title of the burdened property.
   b. an unauthorized physical intrusion of one property into another.
   c. a right granted by a property owner to the owner of an adjoining property to build a structure that protrudes across the property boundary.
   d. a structure that does not comply with a zoning ordinance.

2.6   A court might grant an easement by prescription if

   a. a town needs to dig a trench across an owner's property to install a sewer line to a neighboring property, and the owner refuses permission.
   b. a property owner sells the front half of a lot and wants to continue using the driveway to access the rear of the lot.
   c. a trespasser has been using an owner's property for a certain period with the owner's knowledge but without permission.
   d. a property owner wants to prevent the owner of an adjoining property from building a an improvement that blocks her view.

2.7　The purpose of a deed restriction is to enable an owner to specify

a. the form of ownership in which a property may be held.
b. how long a property must be owned before it can be legally transferred.
c. what groups of people are legally excluded from future ownership of a property.
d. how a property may be used and what improvements may be built on it.

2.8　Melinda purchases a house and finances it. The lender in turn places a lien on Melinda's title. The lien in this mortgage transaction is

a. evidence of debt incurred by a property owner.
b. a promissory note granted by a property owner as security for a debt.
c. the creditor's claim against the property as collateral security for the loan.
d. the document required to clear clouded title.

2.9　In a lien-theory state, what kind of interest does a mortgage lender have in the liened property?

a. A possessory interest.
b. A tenancy-by-mortgagee interest.
c. A legal interest in a pro rata share of the property.
d. An equitable interest.

2.10　How is a lien terminated?

a. Payment of the debt that is the subject of the lien and recording of the satisfaction.
b. Transfer of the property that has the lien.
c. Recording of another lien that is superior.
d. Death of the lienor or lienee.

2.11　A judge rules in favor of the creditor in a court proceeding and places a judgment lien against all the debtor's assets, including his real property. This is an example of a(n)

a. voluntary junior lien.
b. involuntary superior lien.
c. involuntary specific lien.
d. involuntary general lien.

2.12　A real estate tax lien, a federal income tax lien, a judgment lien, and a mortgage lien are recorded against a property. Which lien will be paid first when the property is sold?

a. Real estate tax lien.
b. Federal income tax lien.
c. Judgment lien.
d. Mortgage lien.

2.13　A lien holder can change the lien priority of a junior lien by agreeing to

a. change the date of recording.
b. lower the amount of the claim.
c. cancel the lien.
d. subordinate the lien.

2.14　Which of the following accurately describes the act of foreclosure?

a. A court-ordered acceleration of loan payments.
b. The final step in a bankruptcy filing.
c. A proceeding to enforce a lien by forcing the sale or transfer of a secured property.
d. A proceeding to take equitable title to a property that was liened as security for a mortgage loan.

2.15 A property is secured by a mortgage that does not contain a "power of sale" clause. To foreclose, the lien holder will have to

a. file a deficiency suit.
b. file a foreclosure suit.
c. file a suit to quiet title.
d. obtain a quit claim deed.

2.16 A homeowner defaults on his mortgage loan. In the subsequent foreclosure action, the lender takes title to the liened property directly instead of initiating a court-ordered public sale. This is an example of

a. strict foreclosure.
b. judicial foreclosure.
c. non-judicial foreclosure.
d. deed in lieu of foreclosure.

2.17 A property owner gives Deanna permission to cross his property as a shortcut to her kindergarten school bus. One day the property owner dies. What right was Deanna granted originally, and will it survive the owner's death?

a. A personal easement in gross, which continues after the owner's death.
b. An easement by prescription, which continues after the owner's death.
c. A license, which continues after the owner's death.
d. A license, which terminates upon the owner's death.

2.18 On two adjacent properties, there is an easement that allows property A to use the driveway that belongs to property B. Here, property A is said to be which of the following in relation to property B?

a. Subservient estate.
b. Servient tenement.
c. Senior tenant.
d. Dominant tenement.

2.19 A property owner who is selling her land wants to control how it is used in the future. She might accomplish her aim by means of

a. an injunction.
b. a deed restriction.
c. an easement.
d. a land trust.

2.20 What distinguishes a lien from other types of encumbrance?

a. It involves a monetary claim against the value of a property.
b. It lowers the value of a property.
c. It is created voluntarily by the property owner.
d. It attaches to the property rather than to the owner of the property.

2.21 Which of the following defines actual notice?

a. It is notice published in a newspaper.
b. It is knowledge one could have or should have obtained.
c. It is notice explicitly stated in a legal document.
d. It is knowledge received or imparted through direct experience.

2.22 Which of the following defines constructive notice?

   a. It is notice published in a newspaper.
   b. It is knowledge one could have or should have obtained.
   c. It is notice explicitly stated in a legal document.
   d. It is knowledge received or imparted through direct experience.

2.23 Ownership of real estate can be transferred voluntarily or involuntarily. The three ways title can be transferred voluntarily are by

   a. grant, deed, and will.
   b. escheat, deed, and covenant.
   c. title certificate, will, and deed.
   d. sale contract, deed, and warrant of seizin.

2.24 What is the function of recording a deed?

   a. It makes the deed valid.
   b. It causes title to pass.
   c. It gives constructive notice of ownership.
   d. It removes all prior recorded encumbrances.

2.25 The only clause that is actually required in a deed is the

   a. habendum clause.
   b. granting clause.
   c. reserving clause.
   d. tenendum clause.

2.26 The type of deed that offers the grantee the fullest protection against claims to the title is the

   a. general warranty deed.
   b. special warranty deed.
   c. quitclaim deed.
   d. bargain and defend deed.

2.27 What is one of the purposes of a lawsuit to "quiet title"?

   a. To force the grantor to defend the title against a third party claim.
   b. To terminate a co-ownership estate when one co-owner is unwilling.
   c. To keep the owner's name out of the title records.
   d. To have an encumbrance removed if the lienholder cannot prove its validity.

2.28 Which of the following best describes the documentary stamp tax?

   a. A transfer tax based on the price of the property being conveyed.
   b. A tax a title company must pay in order to examine title records in the recorder's office.
   c. A tax collected by attorneys and paid to the state when transfer documents are prepared.
   d. A tax on stamps used to certify the authenticity of a conveyance.

2.29 The court proceeding that generally settles a decedent's estate is called

   a. testate.
   b. probate.
   c. escheat.
   d. distribution.

2.30   If an owner of real property dies intestate and has no legal heirs, what will happen to the property?

a. It will escheat to the state or county.
b. It will transfer to the decedent's executor.
c. It will be divided equally among adjoining property owners.
d. It will become a public easement.

2.31   A municipality wants to build a sewage treatment facility which will require the acquisition of several parcels of privately owned land. What legal power enables the municipality to buy the necessary properties, even against the owners' wishes?

a. Estoppel.
b. Escheat.
c. Alienation.
d. Eminent domain.

2.32   An adverse possessor must be able to successfully demonstrate that he or she has been

a. openly possessing and claiming the property without the owner's consent.
b. occupying the property without an occupancy permit.
c. using the property intermittently and without permission over a period of years.
d. building a permanent structure on the property.

2.33   A buyer has signed a contract to purchase a property, but is uncertain of the condition of the title. Which of the following parties is legally responsible for knowing the condition of the title?

a. The County Recorder.
b. The seller's agent.
c. The buyer.
d. The mortgage lender.

2.34   A break in the chain of title to a property results in

a. a clouded title.
b. a title plant.
c. a lien of indeterminate ownership.
d. a duplicate title.

2.35   Wayne and Leota obtain an insurance policy that protects them from liabilities and losses resulting from title defects. The kind of policy they bought is a

a. homeowner's insurance policy.
b. standard owner's title insurance policy.
c. lender's title insurance policy.
d. private mortgage insurance policy.

2.36   An owner transfers title to a property to a buyer in exchange for a motorcycle. This is an example of

a. voluntary alienation.
b. involuntary liquidation.
c. hypothecation.
d. 1031 exchange.

2.37   A person wishes to convey any and all interests in a property to another without assurance of the property's marketability. This party would most likely use which of the following types of deed?

a. A sheriff's deed.
b. A special warranty deed.
c. A partition deed.
d. A quitclaim deed.

2.38   Jennifer owns a one-half interest in a condominium as a tenant in common with her business partner. If Jennifer has several heirs and dies without a will, the property will

a. pass to the heirs by the laws of descent and distribution.
b. escheat to the state.
c. pass to the surviving spouse based on homestead law.
d. pass to the surviving heirs according to the provisions of the will.

2.39   A drifter secretly lives in an abandoned shack on a large ranch property. After twenty years, the person makes a claim of ownership to the shack and the land immediately surrounding it that he had cleared. This claim will likely be

a. upheld through adverse possession.
b. upheld because of the length of possession.
c. declined through the doctrine of prior appropriation.
d. declined because possession was secretive.

2.40   To be marketable, title must be

a. insured.
b. free of undisclosed defects and encumbrances.
c. abstracted by an attorney.
d. guaranteed by a title certificate.

2.41   Which of the following types of leasehold estate lacks a specific term?

a. Estate for years.
b. Estate from period-to-period.
c. Estate at will.
d. Estate by the entireties.

2.42   A landlord generally has the right to enter the leased premises

a. at any time without notice.
b. for specified reasonable purposes.
c. provided the tenant gives prior permission.
d. only thirty days prior to lease expiration.

2.43   When a tenant rents an apartment, he or she is usually responsible for

a. compliance with the rules and regulations of the building.
b. payment for any alterations to the leased space.
c. recording the lease in title records.
d. occupying the premises throughout the lease term.

2.44   Under landlord-tenant laws, landlords must treat tenants fairly and honestly. In a residential leasehold, this requirement would include

a. insuring the tenant against loss of personal property.
b. providing required building support and services.
c. guaranteeing that a fair rent is being charged.
d. insuring the property for the value of the leasehold.

2.45   While a one-year lease is in effect, the tenant dies of a sudden illness. In this situation,

a. the lease automatically terminates.
b. the tenant's estate has the option of canceling the contract.
c. the landlord can record a lien against the leased fee interest.
d. the tenant's estate is still obligated under the lease.

2.46 Three students rent a house together, and all three sign a one-year lease. Six months later, two students move out. Which of the following is true of the remaining rent obligation?

a. The remaining tenant is responsible for the full rent obligation.
b. The remaining tenant is responsible for one third of the rent obligation.
c. The lease is cancelled due to abandonment. Therefore, the rent obligation is extinguished.
d. The departing tenants have no further rent obligation.

2.47 A tenant transfers a portion of the leasehold interest to another party. The instrument that accomplishes this transfer is a(n)

a. deed.
b. novation.
c. sublease.
d. reconveyance

2.48 Vijay enters into a lease for his new store. The provisions of the lease require Vijay to pay the operating expenses of the premises such as janitorial and repair expenses. This is an example of a

a. gross lease.
b. percentage lease.
c. land lease.
d. net lease.

2.49 A tenant obtains a full-service lease where the landlord agrees to pay all operating expenses in exchange for an additional $5.00 rent per square foot. Another term for this lease is a(n)

a. gross lease.
b. proprietary lease.
c. exchange lease.
d. full service net lease.

2.50 Which of the following circumstances is the most likely scenario for a ground lease?

a. A developer wants to acquire a necessary parcel that separates two parcels she already owns.
b. An owner-developer wants to retain ownership of the land portion of the improved real property.
c. A fast food company wants to place a restaurant in an existing building without buying either land or improvement.
d. A farmer wants to sell his property to a mining company.

2.51 A tenancy at will can usually be terminated by

a. either party giving proper notice.
b. either party without notice.
c. a sublease, with the lessor's approval.
d. an assignment by the lessor.

2.52 Under the Uniform Residential Landlord and Tenant Act, if a lease does not state a clear expiration date, the lease is regarded as

a. invalid.
b. a tenancy from period-to-period.
c. a tenancy at will.
d. a tenancy for years.

2.53　The Uniform Residential Landlord and Tenant Act generally does not apply to

　　　a. a hotel.
　　　b. a single-family residence.
　　　c. a unit in an apartment building that has fewer than ten units.
　　　d. a duplex in which the owner occupies one of the units.

2.54　In executing a condominium lease, a tenant has acquired

　　　a. a temporary transfer of legal title.
　　　b. a limited freehold interest in the air space of her unit.
　　　c. a temporary possessory interest.
　　　d. a title conveyance in exchange for rent.

2.55　When a tenant acquires a leasehold estate through a lease, what does the property owner acquire?

　　　a. A freehold estate for years.
　　　b. A reduced leasehold estate.
　　　c. A defeasible estate.
　　　d. A leased fee estate.

2.56　When an owner leases her property, she temporarily relinquishes the right to

　　　a. transfer the property.
　　　b. encumber the property.
　　　c. occupy the property.
　　　d. maintain the property.

2.57　Which of the following happens when a leased property is sold?

　　　a. The buyer acquires title subject to the lease, which remains in effect.
　　　b. The lease is cancelled.
　　　c. The lease expires within thirty days unless renewed.
　　　d. A new lease is automatically executed.

2.58　If a lease does not state a specific ending date, when does it terminate?

　　　a. Immediately, since it is an invalid lease.
　　　b. After one year.
　　　c. When either party gives proper notice.
　　　d. Whenever the property is sold.

2.59　In accordance with the statute of frauds,

　　　a. leases in excess of one year must be recorded to be enforceable.
　　　b. oral leases are not enforceable.
　　　c. a five-year lease must be in writing to be enforceable.
　　　d. an unwritten lease is fraudulent.

2.60　Which of the following is true of a sublease?

　　　a. The subtenant takes over sole responsibility for performance of the original lease contract.
　　　b. The original tenant retains primary responsibility for performance of the original lease contract.
　　　c. It does not convey any of the leasehold interest.
　　　d. It conveys the entire leasehold interest.

2.61 A homeowner goes bankrupt and the lender forecloses on her residence. In the foreclosure sale, the proceeds are insufficient to pay off the loan, and the court orders other property sold to cover the shortfall. This action is called a(n)

a. strict foreclosure.
b. suit for specific performance.
c. equity foreclosure judgment.
d. deficiency judgment.

2.62 To make a successful claim of adverse possession, the adverse possessor must satisfy which of the following criteria?

a. The possession must have been concealed, without permission, and for a statutory period of time.
b. The possession must have been unconcealed, for the necessary length of time, and without permission.
c. The possession must be with intent, secretive, notorious and hostile.
d. The possession must be open, without permission, for the statutory period of time, and within the number of permitted intervals.

2.63 One of the primary benefits of recording conveyances is to give evidence to the public that the new owner actually owns the property. What is another benefit of recording to the homeowner?

a. Recording instruments establishes the title's marketability.
b. Recording the deed prevents any future clouds on title.
c. Recording prevents lienholders from illegal credit practices.
d. Recording the deed of conveyance nullifies any and all claims of adverse possession.

2.64 Broker Yvonne successfully closed on her listing, but the seller refused to pay the commission. What is one legitimate course of action available to Yvonne?

a. A vendor's lien
b. An intangible lien
c. A broker's lien
d. A mechanic's lien

2.65 One of the key characteristics of a short sale is that the transaction typically takes much longer to close. What is another anomaly of a short sale that makes it a unique conveyance alternative?

a. The lender must approve of the modified loan and selling terms.
b. The Real Estate Commission may intervene to protect the broker from seller default.
c. The broker must take a discount on the conventional commission scale.
d. The IRS must audit any loan modification.

Test 3: Land Use; Legal Descriptions; Contract Law

3.1   Which of the following is true regarding master planning and zoning?

      a. The aggregate of zoning ordinances is the master plan.
      b. A master plan eliminates the need for zoning ordinances.
      c. Master planning is a county-level function; zoning is limited to the city level.
      d. Zoning ordinances are a primary means of keeping land use in harmony with the master plan.

3.2   The basic intent of zoning ordinances is to

      a. establish the basis for public ownership of land for the common good.
      b. establish subdivision rules and regulations.
      c. specify usage for every parcel within the zoning authority's jurisdiction.
      d. restrict development in unincorporated areas.

3.3   Why do zoning authorities create different types of zones?

      a. To ensure that a variety of building structures are available in the community.
      b. To separate land uses so that they do not interfere with each other.
      c. To preserve high density land uses.
      d. To discourage industrial and commercial users from relocating.

3.4   The key consideration in granting a zoning exception known as a special exception is which of the following?

      a. Hardship
      b. Change of zones
      c. The public interest
      d. The use was legal prior to the new zone creation

3.5   The intensity of land usage generally refers to what?

      a. The number of residential building lots per acre.
      b. The number of people per square mile.
      c. The number of building permits issued per year within a zoning jurisdiction.
      d. The area of a commercial or industrial facility in relation to the size of the site.

3.6   How does Planned Unit Development zoning vary from ordinary zoning?

      a. It applies only to office parks.
      b. It incorporates a number of different zones within a single property boundary.
      c. It requires that multiple tracts of land be developed according to a single design.
      d. It requires developers to obtain a separate building permit for every structure.

3.7   Which of the following situations is most likely to represent an illegal nonconforming use?

      a. A homeowner in a residential zone converts her residence to a private school.
      b. A homeowner builds a toolshed in a neighborhood where there are no toolsheds.
      c. A storeowner remodels a storefront in accordance with regulations, and then the zoning is changed to residential.
      d. A new zoning ordinance outlaws two-story additions after a homeowner completes an addition.

3.8   What is the difference between a variance and a nonconforming use?

    a. A variance, once granted, is unconditional and permanent.
    b. A variance is granted by the zoning board if the owner has a justifiable reason.
    c. A nonconforming use is allowed if the owner requests it in advance of building.
    d. A nonconforming use violates current zoning, but a variance does not.

3.9   A document certifying that a structure complies with building codes and is ready for use is referred to as a(n)

    a. inspection report.
    b. satisfaction bond.
    c. certificate of occupancy.
    d. user permit.

3.10   Which of the following is true of an eminent domain proceeding?

    a. It cancels the property owner's mortgage loan balance.
    b. It leaves the property owner with equitable title in place of legal title.
    c. It conveys legal title to the acquiring entity.
    d. It clouds the chain of title by canceling the original grant.

3.11   Among other provisions, the Superfund Act (CERCLA) and Superfund Amendment and Reauthorization Act of 1986 provided that

    a. large development projects undergo an environmental impact survey immediately after completion of construction.
    b. industrial users of real estate comply with air quality standards.
    c. the EPA would give financial help to homeowners to remedy any hazardous situation resulting from radon, asbestos, or lead-based paint.
    d. parties responsible for improper disposal of hazardous waste could be charged for the cleanup costs.

3.12   Public land use planning strives to balance which of the following potentially conflicting interests?

    a. Individual property rights and the public's interest.
    b. Public policy makers and community business leaders.
    c. Tenant occupancy specifications and construction contractors.
    d. Individual property owners and municipal planning agencies.

3.13   Zoning, building codes, and environmental restrictions are forms of local land use control known as

    a. master planning.
    b. preemption.
    c. police power.
    d. concurrency.

3.14   If a municipality exerts its power of eminent domain against a certain property owner, what happens?

    a. The owner must pay higher property taxes or give up the property.
    b. The owner must cede an easement without receiving any compensation.
    c. The municipality annexes the property.
    d. The owner must sell the property in exchange for market-value compensation.

3.15 To be valid, a local zoning ordinance must

a. reasonably promote community health, safety and welfare.
b. comply with federal zoning laws.
c. apply only to unique properties.
d. published periodically in the local newspaper.

3.16 Why do communities require building permits?

a. To promote development.
b. To establish the basis for an inspection.
c. To promote certificates of occupancy.
d. To ensure that improvements comply with codes.

3.17 What is the purpose of residential zoning?

a. To increase home values in a neighborhood.
b. To regulate the density of dwellings in the residential zone.
c. To prevent families from residing in commercial and industrial sites.
d. To maximize intensity of usage.

3.18 A non-profit organization wants to erect an urgent care facility in a residential zone. Given other favorable circumstances, the local authorities may grant permission by allowing

a. a special exception.
b. an illegal nonconforming use.
c. an easement.
d. a license.

3.19 A property that conformed with zoning ordinances when it was developed but does not conform to new ordinances is said to be

a. an illegal special exception.
b. a variance.
c. a legal nonconforming use.
d. unmarketable.

3.20 The approval process for development of multiple properties in an area includes submission of

a. a covenant of restriction.
b. a plat of subdivision.
c. a court order.
d. a developer's pro forma.

3.21 A legal description of a property is one which

a. accurately identifies the boundaries of the property as distinct from all other properties.
b. accurately describes the location and dimensions of the lot and improvements on the property.
c. is accepted by a licensed surveyor as suitable for inclusion in a survey of the property.
d. is written by an attorney licensed to practice real estate law in the state in which the property is located.

3.22 The essential elements of the metes and bounds system are

a. parallels, base lines, and meridians.
b. boundaries, distances, and a base line.
c. reference points, angles, and distances.
d. lot numbers, sections, and ranges.

3.23 In the Rectangular Survey System, a range is the area in between

a. any row of sections in a township.
b. two consecutive meridians.
c. a principal meridian and a base line.
d. a parallel and a meridian.

3.24 In the Rectangular Survey System, a tier is defined by

a. six consecutive sections of a township.
b. two consecutive meridians.
c. two consecutive parallels.
d. a parallel and a meridian.

3.25 In the Rectangular Survey System, what are the dimensions of a township?

a. One mile square.
b. Six miles by six miles, or 6 miles square.
c. Thirty-six miles square.
d. The north and south boundaries are one mile apart; the east and west boundaries are indeterminate.

3.26 What portion of a section is ten acres?

a. 1/8.
b. 1/16.
c. 1/32.
d. 1/64.

3.27 The lot and block system of legally describing property is used for

a. farm properties.
b. any property in an unincorporated area.
c. properties where metes and bounds is not acceptable.
d. properties in a subdivision.

3.28 A certain legal description contains the phrase, "...northwesterly along Erie Road to the POB...".
What kind of description is this?

a. Plat survey.
b. Government grid.
c. Metes and bounds.
d. Rectangular survey.

3.29 How many sections are there in a township?

a. One.
b. Six.
c. Twelve.
d. Thirty-six.

3.30 In the Rectangular Survey System, a section contains how many acres?

a. 640.
b. 320.
c. 160.
d. 40.

3.31 The valuable consideration necessary to make a contract valid must be

    a. money.
    b. something tangible.
    c. something of value traded in exchange for something of value.
    d. something of equal value with whatever is received in exchange.

3.32 A real estate sales contract, to be enforceable, must

    a. contain a legal description of the property.
    b. be written on a form approved by the state bar association.
    c. be acknowledged by three witnesses.
    d. be recorded within three days to be enforceable.

3.33 How much time does a seller have to accept a buyer's offer?

    a. Forty-eight hours from the time of the offeror's signing of the offer.
    b. Twenty-four hours from the time of the offer's delivery to the seller.
    c. Within 24 hours following the stated expiration.
    d. A reasonable time, or until the expiration date on the offer.

3.34 A buyer submits an offer to a seller and then dies in a car accident. Before learning of the buyer's death, the seller accepts the offer. Which of the following is true?

    a. The seller can force the buyer's estate to go through with the purchase.
    b. The buyer's death terminated the offer.
    c. The seller must make a new offer with the same terms to the buyer's heirs.
    d. The buyer's heirs have the option of enforcing the contract.

3.35 Which of the following contracts can be assigned to another party?

    a. An exclusive listing agreement.
    b. A personal services agreement.
    c. A contract for the sale of undeveloped land.
    d. An employment contract between a broker and a salesperson.

3.36 An implied agency relationship may be deemed to exist if

    a. the parties do not disavow an express contract that has expired.
    b. the parties act is if there is a contract.
    c. an offering party does not receive written notice that the offer has been rejected.
    d. the parties promise to perform their part of the agreement if the other party performs.

3.37 Which of the following is an executory contract?

    a. An expired lease.
    b. A sale contract before closing.
    c. A recorded sale contract.
    d. An option to buy after it is exercised.

3.38 A bilateral contract is one in which

    a. both parties promise to do something in exchange for the other party's performance.
    b. both parties receive equal consideration.
    c. two parties agree to perform a service together.
    d. both parties promise to do something if the other party performs first.

3.39 A homeseller signs a listing agreement with a broker then subsequently revokes the listing. Which of the following is true?

a. The seller continues to have contractual obligations to the broker.
b. The contract remains in full force until the expiration date.
c. The broker may have a claim for marketing expenses expended during the listing term.
d. The seller cannot sign a listing agreement with another broker.

3.40 A breach of contract is

a. a termination of the contract by the mutual consent of the parties.
b. financial damage suffered by a party because another party has nullified a contract provision.
c. a lawsuit to force a party to discharge the contract.
d. the failure of a party to perform according to the terms of the contract.

3.41 What is rescission?

a. The act of withdrawing an offer before it has been accepted.
b. The act of declaring that a contract is no longer in effect for a given party.
c. The act of declaring a contract unenforceable.
d. The act of modifying the terms of an offer.

3.42 To be valid, a valid contract must

a. reflect a mutual understanding or agreement.
b. use precise wording in a document.
c. not be executable.
d. be created only by an attorney.

3.43 Two parties enter into a contract. The agreement fulfills all the requirements for a valid contract, with no disqualifying circumstances. Given this situation, it is still possible that the contract may be

a. void.
b. illegal.
c. unenforceable.
d. voidable.

3.44 The guardian for a mentally incompetent party enters into an oral contract with another party to buy a trade fixture on behalf of the incompetent party. This contract

a. does not meet validity requirements.
b. is possibly valid and enforceable.
c. must be in writing to be valid.
d. is valid but unenforceable.

3.45 A prospective homebuyer submits a signed offer with the condition that the seller pay for the inspection at closing. The seller disagrees, crosses out the provision, then signs and returns the document to the buyer. At this point, assuming all other contract validity items are in order, the original offer is now

a. an accepted offer, therefore a valid contract.
b. an executable option.
c. a counteroffer.
d. an invalid offer.

3.46 A construction contractor executes a contract with a buyer. In the agreement, the contractor promises to complete construction by November 20. This promise can be construed as

a. an option.
b. mutual consent.
c. a meeting of the minds.
d. valuable consideration.

3.47 A seller contracts to sell a property that she does not own. The sale contract for this transaction

a. is executable.
b. must be in writing.
c. is void.
d. is illegal yet potentially enforceable.

3.48 The statute of limitations requires that parties to a contract who have been damaged or who question the contract's provisions

a. must act within a statutory period.
b. must select a specific, limited course of action for recouping their losses.
c. must arbitrate prior to taking court action.
d. must wait a statutory period before they may take legal action.

3.49 The purpose of the statute of frauds is to

a. invalidate certain oral contracts.
b. require certain conveyance-related contracts to be in writing.
c. nullify oral leases and listing agreements.
d. eliminate fraud in real estate contracts.

3.50 A seller immediately accepts a buyer's offer but waits ten days before returning the accepted document to the buyer. Meanwhile, the offer has expired. Which of the following is true?

a. The buyer is bound to the contract since it was accepted immediately.
b. The buyer has no obligations to the seller whatsoever.
c. The buyer may not rescind the expired offer.
d. The seller may sue for specific performance.

3.51 A deed restriction limits how owners may use a property within a given subdivision. One key characteristic of a deed restriction is that it

a. may be revoked by an owner.
b. may be exempt from ADA restrictions.
c. may not be discriminatory.
d. may not apply to protected classes, vis a vis fair housing laws.

4.1   The agency relationship is defined by

    a. the Realtor Code of Ethics.
    b. the laws of agency, or in some states, by statute.
    c. the law of real estate contracts.
    d. the agreement between a principal and an agent.

4.2   Which of the following is true of the connection between compensation and the agency relationship?

    a. An agreement to give and receive compensation creates an agency relationship.
    b. If an agency relationship exists, the principal must provide valuable consideration to the agent.
    c. The relationship is independent of any compensation arrangement.
    d. If an agency relationship exists, the agent is entitled to compensation.

4.3   One of the parties to an agency relationship defaults, and the agreement terminates. Which of the following is true?

    a. All obligations are extinguished.
    b. Both parties must continue to perform all other obligations of the agreement.
    c. The defaulting party may have a financial consequence.
    d. The damaged party has no claim against the defaulting party.

4.4   Among the fiduciary duties imposed on a real estate agent is the requirement to

    a. refuse offers the agent knows will be unacceptable to the principal.
    b. present all offers to the principal regardless of their amount.
    c. advise the principal against accepting an offer that is below full price.
    d. advise a prospect that the principal will not accept the prospect's offer in order to elicit a better offer.

4.5   One of the agent's fiduciary duties that continues even after a listing agreement expires is

    a. obedience.
    b. diligence.
    c. confidentiality.
    d. disclosure.

4.6   The standard of care and competence that a principal can expect from an agent is generally that which is

    a. specified in the agency agreement.
    b. necessary to earn the promised compensation.
    c. necessary to procure a customer.
    d. comparable to that of other practitioners in the area.

4.7   Agent Michael is showing his new listing to a buyer who informs him that he has just inherited five million dollars. Michael is now bound by fiduciary duty to

    a. keep the information in confidence.
    b. disclose the information to the buyer's agent.
    c. disclose the information to the seller.
    d. verify the buyer's statements before disclosing them to the client.

4.8   Agent Gerry has executed an exclusive buyer broker agreement with the Andersons. The agent subsequently places an offer with Melinda, the exclusive selling agent for the Lincolns, to buy their lakefront property. The offer contains provisions for the Lincolns to pay the brokerage commission, which the Lincolns agree to. Given this set of circumstances, Gerry owes the full set of fiduciary duties to

a. the Andersons.
b. the Lincolns.
c. Gerry's broker.
d. Melinda's broker.

4.9   A subagent is the agent of

a. the seller.
b. the buyer.
c. a broker who has an agency relationship with a client.
d. the client's and the customer's agents.

4.10   Which of the following is a dual agency situation?

a. Two agents share the exclusive right to represent the same client on all transactions.
b. One agent represents both sides in a transaction.
c. A selling agent from one brokerage works with a listing agent from another brokerage to complete a transaction.
d. One agent represents two sellers at the same time.

4.11   The duties of a transaction broker or facilitator include

a. preserving the confidentiality of information received from either party.
b. helping the two parties achieve their respective objectives.
c. disclosing material facts that affect the value of the property to both parties.
d. choosing to obey the instructions of one party and informing the other party of the decision.

4.12   In which of the following contact situations would a seller's agent be expected to disclose his agency relationships?

a. The agent is showing the client's property to a prospective buyer.
b. The agent tells an acquaintance at a party about the client's property.
c. The agent answers questions about the client's property for a telephone caller responding to a newspaper ad.
d. The agent is showing a potential buyer houses in a certain price range in the multiple listing book.

4.13   The essential foundation of the agency relationship consists of

a. mutual respect, compensation, and confidentiality.
b. diligence, results, and compensation.
c. service, marketing, and respect.
d. good faith, trust and confidence.

4.14   Audrey wants to take a vacation. To do so, she authorizes an agent to conduct the operations of one of her business enterprises. The kind of agency she has established is

a. limited.
b. general.
c. universal.
d. special.

4.15 A property seller empowers an agent to market and sell a property on his behalf. The kind of agency represented is

a. general.
b. special.
c. universal.
d. no agency.

4.16 Implied agency arises when

a. an agent accepts an oral listing.
b. a principal accepts an oral listing.
c. a party creates an agency relationship outside of an express agreement.
d. a principal agrees to all terms of a written listing agreement, whether express or implied.

4.17 An agency relationship may be involuntarily terminated for which of the following reasons?

a. Condemnation of the property.
b. Mutual consent.
c. Full performance.
d. Renewal of the agent's license.

4.18 A principal discloses that she would sell a property for $500,000. During the listing period, the house is listed and marketed for $530,000. No offers come in, and the listing expires. Three weeks later, the agent confides to a customer that the seller would have sold for less than the listed price. Which of the following is true?

a. The agent has violated the duty of confidentiality.
b. The agent has fulfilled all fiduciary duties, since the listing has expired.
c. The agent is violating the duties owed this customer.
d. The agent has created a dual agency situation with the customer.

4.19 A principal instructs an agent to market a property only to families on the west side of the university campus. The agent refuses to comply. In this case,

a. the agent has violated fiduciary duty.
b. the agent has not violated fiduciary duty.
c. the agent is liable for breaching the listing terms.
d. the agent should obey the instruction to salvage the listing.

4.20 An owner's agent is showing a buyer a residential property for sale. The buyer notices water stains on the foundation walls and floor, and informs the agent. The appropriate course of action for the agent is to

a. immediately contract to paint the ceiling.
b. immediately contract to repair the roof.
c. suggest the buyer make a lower-price offer.
d. inform the seller.

4.21 The meaning and salient characteristics of the agency relationship should be disclosed to the client

a. prior to completing a listing agreement.
b. prior to or upon completion of an offer.
c. upon the initial contact with the person.
d. prior to showing properties.

4.22   When must a listing agent disclose his or her agency relationship to prospective tenants or buyers?

a. Immediately prior to the initial contact.
b. Upon initial contact.
c. Whenever substantive communication is made beyond casual conversation.
d. Immediately following any offer executed by the customer.

4.23   A buyer agent or tenant representative should disclose his or her agency relationship to the owner's agent

a. immediately prior to the initial contact.
b. upon initial contact.
c. immediately prior to substantive contact.
d. immediately following any offer executed by the landlord.

4.24   An agent is operating as a disclosed dual agent on a transaction. In this case, the agent

a. may not represent one party's interests to the detriment of the other.
b. must operate without a listing agreement.
c. must be obedient and loyal to both parties.
d. must require that the principals refrain from disclosing any material facts to him.

4.25   An agent informs a buyer that a provision in a contract is very commonplace. After explaining the clause, the agent assures the buyer that the clause does not mean anything significant. If something goes wrong with the transaction, the agent could be liable for

a. violating duties owed a customer.
b. misinterpreting the clause.
c. intentional misrepresentation.
d. practicing law without a license.

4.26   When a broker enters into a listing agreement, the broker has agreed to accept which of the following?

a. Fiduciary and contractual obligations with the client.
b. Fiduciary relationships with client and customer.
c. Contractual obligations with cooperating brokers.
d. Fiduciary obligations with the customer.

4.27   The degree of authority granted by a residential brokerage listing agreement generally allows the agent to

a. create contractual obligations for the client.
b. negotiate the selling price between client and customer.
c. hire inspectors, and other individuals to prepare the property for marketing.
d. market, sell and show the property.

4.28   A salesperson, without an oral or written listing agreement, brings potential buyers to the seller. The seller says, "You can bring me buyers if you want, but I'm not paying you a commission." The salesperson then continues to direct buyers to the property. Which of the following is true about this situation?

a. There is no agency relationship, and therefore the seller will owe no commission if one of the salesperson's buyers buys the property.
b. An implied agency may have been created, with obligations to perform for both seller and agent.
c. The seller and agent have an illegal, undisclosed agency relationship.
d. The agent has an open exclusive agency listing with no commission agreement, and therefore owes no fiduciary duties to the seller.

4.29 An agent enters into a listing agreement with a homeseller, but then becomes too busy to professionally fulfill the terms of the agreement. To solve the dilemma, the agent assigns the agreement to another licensee in the office. Which of the following is true about this situation?

a. The agent cannot assign the listing agreement.
b. The new listing agent acquires the full set of fiduciary duties owed to the client.
c. The new broker has to split any commission that results with the assigning broker.
d. The original broker has to disclose the assignment to the seller.

4.30 From an agent's point of view, the most desirable form of listing agreement is a(n)

a. exclusive agency.
b. exclusive right to sell.
c. open listing.
d. net listing.

4.31 What is a multiple listing?

a. A listing shared by a listing agent and a selling agent.
b. A listing that a listing agent delegates to a subagent.
c. A listing that is entered in a multiple listing service.
d. A listing that authorizes a listing agent to market more than one property for a seller.

4.32 Which of the following conditions is necessary for a customer to qualify as "ready, willing, and able" in the context of a commissionable transaction?

a. The customer's offer must be accepted.
b. The customer must be legally competent to undertake the transaction.
c. The customer must have a commitment from a lender.
d. The customer must have no business relationship with the agent.

4.33 Although a listing broker may delegate listing tasks to an employed licensee, the broker may not delegate the authority to

a. obtain and distribute compensation.
b. provide cooperating brokers with information about the property.
c. advertise the property.
d. inspect the property for hazardous substances.

4.34 Agent Peter has an open listing with Frank. Paul is Peter's broker. Agent Perry's customer buys Frank's house. Patrick has a commission agreement with Frank. Who is most likely to be compensated in this scenario?

a. Peter, since he has a written listing agreement.
b. Paul, since he is Peter's broker
c. Perry, since he found the customer.
d. Patrick, since he has a commission agreement.

4.35 If an agent has an exclusive listing to sell a property, and the property is then taken by eminent domain, what is the status of the listing?

a. The seller's obligations under the listing are assigned to the agency that takes the property.
b. It becomes a voidable contract.
c. The commission clause of the agreement is canceled.
d. It may be terminated against the agent's will.

4.36 A broker obtains an exclusive listing to sell a house, but after two months, he abandons the listing because the seller is too demanding and hot-tempered. What can the seller do in this situation?

a. Have the licensee's license revoked for negligence.
b. Sue the broker for money damages.
c. Sign a listing agreement with another broker and force the first broker to pay the commission.
d. Force the broker to perform the contract without compensation.

4.37 An owner agrees to pay a broker for procuring a tenant unless it is the owner who finds the tenant. This is an example of a(n)

a. exclusive right-to sell agreement.
b. exclusive agency agreement.
c. open listing.
d. net listing.

4.38 A landlord promises to compensate a broker for procuring a tenant, provided the broker is the procuring cause. This is an example of a(n)

a. exclusive right-to rent agreement.
b. exclusive agency agreement.
c. open rental listing.
d. net lease listing.

4.39 A property owner agrees to pay a broker an open-ended commission as the difference between the sale price and a net amount, provided the owner receives a minimum amount of proceeds from the sale at closing. This is an example of a(n)

a. exclusive right-to sell agreement.
b. exclusive agency agreement.
c. open listing.
d. net listing.

4.40 In the context of agency law, the legal difference between an owner representation agreement and a buyer representation agreement is

a. the client.
b. the commission amount.
c. fiduciary duties.
d. regulatory approvals.

4.41 A multiple listing authorization gives a broker what authority?

a. To list the owner's property in a multiple listing service.
b. To sell several properties for the owner at once.
c. To represent both seller and buyer, if necessary, in selling the property.
d. To delegate the listing responsibilities to other agents.

4.42 Which of the following relationships characterizes a designated agency relationship?

a. A broker assign a preferred subagent from other firms to represent each party.
b. There is no such duty as maintaining confidentiality.
c. The broker primarily represents the seller.
d. The broker assigns who is to represent the buyer and seller.

Test 5: Brokerage Business; Sale Contracts

5.1   Which of the following business entities is generally prohibited from brokering real estate?

   a. Sole proprietorship.
   b. Partnership.
   c. Corporation for profit.
   d. Non-profit corporation.

5.2   A joint venture may generally broker real estate if the co-venturers

   a. form a business trust.
   b. form a co-operative association.
   c. are properly licensed.
   d. are limited partners.

5.3   A licensed salesperson may work only for

   a. a client who has signed a listing agreement with a licensed broker.
   b. a single employing broker who has an active broker's license.
   c. a client who has signed an authorization agreement with a licensed salesperson.
   d. an employer who has an active or inactive broker's license.

5.4   Which of the following activities is a licensed salesperson allowed to engage in?

   a. Accept a listing that is in an associate's name.
   b. Accept a commission directly from the MLS.
   c. Offer a property for lease on behalf of the employing broker.
   d. Sign a contract with a management company on behalf of a client.

5.5   If a salesperson has worked on a completed transaction that involved a listing agent, a selling agent, and several subagents for each of these, from whom will the salesperson receive any compensation that is due?

   a. The listing agent.
   b. The selling agent.
   c. The seller.
   d. The employing broker.

5.6   A property has sold for $380,000. The listing agreement calls for a commission of 6.5%. The listing broker and seller have agreed the listing broker will share the commission equally with the buyer broker. What will the listing agent receive if the agent is scheduled to get a 40% share?

   a. $4,445.
   b. $3,556.
   c. $2,667.
   d. $4,940.

5.7   A real estate salesperson finds a buyer to a For Sale By Owner property. The home sells for $245,000, and the seller agrees to pay a commission of 3%. The salesperson is on a 65% commission schedule with her broker, who pays her 65% minus office expenses of $500. How much will the salesperson receive from this transaction?

   a. $4,778.
   b. $4,452.
   c. $4,278.
   d. $3,175.

5.8   A salesperson makes a listing presentation to a homeseller and obtains a signed listing agreement. The first thing the salesperson must now do is

a. make a final pricing determination for the property.
b. negotiate the commission with the client.
c. complete the signing of the listing.
d. explain the agency relationship to the client.

5.9   Juan shows a customer a property that is listed by another brokerage firm. He obtains an offer that is $15,000 less than the listing price. How should Juan deal with this offer?

a. Advise the buyer that the offer will be rejected.
b. Present the offer to the seller at the earliest possible moment.
c. Ask the listing broker to lower the listing price.
d. Counter the offer.

5.10 A broker receives an earnest money deposit from a buyer and signs the check over to the listing agent as a partial commission advance. What is wrong with this procedure?

a. Nothing, provided the deposit clears the bank and doesn't bounce.
b. The broker and the agent are guilty of price fixing.
c. The broker has illegally converted security funds for business use.
d. The agent may not be able to return the advance if the transaction falls through.

5.11 Under what circumstance may a property listed for sale with a brokerage be advertised without identifying the broker?

a. When the salesperson is an out-of-state licensee.
b. When the ad is restricted to the brokerage's website.
c. When the advertisement is a silent ad.
d. Never.

5.12 Competing brokers in a county seat agree on a standard commission rate for principals within the county. This is a possible violation of

a. fair trade and anti-trust laws.
b. the Statute of Frauds.
c. contract law.
d. the Uniform Commercial Code.

5.13 What is co-brokerage?

a. An owner agent and a buyer agent combine efforts to complete a sale.
b. Outside brokers assist a listing agent in procuring a buyer.
c. An owner or buyer lists with several brokers to complete a transaction.
d. Agents from a single agency cooperate to generate listings for the broker.

5.14 Which of the following may associate his or her name or title with the term "Realtor®"?

a. Any active or inactive broker in the country.
b. Any duly licensed, active agent or broker.
c. Any member in good standing in a properly chartered real estate trade organization.
d. Only members of the National Association of Realtors®.

5.15 Real estate sales agents are legally authorized to

a. represent their employing broker in procuring clients and customers.
b. act directly on a client's behalf to discharge the broker's listing responsibilities.
c. negotiate and execute contracts for sale on behalf of the client.
d. take on the listing responsibilities for other listings in MLS.

5.16 How does the position of an independent contractor licensee (IC) differ from that of an employee licensee?

a. The IC is responsible for his or her own taxes; the broker does not withhold.
b. The IC must obtain his or her own training; it is not provided by the broker.
c. The employee is not entitled to company benefits.
d. The IC must abide by all office meeting schedules.

5.17 A salesperson's commission rate and structure is established by

a. state regulation.
b. competitive conditions.
c. agreement with other brokers in the market.
d. negotiations with the client.

5.18 In obtaining offers from a buyer, an agent must be careful to

a. pursue only those offers which are at or near the listed price.
b. balance the owner's price expectations with the buyer's opinion of value.
c. avoid disclosing what price the owner will accept.
d. avoid completing offers that are beneath market value.

5.19 Commingling is the practice of

a. blending escrow funds on a number of properties in one escrow account.
b. mixing socially with prospects at open houses or other marketing functions.
c. allocating commission funds from a transaction for use in the agency's business.
d. mixing escrow funds with the broker's operating funds.

5.20 Three leading agencies charge identical commission rates for brokering office properties in Phoenix. Based on this information alone, which of the following is true?

a. There is insufficient evidence of anything other than a normal business practice.
b. The brokers have engaged in legal collusion.
c. The brokers have allocated the Phoenix market.
d. The brokers have illegally fixed prices.

5.21 A real estate sale contract is an executory contract until

a. the completed sale transaction is recorded.
b. the buyer and seller have agreed to all provisions and have signed the contract.
c. all the obligations and promises are performed and the transaction is closed.
d. the loan has been approved, the title insurance has been obtained, and the closing date is set.

5.22 In assisting a buyer or seller to complete an offer to purchase, what should an agent do to reduce the risk of committing an unauthorized practice of law?

a. Use a standard contract promulgated by a state agency or a real estate board.
b. Observe ethical standards promulgated by real estate trade organizations.
c. Offer legal advice only on points of the contract that the agent is absolutely certain about.
d. Write contract terms that are fair to both buyer and seller.

5.23 To be enforceable, a contract for the conveyance of real estate must

a. be acknowledged by witnesses.
b. be written.
c. be recorded.
d. have an expiration date.

5.24 A buyer makes an offer to purchase a house, and the seller accepts the offer. However, before the salesperson can inform the buyer of the seller's decision, the buyer delivers a written notice that she is opting out and cancelling the agreement. At this point, which of the following is true?

a. The contract has been legitimately cancelled and is null and void.
b. The seller must give the buyer an opportunity to make a new offer.
c. The buyer must perform under the terms of the contract
d. The seller must notify the buyer in writing that the buyer is in default.

5.25 Which of the following is an essential element of a valid contract for the sale of real estate?

a. A valid blank form that the contract is written on.
b. A habitable property.
c. An offer and acceptance.
d. A marketable title.

5.26 What kind of interest does the buyer acquire once a real estate sale contract is signed by the principal parties?

a. Legal title.
b. Lienholder interest.
c. Reversionary interest.
d. Equitable title.

5.27 A contingency in a sale contract is

a. a promise by buyer or seller to perform a specific action.
b. a condition that, if unmet, renders the contract unenforceable.
c. one of several alternative actions that buyer or seller may take to satisfy contract requirements.
d. an optional, unilateral action that either party may take at the request of the other party.

5.28 A clause in a sale contract stipulates that the seller must provide evidence that the property is free of active termite infestation. On the day of closing, the buyer learns that inspection service did not provide the required written documentation. The buyer then proceeds to declare that the sale is off. Which of the following is true of this situation?

a. The seller can sue for specific performance.
b. The buyer will be in default, and liable for damages, if he does not complete the transaction.
c. The buyer may be able to have the contract canceled.
d. The contract is automatically void.

5.29 A buyer signs an earnest money agreement and gives it to the broker who showed her the property she is buying. After leaving the broker's office, she reconsiders and decides she prefers a different property. How long does she have to take back her offer?

a. Until the seller communicates acceptance of the offer.
b. Until the earnest money deposit check is cashed.
c. She can take it back at any time, but must forfeit the earnest money.
d. She cannot take it back until after the expiration date of the offer.

5.30 On Wednesday, Fred offers to sell his property to Jack for $275,000, with the offer to remain open until 5 p.m. the next day. On Thursday morning, Sally offers Fred $280,000 for the property and Fred accepts. At 1 p.m. on Thursday afternoon, Jack accepts. Which of the following is true of this situation?

a. The acceptance by Sally creates a contract and terminates Fred's offer to Jack.
b. Fred has entered into contracts with both Jack and Sally to sell the same property.
c. Fred's acceptance of Sally's offer is invalidated by Jack's acceptance, because Fred's offer to Jack was made prior to Sally's offer to Fred.
d. No contract has been created because it is impossible to have two valid sale contracts for the same property.

5.31 Among the items that normally must be disclosed in a sale contract or its addenda is/are the

a. buyer's financial capability.
b. buyer's source of funds for the down payment.
c. seller's acceptable price range.
d. agency relationships and property condition.

5.32 To create an enforceable option-to-buy contract, there must be an exchange of

a. a promise to sell and a promise to buy.
b. valuable consideration and a right to buy.
c. valuable consideration and a promise to buy.
d. a down payment and a post-dated contract for sale.

5.33 Mary Carboy buys a house from Jim Schmidt and at the same time obtains an option to purchase the adjoining vacant lot for $10,000 within one year. A few months later, Carboy informs Schmidt that she is ready to exercise her option, but finds that Schmidt has received an offer of $12,000 from another party. Schmidt states that he will accept the offer unless Carboy is willing to match the $12,000 offer. Which of the following is true of this situation?

a. Schmidt must sell to Carboy for $10,000.
b. Carboy must pay $12,000 or lose the property.
c. Schmidt may sell to Carboy or the other party, but the price cannot exceed $10,000.
d. If the other party delivers payment before Carboy does, the option is canceled.

5.34 Which of the following is true regarding the assignability of an option?

a. It is assignable only if the contract specifically allows assignment.
b. It is never assignable.
c. It is assignable only if the option is exercised.
d. It is always assignable unless the contract prohibits assignment.

5.35 Which of the following is true of a contract for deed transaction?

a. At the end of the contract period, the vendee receives equitable title, provided all required periodic payments have been made.
b. The vendee has no right to possess or occupy the property during the contract period.
c. At the end of the contract period, the vendor conveys legal title, provided the vendee has fulfilled all obligations.
d. The vendor may cancel the contract at any time before the final payment has been received.

5.36 Several buyers are competing for the last available home in a desirable new subdivision. One buyer calls the owner-developer directly on the phone and offers $20,000 over and above the listed price. The developer accepts the offer. At this point,

a. the parties have a valid, enforceable sale contract on the home.
b. the parties have completed a verbal, executory contract.
c. the parties may not cancel their contract.
d. the developer could not entertain other offers on the property.

5.37 An owner completes a sales contract on her property with a buyer. Before closing, the seller runs into financial trouble and assigns the contract to her principal creditor. The buyer cries foul, fearing the property will be lost. Which of the following is true?

a. The buyer can sue the assignee to disallow the illegal assignment.
b. The buyer can take legal action against the assignor.
c. The assignor has completed a legal action.
d. The sale contract is nullified.

5.38. A due-on-sale clause in a sale contract puts parties on notice that

a. the full price of the property is due to the seller at closing.
b. any loans surviving closing become immediately payable.
c. all of the seller's debts must be retired before or upon closing.
d. any conveyance may trigger an acceleration of any loans secured by the property.

5.39 A tenant has an option-to-purchase agreement with the landlord that expires on June 30. On July 1, the tenant frantically calls the landlord to exercise the option, offering the apology that she was busy with a death in the family. Which of the following is true?

a. Since options contain grace periods, the landlord must sell.
b. The tenant loses the right to buy, but can claim the money paid for the option from the landlord.
c. The landlord does not have to sell, but must renew the option.
d. The option is expired, and the tenant has no rightful claim to money paid for the option.

5.40 Two parties enter into a contract for deed agreement. In this form of agreement,

a. title is conveyed to the buyer, but the seller retains possession for a stipulated time period.
b. the buyer contracts to pay all cash at closing in exchange for the deed.
c. the seller retains legal title while the buyer makes partial payments until the contract is fully executed.
d. the buyer immediately acquires legal title and takes possession.

5.41 The federal law that produced the Do-Not-Call list and related protections is referred to as the

a. Solicitation Regulation Act.
b. Telemarketing Prohibition Act.
c. CAN-SPAM Act.
d. Telephone Consumer Protection Act

5.42 New federal regulation in advertising requires email advertisers to give recipients an option to discontinue receiving emails from such advertiser. This legislation is called

a. the CAN-SPAM Act.
b. the Truth-in-Advertising Act
c. the Telephone Consumer Protection Act
d. the Email Advertising Prohibition Act, or EAPA.

5.43 Which of the following is NOT a trust fund violation?

    a. Using operating funds to reimburse a tenant's lease deposit if spent by the broker.
    b. Keeping enough operating funds in a trust account to cover bank fees.
    c. Depositing trust funds in an operating account.
    d. Returning trust funds to a buyer if approved by all parties.

5.44 In the village of Bobcat Heights, a group of brokers in the MLS mutually agree to not show broker Nguyen's listings. This would be considered a violation of

    a. fair trade practices.
    b. redlining.
    c. housing discrimination.
    d. sandbagging.

6.1   If the price of an item is increasing, one can usually assume that

a. demand for the item is decreasing in relation to supply of the item.
b. demand for the item is increasing in relation to supply of the item.
c. supply of the item is increasing.
d. demand for the item and supply of the item are increasing.

6.2   When the market for an item has achieved market equilibrium, which of the following statements is true?

a. New suppliers will enter the market and drive the price down.
b. Demand will slowly taper off, driving the price down.
c. Unmet demand for the item is directed toward demand for some other item.
d. Supply and demand are equal, and price and value are equal.

6.3   As an economic product, real estate is distinguished by

a. its homogeneity.
b. its variety.
c. the uniqueness of every parcel.
d. its ability to appreciate in value.

6.4   The city of Stevensville has declared a moratorium on new construction. If demand is increasing, what will be the likely effect on real estate prices in the area?

a. Prices level off.
b. Prices continue to follow the trend that preceded the moratorium.
c. Prices fall.
d. Prices rise.

6.5   If Okapi, Inc., a company that markets its sports clothing worldwide, moves into Stevensville and hires 100 employees, it is reasonable to expect that the town will experience

a. an immediate rise in the demand for industrial real estate, but no other changes in the real estate market.
b. an increase in demand for all types of real estate.
c. a housing boom, but no other changes in the real estate market.
d. an immediate increase in the prices for industrial and office real estate, but no impact on the residential market.

6.6   What is "absorption?"

a. The amount of new space that is added to available space over a period of time.
b. The number of houses that are built over a period of time.
c. The amount of space that is occupied at any given time.
d. The number of available units that become occupied over a period of time.

6.7   When vacancies are declining in a real estate market, it is common for the market to experience

a. rising prices.
b. falling prices.
c. falling construction activity.
d. falling absorption.

6.8   The price for any product is a function of four fundamental determinants of value. These are

a. durability, feasibility, mobility, and location.
b. desire, utility, scarcity, and purchasing power.
c. popularity, recognizability, promotion, and rebate.
d. fungibility, costs, convenience, and uniqueness.

6.9   A town is rapidly growing, but all the buildable vacant lots in the most desirable area have already been occupied. In this case, it is likely that the price of existing homes in that area

a. will stabilize, since the population must stabilize.
b. will increase.
c. will decline, since no further building can take place.
d. will not show any predictable movement.

6.10   If there is a significant undersupply of homes in a market, construction will tend to increase. This is an example of

a. supply outstripping demand.
b. demand outstripping value.
c. consumer optimism.
d. the market tending toward equilibrium.

6.11   If commercial real estate rental prices are falling in a market, it is likely that

a. demand has outstripped supply of space.
b. the market is in equilibrium.
c. the market is over-supplied.
d. employment is increasing.

6.12   A construction boom in a market is an indication that prices

a. have been increasing.
b. have been declining.
c. have been in equilibrium.
d. have exceeded supply.

6.13   Why is real estate traditionally considered a relatively illiquid economic product?

a. Its physical form is fixed.
b. Real estate is defined as land, not water.
c. It is often difficult to convert to cash.
d. It cannot be moved.

6.14   What does "base employment" refer to in the context of real estate demand?

a. The lowest category of employment in terms of wages and desirability
b. The number of persons employed in base industries in an area
c. The number of persons employed on military bases in an area
d. The labor pool available for employment in all industries in an area

6.15   What is "vacancy" in real estate market economics?

a. A property that has no owner-occupant
b. The total number of properties of a certain type that are on the market at a given time
c. The absence of certain types of users in a given market area
d. The total existing space of a certain type that is unoccupied at a given time

6.16 A moratorium on new construction is an example of

    a. local government influencing the real estate market, regardless of demand.
    b. the natural result of demand exceeding supply in a local market.
    c. government promotion of the free market concept in the local real estate market.
    d. a government policy that aims to restrain a trend of rising prices in the local real estate market.

6.17 Of the following potential influences on a local real estate market, which one would be considered local, rather than regional, national, or global?

    a. Changes in money supply
    b. Federal Reserve interest rates
    c. In- and out-migrations of major employers
    d. Trade imbalances with foreign trading partners

6.18 There is a lot of new construction going on in the town of Florence. Which of the following would most likely be the immediate effect on the real estate market?

    a. Demand increases and prices rise.
    b. Vacancy rises and prices fall.
    c. Absorption and vacancy decrease.
    d. Supply decreases relative to demand.

6.19 What kind of real estate users are most concerned with neighborhood quality, access to services, property amenities, and quality of life in their demand for real estate?

    a. Retail
    b. Office
    c. Industrial
    d. Residential

6.20 One distinguishing feature of real estate as an economic product is

    a. its easy convertibility to cash.
    b. its quick response to changes in supply-demand balance.
    c. its susceptibility to swings in the local economy.
    d. the easy substitutability of one item for another.

6.21 Bill Parsons paid $450,000 for a house to operate as a rental property, figuring that he could rent it out at a rate of $2,700 a month. In paying a price based on the property's ability to generate a desired future income, Parsons was motivated by the economic principle known as

    a. substitution.
    b. anticipation.
    c. supply and demand.
    d. utility.

6.22 Which of the following situations illustrates the principle of contribution?

    a. A homebuyer makes a down payment of 20% instead of the 10% the lender requires.
    b. A homeowner adds a third bathroom to a house and thereby increases the appraised value by $10,000.
    c. The appraised value of a house goes up by $20,000 over a two-year period because of the prices recently paid for other houses in the neighborhood.
    d. Because of a decline in mortgage interest rates, a homeowner in a certain market is able to list her house at a higher price.

6.23   When a property owner combines two adjacent properties to create a single property with a higher value than the sum of the values of the two separate properties, the applicable principle of value is called

    a. assemblage.
    b. accretion.
    c. progression.
    d. subdivision.

6.24   What is the difference between market value and market price, if any?

    a. There is no difference.
    b. Market value is a broker's estimate; market price is a precise number derived by a licensed appraiser.
    c. Market value is an average price derived from comparable sales; market price is a price based on the cost of creating the property.
    d. Market value is an estimate; market price is the price at which a property sold.

6.25   Which of the following is a valid requirement for defensibly characterizing a property's living area?

    a. Countable living area must be attached to the main house.
    b. Closets must be excluded from gross living area.
    c. The property must be finished, i.e., have completed studwork and sub-flooring.
    d. Enclosed porches and stairways cannot be counted as living area.

6.26   How is a property's gross living area generally measured?

    a. From the lot's area, minus the area of improved buildings
    b. From the exterior walls, above grade, excluding open areas
    c. By measuring the interior rooms
    d. By measuring area of all enclosed rooms, minus the basement and attic

6.27   Which of the following statements properly describes the central concept of the sales comparison approach?

    a. Find the median price of recently sold comparable properties and add or subtract dollar amounts in the subject property to account for competitive differences.
    b. Make dollar adjustments to the sale prices of comparable properties to account for competitive differences with the subject.
    c. Find at least three comparable properties that are currently for sale and make dollar adjustments to the listing prices to account for competitive differences with the subject.
    d. Apply an appreciation factor to the price at which the subject property most recently sold and make dollar adjustments to account for competitive differences with comparable properties currently for sale.

6.28   One of the strengths of the sales comparison approach is that it

    a. takes into account the subject property's investment value.
    b. reveals the profit margin of the builder or developer of the subject property.
    c. discovers the underlying value of the subject property apart from the influence of competing properties.
    d. takes into account the competitive value of specific amenities of the subject property.

6.29   In making dollar adjustments in the sales comparison approach, the appraiser

    a. adds value to a comparable that is inferior to the subject property.
    b. adds value to the subject property if it is inferior to a comparable.
    c. subtracts value from a comparable that is inferior to the subject property.
    d. subtracts value from the subject property if it is inferior to a comparable.

6.30   The best comparable property for use in the sales comparison approach is the one that

a. requires the most and largest adjustments.
b. requires the fewest and smallest adjustments.
c. sold most recently at the highest price.
d. is located closest to the subject property.

6.31   A house is being appraised using the sales comparison approach. The house has three bedrooms, two bathrooms, and a patio. The appraiser selects a comparable house that has three bedrooms, 3 bathrooms, and no patio. The comparable house just sold for $400,000. A bath is valued at $7,000, and a patio at $2,000. Assuming all else is equal, what is the adjusted value of the comparable?

a. $402,000.
b. $407,000.
c. $395,000.
d. $405,000.

6.32   Which of the following statements properly describes the central methodology of the cost approach to appraisal?

a. Apply a depreciation factor to the reported actual cost of acquiring and improving the subject property.
b. Estimate the cost of building the improvements on the subject property.
c. Estimate the land value and add to this the actual cost of the improvements adjusted for competitive differences with similar properties.
d. Add the estimated land value and cost of improvements and subtract the accrued depreciation of the improvements.

6.33   One of the strengths of the cost approach is that it

a. takes into account the amount of money required to develop a similar property.
b. is very accurate for a property with new improvements that represent the highest and best use.
c. results in an actual price in dollars instead of an estimated value.
d. reveals the owner's return on money invested in the cost of development.

6.34   The principle underlying depreciation from physical deterioration is that

a. eventually, a property loses all of its value.
b. a property loses a portion of its value each year because of economic obsolescence.
c. a property loses the same increment of value each year over the economic life of the property.
d. the value lost to depreciation is incurable.

6.35   A property is being appraised by the cost approach. The appraiser estimates that the land is worth $150,000 and the replacement cost of the improvements is $475,000. Total depreciation from all causes is $50,000. What is the indicated value of the property?

a. $675,000.
b. $650,000.
c. $625,000.
d. $575,000.

6.36   Which of the following statements properly describes how to apply the income capitalization approach to appraisal?

a. Apply a rate of return to the price paid for an income property.
b. Divide the income a property generates by a rate of return.
c. Estimate the amount of income a property must generate to return the capital amount invested in it.
d. Estimate the rate of return a property owner receives from income generated by the property.

6.37 A strength of the income capitalization approach is that it

a. uses a rate of return that is required for all potential purchasers in a market.
b. yields an accurate projection of investment income.
c. uses a method that is also used by investors to determine how much they should pay for an investment property.
d. can be used with any type of property in any market.

6.38 A property is being appraised using the income capitalization approach. Annually, it has an estimated gross income of $60,000, vacancy and credit losses of $3,000, and operating expenses of $20,000. Using a capitalization rate of ten percent, what is the indicated value (to the nearest $1,000)?

a. $370,000.
b. $400,000.
c. $570,000.
d. $600,000.

6.39 An apartment building that sold for $450,000 had monthly gross rent receipts of $3,000. What is its monthly gross rent multiplier?

a. 12.5
b. .01.
c. .08.
d. 150.

6.40 A rental house has monthly gross income of $2,400. A suitable gross income multiplier derived from market data is 14.1. What estimated sale price (to the nearest $1,000) is indicated?

a. $338,000.
b. $204,000.
c. $406,000.
d. $346,000.

6.41 A certified appraiser is one who has received certification by

a. a licensed real estate school.
b. the Appraisal Institute.
c. the state in which the appraiser operates.
d. the Appraisal Review Board.

6.42 The act that required federally-related appraisals to be conducted by a certified appraiser is known as

a. The Financial Institutions Reform, Recovery and Enforcement Act (FIRREA).
b. The Uniform Standards of Professional Appraisal Practice Act (USPAPA).
c. The Appraisal Foundation Authorization and Reform Act (AFAR).
d. The Federal Institution for Regulation and Enforcement of Appraisal Act (FIREAA).

6.43 As a component of real estate value, the principle of substitution states that

a. if two similar properties are for sale, a buyer will purchase the cheaper of the two.
b. if one of two adjacent homes is more valuable, the price of the other home will tend to rise.
c. if too many properties are built in a market, the prices will tend to go down.
d. people will readily move to another home if it is of equal value.

6.44 Highest and best use of a property is that use which

a. is physically and financially feasible, legal, and the most productive.
b. is legal, feasible, and deemed the most appropriate by zoning authorities.
c. entails the largest building that zoning ordinances will allow developers to erect.
d. conforms to other properties in the area.

6.45 Lynne just bought a house. She paid $375,000, for it, even though it had been listed at $390,000. An adjoining property owner, Ken, had tried to buy the property for $370,000, but had been refused. He now offers Lynne $380,000 for the house. Lynne is interested, so she hires an appraiser. The appraiser returns an estimate of value of $400,000. Which of these numbers can be called the market value?

    a. $375,000.
    b. $380,000.
    c. $390,000.
    d. $400,000.

6.46 A notable weakness of the sales comparison approach to value is that

    a. there may be no recent sale price data in the market.
    b. the approach is not based on the principle of substitution.
    c. the approach is only accurate with unique, special purpose properties.
    d. sale prices cannot be compared, since all real estate is different.

6.47 In the market data approach, an appraiser

    a. chooses nearby comparables, adjusts the subject for differences, and estimates the value.
    b. gathers relevant price data, applies the data to the subject, and estimates the value.
    c. selects comparable properties, adjusts the comparables, and estimates the value.
    d. identifies the price previously paid, applies an appreciation rate, and estimates the value.

6.48 In the sales comparison approach, an adjustment is warranted if

    a. the buyer obtains conventional financing for the property.
    b. the seller offers below-market seller financing.
    c. a comparable is located in another, albeit similar neighborhood.
    d. one property has a hip roof and the other has a gabled roof.

6.49 To complete the sales comparison approach, the appraiser

    a. averages the comparable values.
    b. weights the comparables.
    c. identifies the subject's value as that of the middle value of the comparables.
    d. identifies the subject's value as that of the nearest comparable.

6.50 One weakness of the cost approach for appraising market value is that

    a. builders may not pay market value for materials or labor.
    b. market value is not always the same as what the property cost.
    c. comparables used may not have similar quality of construction.
    d. new properties have inestimable costs and rates of depreciation.

6.51 The cost of constructing a functional equivalent of a subject property is known as

    a. reproduction cost.
    b. replacement cost.
    c. restitution cost.
    d. reconstruction cost.

6.52 An office building lacks fiber optic cabling to accommodate the latest communications equipment. This is an example of

    a. physical deterioration.
    b. economic obsolescence.
    c. incurable depreciation.
    d. functional obsolescence.

6.53 A home is located in a neighborhood where homeowners on the block have failed to maintain their properties. This is an example of

a. curable external obsolescence.
b. incurable economic obsolescence.
c. functional obsolescence.
d. physical deterioration.

6.54 In appraisal, loss of value in a property from any cause is referred to as

a. deterioration.
b. obsolescence.
c. depreciation.
d. deflation.

6.55 In the cost approach, after estimating the value of the land and the cost of the improvements, the appraiser

a. estimates depreciation, subtracts depreciation from cost, and adds back the land value.
b. subtracts deterioration from cost, estimates land depreciation, and totals the two values.
c. estimates depreciation of land and improvements and subtracts the total from original cost.
d. estimates obsolescence and subtracts from the cost of land and improvements.

6.56 Which regulatory entity/code establishes standards for an appraiser's methods, reporting methods and disclosures?

a. Financial Institutions Reform, Recovery, and Enforcement Act (FIRREA)
b. Uniform Standards of Professional Appraisal Practice (USPAP)
c. National Association of Realtors®' Code of Ethics
d. Federal Appraisal Regulation and Licensing Board.

7.1   What is a lien-theory state?

a. A state in which a mortgagee holds legal title to a secured property.
b. A state in which a mortgagee has equitable title to a secured property.
c. A state that allows a real estate owner's creditors to record liens against the owner's property.
d. A state in which a lien is considered as a conveyance.

7.2   What is the function of a note in a mortgage or trust deed financing arrangement?

a. It is the lender's security instrument in the collateral property.
b. It is evidence of ownership of the mortgage or trust deed.
c. It contains the borrower's promise to maintain the value of the property given as collateral for a loan.
d. It is evidence of the borrower's debt to the lender.

7.3   When homebuyer Henry pledges his newly purchased home as collateral for a mortgage loan, the evidence of the pledge is the

a. trust deed or mortgage.
b. promissory note.
c. loan commitment.
d. loan receipt.

7.4   The borrower in a mortgage loan transaction is known as the

a. mortgagee.
b. mortgagor.
c. lienor.
d. trustee.

7.5   If a borrower obtains an interest-only loan of $200,000 at an annual interest rate of 6%, what is the monthly interest payment?

a. $1,200.
b. $600.
c. $500.
d. $1,000.

7.6   If a borrower's monthly interest payment on an interest-only loan at an annual interest rate of 6% is $5,000, how much was the loan amount?

a. $720,000.
b. $1,000,000.
c. $1,200,000.
d. $500,000.

7.7   A borrower of a $250,000 interest-only loan makes annual interest payments of $18,750. What interest rate is the borrower paying?

a. 7.5%.
b. .75%.
c. 3.75%.
d. 8.5%.

7.8   Maria borrows $600,000 and pays two points for the loan. How much does she pay in points?

      a. $1,200.
      b. $12,000.
      c. $7,200.
      d. It depends on the interest rate.

7.9   Which of the following is true of an amortizing loan?

      a. The amount of annual interest paid is the same for every year of the loan term.
      b. Part of each periodic payment is applied to repayment of the loan balance in advance and part is applied to payment of interest in arrears.
      c. Except for any points that may be paid, the interest on the loan balance is usually paid in advance.
      d. The interest rate is reduced each year to maintain equal payments even though the outstanding loan balance is smaller.

7.10 For a loan that is not backed by the Federal Housing Administration or Veterans Administration, and for which the borrower is making a down payment of less than 20%, the lender is likely to require the borrower to obtain

      a. a subrogation agreement.
      b. private mortgage insurance.
      c. a letter of credit.
      d. a co-signer on the note.

7.11 What is a loan-to-value ratio?

      a. The percentage of a lender's portfolio that is composed of mortgage loans.
      b. The ratio of borrowed principal plus total interest to the appraised value of the collateral property.
      c. The ratio of a lender's return on a mortgage loan to the value of the collateral property.
      d. The fraction of the appraised value of the property offered as collateral which the lender is willing to lend.

7.12 The difference between what a borrower has to pay to purchase a property and the amount a lender will lend on the property is the

      a. mortgage insurance coverage amount.
      b. lender's profit margin.
      c. buyer's down payment.
      d. origination fee.

7.13 The Equal Credit Opportunity Act prohibits a lender from

      a. refusing a loan because the borrower does not match the lender's target market.
      b. including income from self-employment in the borrower's qualifying income.
      c. requiring both spouses to sign the loan application form.
      d. refusing a loan because a borrower has a defective credit report.

7.14 A loan applicant has an annual gross income of $72,000. How much will a lender allow the applicant to pay for monthly housing expense to qualify for a loan if the lender uses an income ratio of 28%?

      a. $2,160.
      b. $1,680.
      c. $1,068.
      d. $840.

7.15 AMC Bank discovers, in considering buyer Bob's application for a mortgage loan, that Bob has borrowed the down payment from an uncle and has to repay that loan. Bob should expect that AMC Bank will

a. refuse the application.
b. adjust the applicant's debt ratio calculation and lower the loan amount.
c. increase the loan amount to enable the borrower to pay off the loan to the relative.
d. require the borrower to make payments to an escrow account for repayment of the relative's loan.

7.16 The Federal Reserve's Regulation Z applies to which loans?

a. All loans.
b. All loans secured by real estate.
c. All loans secured by a residence.
d. All loans over $25,000.

7.17 If a particular loan falls under Regulation Z's right of rescission provision,

a. the lender has the right to change the terms of the loan within a certain period.
b. the lender has the right to accelerate repayment of the loan because of a change in the borrower's credit status.
c. the borrower has the right to pay off the loan ahead of schedule with no penalty.
d. the borrower has a limited right to cancel the transaction within a certain period.

7.18 Under the Equal Credit Opportunity Act, a lender, or a real estate agent who assists a seller in qualifying a potential buyer, may not

a. tell a rejected loan applicant the reasons for the rejection.
b. ask the buyer/borrower about his/her religion or national origin.
c. ask the buyer/borrower to explain unconventional sources of income.
d. use a credit report that has not been provided to the borrower.

7.19 A conventional mortgage loan is one that is

a. backed by the Federal National Mortgage Association.
b. insured under Section 203(b) of the Federal Housing Administration loan program.
c. guaranteed by the Government National Mortgage Association.
d. not FHA-insured or VA-guaranteed.

7.20 The assumability of an FHA-insured loan is

a. unrestricted.
b. limited by when the loan was originated.
c. limited to owner-occupied properties.
d. prohibited on all existing loans under current regulations.

7.21 A VA certificate of eligibility determines

a. how long an individual served in the military.
b. the maximum loan amount an approved lender can give to veterans.
c. how much of a loan the VA will guarantee.
d. whether a lender is approved to issue VA-guaranteed loans.

7.22 A borrower obtains a 30-year, fully amortizing mortgage loan of $450,000 at 8%. What is the principal balance at the end of the loan term?

a. $36,000.
b. $450,000.
c. $4,220.
d. Zero.

7.23 Which of the following describes a purchase money mortgage financing arrangement?

a. A bank gives a buyer a senior mortgage loan that fully covers the cost of purchasing the property.
b. The buyer gives the seller a mortgage and note as part of the purchase price of the property.
c. A land trust holds title to the property while the buyer makes periodic installment payments to the seller.
d. The seller uses the purchase money obtained from the buyer's mortgage loan to repay the seller's outstanding loan balance.

7.24 A homeowner borrows money from a lender and gives the lender a mortgage on the property as collateral for the loan. The homeowner retains title to the property. This is an example of

a. intermediation.
b. forfeiture.
c. hypothecation.
d. subordination.

7.25 Which of the following correctly describes the flow of money and documents in a mortgage loan transaction?

a. The borrower gives the lender a note and a mortgage in exchange for loan funds.
b. The lender gives the borrower a mortgage and receives a note in exchange for loan funds.
c. The borrower receives a note in exchange for a mortgage from the lender.
d. The lender gives the borrower a note, loan funds and a mortgage.

7.26 In a deed of trust transaction, which of the following occurs?

a. The beneficiary conveys title to a trustee in exchange for loan funds.
b. The trustee conveys title to a beneficiary in exchange for loan funds.
c. The trustor conveys title to a trustee in exchange for loan funds from the beneficiary.
d. The trustee conveys title to a trustor in exchange for loan funds from the beneficiary.

7.27 A lender lends money to a homeowner and takes legal title to the property as collateral during the payoff period. They are in a

a. title-theory state.
b. lien-theory state.
c. state allowing land trusts.
d. state where hypothecation is illegal.

7.28 A lender who charges a rate of interest in excess of legal limits is guilty of

a. redlining.
b. usury.
c. profit-taking.
d. nothing; there are no legal limits to interest rates.

7.29 A lender is charging 2.5 points on a $300,000 loan. The borrower must therefore pay the lender an advance amount of

a. $3,600.
b. $750.
c. $7,500.
d. $6,000.

7.30 The difference between a balloon loan and an amortized loan is

    a. an amortized loan is paid off over the loan period.
    b. a balloon loan always has a shorter loan term.
    c. an amortized loan requires interest-payments.
    d. a balloon loan must be retired in five years.

7.31 A distinctive feature of a promissory note is that

    a. it is not assignable.
    b. it must be accompanied by a mortgage.
    c. it is a negotiable instrument.
    d. it may not be prepaid.

7.32 When the terms of the mortgage loan are satisfied, the mortgagee

    a. may retain any overage in the escrow account.
    b. may inspect the property before returning legal title.
    c. may be entitled to charge the borrower a small fee to close the loan.
    d. may be required to execute a release of mortgage document.

7.33 In addition to income, credit, and employment data, a mortgage lender requires additional documentation, usually including

    a. an appraisal report.
    b. a criminal record report.
    c. a subordination agreement.
    d. a default recourse waiver.

7.34 The three overriding considerations of a lender's mortgage loan decision are

    a. points, interest rate, and loan term.
    b. the location of the mortgaged property, the borrower's cash, and the amount of the borrower's equity.
    c. the ability to re-pay, the value of the collateral, and the profitability of the loan.
    d. the amount of the loan, the borrower's income, and the down payment.

7.35 The reason lenders consider the loan-to-value ratio important in underwriting is that

    a. they don't want to lend borrowers any more money than necessary.
    b. they want to ensure there is more than enough collateral to cover the loan amount.
    c. borrowers can only afford to borrow a portion of the entire purchase price.
    d. the higher the loan-to-value ratio, the more profitable the loan.

7.36 The Equal Credit Opportunity Act (ECOA) requires lenders to

    a. extend equal credit to all prospective borrowers.
    b. consider the income of a spouse in evaluating a family's creditworthiness.
    c. discount the income of a person involved in child-rearing or child-bearing.
    d. specialize in lending activity by geographical area for improved customer service.

7.37 Lenders use an income ratio in qualifying to

    a. insure a borrower has the earning power to make the loan payments.
    b. compare a borrower's earnings to the borrower's short-term debt.
    c. identify the highest possible interest rate that the borrower can afford.
    d. quantify the borrower's assets to the fullest extent.

7.38 The debt ratio formula used to qualify borrowers is

    a. total debt divided by debt payments.
    b. gross income divided by assets.
    c. gross income divided by debts.
    d. debt payments divided by gross income.

7.39 At the closing of a mortgage loan

    a. the borrower pays off the note and receives clear title.
    b. the lender issues a firm loan commitment.
    c. the parties complete all loan origination documents and the loan is funded.
    d. the borrower's loan application is complete and the file closed.

7.40 Which laws or regulations require mortgage lenders to disclose financing costs and annual percentage rate to a borrower before funding a loan?

    a. The Equal Credit Opportunity Act.
    b. Truth-in-Lending laws and Regulation Z.
    c. The Real Estate Settlement and Procedures Act.
    d. Federal Fair Housing Laws.

7.41 Which laws or regulations prevent mortgage lenders from discriminating in extending credit to potential borrowers?

    a. The Equal Credit Opportunity Act.
    b. Truth-in-Lending laws.
    c. The Real Estate Settlement and Procedures Act.
    d. Federal Fair Housing Laws.

7.42 Which laws or regulations require mortgage lenders to provide an estimate of closing costs to a borrower and forbid them to pay kickbacks for referrals?

    a. The Equal Credit Opportunity Act.
    b. Truth-in-Lending laws.
    c. the Real Estate Settlement and Procedures Act.
    d. Federal Fair Housing Laws.

7.43 Which of the following are methods used by the Federal Reserve System to regulate the money supply?

    a. Selling securities, printing money, and controlling lending underwriting requirements.
    b. Buying securities, changing the discount rate, and controlling banking reserves.
    c. Printing money, changing interest rates, and selling T-bills.
    d. Controlling the prime rate, trading securities, and purchasing loans.

7.44 How does the secondary mortgage market aid borrowers seeking a mortgage loan?

    a. It cycles funds back to primary lenders so they can make more loans.
    b. It issues second mortgages and sells them in the home equity market.
    c. It lends funds to banks so they can make more loans.
    d. It pays off defaulted loans made by primary mortgage lenders.

7.45 The major organizations operating in the secondary mortgage market are

    a. Fannie Mae, Freddie Mac, and Ginnie Mae.
    b. Fannie Mae, GMAC, and MGIC.
    c. Freddie Mac, FHA, and VA.
    d. Fannie Mae, Freddie Mac, and the Federal Reserve.

7.46   What is the role of Fannie Mae in the secondary mortgage market?

   a. It guarantees FHA-backed and VA-backed loans.
   b. It insures FHA-backed and VA-backed loans.
   c. It purchases FHA-backed and VA-backed loans.
   d. It originates FHA-backed and VA-backed loans.

7.47   What is the role of the Federal Housing Authority in the mortgage lending market?

   a. It guarantees loans made by approved lenders.
   b. It insures loans made by approved lenders.
   c. It purchases loans made by approved lenders.
   d. It originates loans made by approved lenders.

7.48   What is the role of the Veteran's Administration in the mortgage lending market?

   a. It guarantees loans made by approved lenders.
   b. It insures loans made by approved lenders.
   c. It purchases loans made by approved lenders.
   d. It originates loans made by approved lenders.

7.49   In a graduated payment mortgage loan,

   a. loan funds are disbursed to the borrower on a graduated basis.
   b. the interest rate periodically increases in graduated phases.
   c. the loan payments gradually increase.
   d. the loan payments gradually increase and the loan term gradually decreases.

7.50   In a buydown,

   a. the lender lowers the interest rate on a loan in exchange for a prepayment of principal.
   b. the borrower pays additional interest at the onset in order to obtain a lower interest rate.
   c. the lender requires the borrower to buy down the price of the property by increasing the down payment.
   d. the borrower pays the lender additional funds to buy down the term of the loan.

7.51   Steve just purchased a house for $750,000 with a $700,000 mortgage loan and $50,000 cash downpayment. Which of the following will Steve's lender most likely require in order to approve this loan?

   a. A personal guarantee
   b. A buydown loan as a second lien
   c. Private mortgage insurance
   d. Additional points

7.52   Who is the primary customer for the Federal Agricultural Mortgage Corporation, or FAMC?

   a. Military veterans from farming families
   b. Primary medical market lenders
   c. Economically liquid farmers
   d. Agribusinesses

8.1　When an investor has to pay a lender more to finance the investment than the investment property generates in income, the investor suffers from

    a. negative amortization.
    b. negative leverage.
    c. a reverse mortgage.
    d. a debt investment.

8.2　Cost recovery is allowed as a federal tax deduction on

    a. principal residences that do not have a home office.
    b. income properties.
    c. land.
    d. commercial properties owned by the federal government.

8.3　A homeowner paid $200,000 for a house three years ago. The house sells today for $239,000. How much has the property appreciated?

    a. 8.4 %.
    b. 6.5 %.
    c. 19.5 %.
    d. 16.3 %.

8.4　The primary tax benefit in owning a non-income property such as a residence is

    a. depreciation of improvements.
    b. appreciation of land.
    c. a deduction for costs of operating the property.
    d. a deduction for mortgage interest.

8.5　A house sold for $250,000. The seller paid a brokerage commission of six percent, legal fees of $600, and had other closing costs of $1,500. What are net proceeds from the sale?

    a. $235,000.
    b. $234,000.
    c. $233,500.
    d. $232,900.

8.6　A homeowner bought a house five years ago for $450,000. Since then, the homeowner has spent $9,000 to pave the driveway and has added a central heating/air conditioning system at a cost of $12,000.　What is the homeowner's adjusted basis if the house is sold today?

    a. $468,000.
    b. $471,000.
    c. $429,000.
    d. $435,000.

8.7　A homeowner sold her house and realized a net proceeds amount of $420,000. Her adjusted basis in the home was $352,000. She immediately bought another house for $400,000. What was her capital gain?

    a. $20,000.
    b. $48,000.
    c. $68,000.
    d. None.

8.8 After five years of owner-occupancy, Simon Wilson sells his principal residence for a gain of $150,000, and the next month buys another principal residence that costs more than the adjusted sale price of the old home. Which of the following is true of the treatment of the tax on gain?

   a. There is no taxable gain.
   b. It must be paid in the year of the sale.
   c. The homeowner may choose to pay it or defer it.
   d. Tax is due on the difference between the cost of the new home and adjusted basis of the old one.

8.9 Ralph Roberts buys a small office building as an investment and participates actively in the management and operation of the building. This is an example of

   a. syndication.
   b. equity investment.
   c. direct investment.
   d. illiquidity.

8.10 Elmo Gilmore owns a small retail property that he inherited from his father. There are no mortgages or interest expenses connected with the property. Elmo takes an annual cost recovery expense of $5,000. The property has a monthly gross income of $1,500 and monthly operating expenses of $500. Elmo's taxable income from this property will be taxed at a rate of 30%. What is the tax liability for the year?

   a. $2,100.
   b. $3,600.
   c. $3,900.
   d. $7,000.

8.11 All investors desire their investments to increase in value. However,

   a. the degree of return is inversely related to the degree of risk.
   b. the more the investor stands to gain, the greater the risk that the investor may lose.
   c. investments requiring intense management have lesser returns.
   d. the more liquid an investment is, the greater the chances are that the investment will not appreciate.

8.12 Two of the financial rewards that investments offer are

   a. income and tax benefits.
   b. negative leverage and appreciation.
   c. appreciation and taxation.
   d. positive leverage and prestige.

8.13 Because a real estate investment can take a long time to sell, real estate investments are considered to be

   a. management intensive.
   b. insensitive to marketing.
   c. vulnerable to seller's markets.
   d. relatively illiquid.

8.14 Compared to a stock portfolio, a real estate investment would be considered

   a. a riskier investment.
   b. a more management-intensive investment.
   c. a shorter-term investment.
   d. a more leveraged investment.

8.15 Six investors purchase a shopping center. One investor manages the tenants and another handles the marketing and leasing. Two investors manage accounting and finance, and the remaining two run the management office. This is a possible example of

a. a general partnership.
b. a limited partnership.
c. a real estate investment trust.
d. an investment conduit.

8.16 The formula for determining taxable income produced by an income property is

a. gross income minus expenses plus land and building depreciation.
b. gross income minus expenses minus land and building depreciation.
c. gross income minus building depreciation plus land depreciation.
d. gross income minus expenses minus building depreciation.

8.17 In deriving taxable income on an investment property, it is generally legal to

a. deduct principal and interest payments from income.
b. deduct principal payments from income.
c. deduct interest payments from income.
d. deduct principal and interest payments from income and capital gain.

8.18 Jake does not use any part of his principal residence as a home office. Which of the following is true of the tax treatment of this property?

a. The owner may deduct the property's interest and principal from ordinary income.
b. The owner may depreciate the property and deduct depreciation expenses from ordinary income.
c. The owner can deduct any capital gain when the property is sold.
d. The owner may be able to avoid capital gain tax when the property is sold.

8.19 An investment property seller pays $14,000 in closing costs. These costs

a. may be deducted from personal income.
b. may be deducted from the property's income.
c. may be deducted from the sale price for gains tax purposes.
d. may be deducted from the adjusted basis for gains tax purposes.

8.20 The formula for calculating capital gain tax is the taxpayer's tax bracket multiplied by

a. the sum of the beginning basis plus gain.
b. the difference between amount realized and adjusted basis.
c. the sum of net sale proceeds and capital gain.
d. the difference between net sale proceeds and capital gain.

8.21 Which of the following entities can legally levy annual real property taxes?

a. The Internal Revenue Service.
b. A utility company.
c. A tax district.
d. A court of law.

8.22 Certain classes of property owner and types of property are exempted or immune from real property taxation in many areas. The protected categories usually include

a. recreational properties.
b. properties owned by a government agency.
c. properties that comply with the Americans with Disabilities Act.
d. properties occupied by single-parent families.

171

8.23   What is the purpose of an equalization factor in ad valorem taxation?

   a. It modifies a local tax rate to bring it into conformity with statutory tax rates.
   b. It changes the assessed value of an individual property to make it reflect the assessed values of other properties in the same neighborhood.
   c. It adjusts assessments in a locality to make them more consistent with an average level for the state or other higher level jurisdiction.
   d. It adjusts the amount of the homestead exemption in a certain area to make it proportionally equivalent to the average homestead exemption in other areas.

8.24   A school district's tax rate is 10 mills. The school district's required revenue from real estate taxes is $20,000,000. What is the tax base of the area?

   a. $20,000,000.
   b. $200,000,000.
   c. $2,000,000,000.
   d. $200,000,000,000.

8.25   A homeowner receives a tax bill that includes an amount for the library district, taxed at $1.00 per $1,000, and the fire protection district, taxed at $2.00 per $1,000. How much does the taxpayer have to pay for these two items if the property's taxable value is $441,000?

   a. $4,701.
   b. $471.
   c. $4,230.
   d. $1,323.

8.26   A town is replacing a sidewalk that serves five homes. The length of the sidewalk is 200 feet. Mary's property has 38 feet of front footage. If the cost of the project to be paid by a special assessment is $30,000, what will Mary's assessment be?

   a. $6,000.
   b. $5,700.
   c. $789.
   d. $1,579.

8.27   What is a tax deed?

   a. A conveyance instrument for a property that is sold to enforce a tax lien.
   b. A document recorded in title records showing that property taxes have been paid.
   c. A notice to a homeowner that a tax lien has been entered against the property.
   d. A document that gives a municipal authority the power to collect an individual tax bill.

8.28   If a property owner has the right to redeem his or her property after a tax sale, the owner has

   a. a legal right of rescission.
   b. an equitable right to acquire title.
   c. a right of homestead exclusion.
   d. a statutory right of redemption.

8.29   The formula for deriving a municipal jurisdiction's ad valorem tax base is

   a. the jurisdiction's annual budget times the tax rate.
   b. the total of all assessed values of properties minus exemptions.
   c. the total amount of ad valorem taxes required by the budget.
   d. the municipality's budget multiplied times the millage rate.

8.30 A homeowner's total tax bill is derived by

a. dividing the tax requirement by the tax base.
b. multiplying each district's tax rate times the market value of the property.
c. multiplying each district's tax rate times the taxable value of the property.
d. averaging the tax rate for each tax district, and multiplying the average tax rate times the assessed value.

8.31 The fair housing law that first protected people against discrimination in housing based on race was the

a. Civil Rights Act of 1866.
b. Civil Rights Act of 1968.
c. Executive Order 11063 of 1962.
d. Title VIII amendment to the Fair Housing Act.

8.32 The classes protected against discrimination by the Fair Housing Act of 1968 are

a. race only.
b. religion and gender only.
c. race, color, religion, and national origin.
d. age and gender only.

8.33 An agent is committing an act of discriminatory advertising by doing which of the following?

a. Telling prospective buyers about the positive and negative aspects of a certain neighborhood.
b. Telling a prospective seller that now would be a good time to put a property on the market.
c. Advertising a property as available to individuals of a particular race.
d. Telling a prospective buyer that the agent is too busy to show the buyer properties personally on a given day.

8.34 Which of the following is an example of blockbusting?

a. An agent shows a minority home buyer properties located in a neighborhood where there are no other minority homeowners.
b. An agent persuades a minority home buyer to avoid looking in a neighborhood where there are no minority homeowners.
c. An agent persuades a family to put their house on the market because ethnic minority families are beginning to move into the neighborhood.
d. An agent persuades a minority home buyer to buy a property located in an area where most of the homeowners belong to minority groups.

8.35 The practice of redlining is specifically prohibited by

a. The Home Mortgage Disclosure Act.
b. The Real Estate Settlement Procedures Act.
c. The Civil Rights Act of 1866.
d. The Americans with Disabilities Act.

8.36 Title VIII of the Civil Rights Act of 1968 applies to the sale of

a. all single-family residences.
b. all privately owned single-family residences.
c. privately owned single-family residences listed with a broker.
d. privately owned single-family residences for sale by owner.

8.37 A broker signs a listing agreement to sell a home for $400,000. An immigrant couple are interested in the house and ask the agent the price. The agent states the price as $420,000. According to the fair housing laws, such an action is

a. illegal, because the agent changed the terms of the sale to discourage this particular couple.
b. illegal, because the agent violated the listing agreement.
c. legal, because the quoted price increase did not exceed 10% of the listing price.
d. legal, because the increased price does not necessarily exclude the couple.

8.38 Which of the following actions is allowed under federal fair housing laws?

a. A broker, following the instructions of the seller, advertises the property as for sale to Christian families only.
b. A home seller, acting without a broker, places a "for sale-- mature, single men only" sign in front of the house.
c. The owner of four rental houses advertises one of the properties for rent to married couples, no children, no pets.
d. The owner of a duplex who resides in one of the units refuses to rent the other unit to a non-Christian.

8.39 Cecily Longstreet believes a real estate agent has kept her from seeing a certain property for rent because she is a woman. What actions should she take if she wants legal satisfaction for her complaint?

a. File charges of illegal discrimination with the police department that has jurisdiction over the local area.
b. File a complaint with HUD and/or file suit against the offending parties in a state or federal court within the prescribed time period.
c. Wait two years and then file a civil suit in federal court.
d. Sue HUD for damages under the Civil rights Act of 1866.

8.40 George Scott hires Shannon Lang to sell his house, with the condition that he will not be the first one in the neighborhood to sell to members of a certain ethnic group. What should Shannon do about this condition?

a. Inform Scott that the condition is illegal and that she cannot comply with it.
b. Note the condition on the listing agreement and have Scott initial it.
c. Pretend that she did not hear the condition and proceed to market the property to all groups.
d. Tell Scott that she will try to discourage members of that group from looking at the property, but that she cannot control cooperating brokers.

8.41 Under federal fair housing laws, the owner of a ten-unit apartment building may legally

a. advertise that the property is not available to anyone requiring wheelchair access.
b. refuse to rent to aliens.
c. require families without children to pay the same security deposit that families with children must pay.
d. require tenants to move out when they become 62 years old.

8.42 Sam Gough wants to rent out his home, but wants to exclude families with children because of his belief that they cause damage. Under what conditions would federal fair housing laws allow Gough to rent on these terms?

a. The owner has a consistent no-children policy in all his rental properties.
b. The owner can prove that costs to repair damage caused by previous tenants with children exceeded the tenants' security deposit.
c. It is a single-family house that is part of a federally-designated planned unit development.
d. It is a single-family house, and the owner owns only one other rental home in addition to his own residence.

8.43   Which of the following laws or rulings extended discrimination to include gender, handicapped status, and family status?

    a. Executive Order 11063.
    b. the Civil Rights Act of 1968.
    c. the Fair Housing Amendments Act of 1988.
    d. Jones v Mayer.

8.44   The Wallaces, a minority family, would like to buy a home in a certain price range. Agent Ambrose shows the family all available properties in a neighborhood of families with similar backgrounds. Ambrose does not mention a number of homes in the family's price range in other neighborhoods. This agent could be liable for

    a. blockbusting.
    b. providing unequal services.
    c. steering.
    d. nothing; his services were legal and acceptable.

8.45   An agent does not like a particular minority buyer, and is very short with the person, refusing to engage in lengthy conversation or show him any properties. A second minority party visits the office the next day. The agent is very forthcoming, and shows the person five prospective properties. This agent could be liable for

    a. providing unequal services.
    b. steering.
    c. misrepresentation.
    d. nothing; both parties were minorities, and therefore no discrimination occurred.

8.46   Following the client's recommendation, an agent conceals the availability of a property from an employed but pregnant and unmarried minority woman. This agent could be liable for

    a. discriminatory misrepresentation by omission.
    b. steering.
    c. violating fiduciary duty.
    d. nothing: an agent may show or not show any property at his or her discretion.

8.47. When must a Property Condition Disclosure Statement be used?

    a. With a newly-constructed single family home
    b. Immediately following the closing of any residential property
    c. Prior to the sale of an occupied 1-4 unit dwelling
    d. Prior to the closing of any commercial or residential re-sale

8.48. If a single-family resident has listed her property with a licensee, the Seller's Property Condition Disclosure form

    a. can be substituted by the licensee's material facts disclosure form.
    b. does not have to be completed prior to closing.
    c. can be completed by either the seller or the licensee.
    d. must still be completed according to local requirements.

8.49. Which of the following would be a non-material fact that would not have to be included in the Seller's Property Condition Disclosure form?

    a. A house has a leaking roof.
    b. A basement floods.
    c. A previous occupant died in the house.
    d. A previous occupant contaminated the house by manufacturing methamphetamine in the basement.

8.50 Jessica wishes to purchase seller Ryan's house. In putting together her offer documents, Jessica includes a handwritten note along with her full-price offer saying how much she loves the property and how she can imagine living at the home for the rest of her life. This personal note included with the offer is typically referred to as a

a. homestead pledge.
b. guaranteed resident assurance.
c. waiver of inspection.
d. love letter.

8.51 Real estate wholesaling is a method of profiting from a real estate transaction without actually buying any real estate. The wholesaler finds a willing seller, puts the property under contract, and finds a third-party buyer willing to buy at a higher price than what the wholesaler has agreed to pay the original seller. How are some states fighting the practice of real estate wholesaling?

a. By requiring the wholesaler to have a real estate license
b. By prohibiting the assignment of contracts within 10 days of closing.
c. By requiring any property to be fully occupied by any particular owner for 300 days
d. By banning wholesaling on transactions of $250,000 or more

9.1 The conditions of an escrow agreement cannot be met and the related transaction cannot be completed. In such a case, the escrow agent

a. levies a fine against the defaulting party.
b. assigns his or her fiduciary responsibilities to the seller's broker.
c. returns funds to the buyer.
d. cancels the sale contract and destroys the transaction documents.

9.2 To avoid violating the Real Estate Settlement Procedures Act, parties who are providing services to the buyer or seller in a transaction must

a. be paid before the closing date for any service they provide.
b. inform the closing agent of the cost of their services at least one week before the closing date.
c. receive payment only from the funds held in escrow, not directly from buyer or seller.
d. disclose in writing any business relationships they have with other parties involved in the transaction.

9.3 A certain item is to be prorated between a buyer and seller. If no outside party is concerned, which of the following statements is true?

a. The item must be prorated and recorded as a debit to one party and a credit to the other party for the same amount.
b. The item must be prorated and recorded as a debit to one party; the remainder is recorded as a credit to the other party.
c. The party who is owed money receives a credit for the entire item and a debit for the prorated amount.
d. The party who owes money receives a debit for the portion owed and a credit for the portion that is not owed.

9.4 An item is said to be paid in arrears if it is normally paid

a. on a monthly or yearly basis.
b. at some time after the expense is incurred.
c. only after it is billed.
d. whenever it is incurred.

9.5 A seller received a rental payment of $900 in advance. At closing, the seller has earned only $320 of this rent. What should appear on the closing statement?

a. A debit to the seller and credit to the buyer for $320.
b. A debit to the seller for $580 and a credit to the buyer for $320.
c. A debit to the seller for $320 and a credit to the buyer for $900.
d. A debit to the seller and credit to the buyer for $580.

9.6 A buyer will receive a water bill for an estimated $100 at the end of the month. At closing, the seller has used an estimated $43 in water. What should appear on the closing statement?

a. A debit to the seller and credit to the buyer for $57.
b. A debit to the seller and credit to the buyer for $43.
c. A debit to the buyer and credit to the seller for $57.
d. A debit to the buyer and credit to the seller for $43.

9.7 A sale transaction closes on April 1, the ninety-first day of the tax year. The day of closing belongs to the seller. Real estate taxes for the year, not yet billed, are expected to be $2,190. According to the 365-day method, what is the seller's share of the tax bill?

a. $1,644.00.
b. $546.00.
c. $959.30
d. $1,364.66.

9.8 A sale transaction closes on July 4 (184th day of the year). The day of closing belongs to the seller. On January 1, the seller paid a hazard insurance premium of $3,750 for the calendar year. According to the 12-month/30-day method, what is the seller's share of the insurance premium?

a. $1,833.33.
b. $1,875.00.
c. $1,890.50.
d. $1,916.67.

9.9 Waldo is buying Marianne's house. The closing date (day belongs to seller) of the sale transaction is September 1 (day 244 of the year). Current Year real estate taxes are $1,100 (will be billed to buyer next year). Use the 365-day method for prorating. What is Marianne's share of the real estate taxes?

a. $364.66.
b. $367.67.
c. $732.33.
d. $735.34.

9.10 Christie is buying John's house. The closing date (day belongs to seller) of the sale transaction is September 1 (day 244 of the year). Existing hazard insurance of $350 has been paid by John through December 31. Use the 365-day method for prorating. What is Christie's share of the existing hazard insurance already paid in full?

a. $116.03.
b. $117.99.
c. $232.01.
d. $233.97.

9.11 Julie is buying Florence's house. The closing date (day belongs to seller) of the sale transaction is September 1 (day 244 of the year). The buyer's loan amount is $787,500 (90%; 30 years @ 8%). The monthly payment on this loan is $5,778.40, with $5,250 going to interest in the first month. At closing, Julie must pre-pay interest for the period of Sept. 2-Sept. 30. Use the 365-day method for prorating. What is Julie's prepaid interest amount?

a. $5,075.00.
b. $5,250.00.
c. $5,431.00.
d. $5,585.80.

9.12 Melissa is buying Raymond's house. Melissa's loan amount is $887,500. She has agreed to pay 2 points at closing. How much will Melissa pay for points?

a. $1,575.
b. $1,775.
c. $17,750.
d. $8,875.

9.13 Tina is buying Terrell's house for $375,000. The broker's commission, to be paid by the seller, is 6%. How much will Terrell pay the broker?

a. $62,500.
b. $5,250.
c. $9,450.
d. $22,500.

9.14 A sale contract stipulates that a buyer is to pay the seller's transfer tax expenses. This practice is not customary in the area. In this case,

a. the buyer and seller must amend the contract before closing.
b. the contract is voidable, since the seller must pay the expense.
c. the buyer may pay or not pay the expense, at his or her option.
d. the buyer must pay the expense.

9.15 What a buyer has to pay at closing is equal to

a. the excess of the buyer's debits over the buyer's credits.
b. the excess of the buyer's credits over the buyer's debits.
c. the excess of the seller's debits over the seller's credits.
d. the excess of the seller's credits over the seller's debits.

9.16 The standard E & O policy covers damages resulting from

a. failure to disclose an environmental condition.
b. antitrust violations.
c. mishandling of earnest money deposits.
d. negligence, error or omission in carrying out professional services.

9.17 Which of the following is a common risk relating to the agency relationship?

a. Failing to inform and disclose properly.
b. Failing to take a personal interest in a transaction.
c. Acting as an exclusive agent without an oral agency agreement.
d. Forgetting to record the listing agreement.

9.18 Even after giving buyer and seller the required information about property condition disclosures, the licensee may still be subject to legal action for

a. failing to detect customer misrepresentations.
b. failing to disclose known adverse facts.
c. relying on publicly available market information.
d. advising the purchaser to exercise due diligence.

9.19 A licensee performing a comparative market analysis must be careful to

a. use the term "market value" whenever possible in the report.
b. show a low suggested selling price to avoid a complaint of misrepresenting the value.
c. include the results of a certified appraisal in the analysis.
d. avoid creating a false impression that the licensee is a certified appraiser.

9.20 One of the major risk areas in fulfilling a listing agreement is

a. finding a buyer who turns out to be unqualified.
b. exceeding the authority of the agreement.
c. showing the property without the presence of the owner.
d. cooperating with other licensees.

9.21 To reduce the risk of committing an error or omission in the contracting process, it is a good idea to

a. use a checklist of all items, contingencies, dates and responsibilities that must be met.
b. delegate some of your responsibilities to the licensee who represents the other party in the contract.
c. call the buyer and seller daily to check on progress.
d. cut the list of necessary tasks down to a few essentials and concentrate on tracking those.

9.22 Regarding contracts and forms,

a. once written and signed they cannot be changed except by a lawyer.
b. real estate licensees may alter forms but not contracts.
c. whoever originates them can make changes without the risk of unauthorized practice of law.
d. the principals may make changes as long as they sign or initial each change.

9.23 Fair housing laws are easily violated. An effective way for agents to minimize the risk of doing so is to

a. deal only with consumers who do not belong to a protected class.
b. obtain education in the content and intent of the laws.
c. make sure there is always a witness present at all meetings with consumers.
d. stay away from transactions involving public housing.

9.24 A licensee risks violating antitrust law by

a. being present at a conversation where the setting of commission rates is discussed.
b. being present at a discussion of antitrust laws.
c. charging a commission rate that happens to be the same as that charged by another firm.
d. cooperating with another firm to do market research.

9.25 How is an intentional misrepresentation penalized?

a. License discipline, fines, and possible incarceration.
b. License discipline and fines, but no incarceration.
c. License discipline only.
d. Fines only.

9.26 Of the following actions, the only one which avoids any risk of committing unintentional misrepresentation is

a. measuring and reporting property dimensions.
b. describing properties and amenities.
c. stating that a client should seek legal counsel.
d. making statements about the presence or absence of hazardous substances.

9.27 To reduce risks inherent in reporting transaction progress to a client, the licensee should

a. make reports orally only, never in writing.
b. leave progress reporting to the inspectors and other experts.
c. advise the client that it is company policy to make no progress reports until the contingency period is over.
d. avoid speculative statements in all reports

9.28 How does sharing the qualifying function with a lender protect a licensee?

a. It guarantees that a buyer will have a loan.
b. It reduces the chance of presenting an offer from an unqualified buyer.
c. It relieves the licensee of his or her due diligence responsibilities.
d. It allows the licensee to avoid asking embarrassing questions.

9.29 The area of agent activity where there is the greatest risk of failing to maintain client confidentiality is

a. trust fund handling.
b. office management.
c. the agency relationship.
d. the closing process.

9.30 The area of agent activity where there is the greatest risk of creating a false impression that the licensee is a certified appraiser is

a. performing a comparative market analysis.
b. writing property advertisements.
c. presenting written offers.
d. researching ownership documents.

9.31 One of the major risk areas in advertising a listed property is that an advertisement will

a. describe the property in excessively glowing terms.
b. fail to appear at the same time in all available media.
c. omit any mention of the owner's main selling points.
d. make a substantial misrepresentation.

9.32 Property managers have a _____ relationship with the property owner.

a. non-binding
b. partnership
c. fiduciary
d. subagency

9.33 One of the property manager's fundamental responsibilities is

a. obtaining construction loans for the principal.
b. financial reporting to the principal.
c. finding a buyer for the property.
d. maintaining good standing in a managers' professional association.

9.34 Effective gross income is defined as

a. the total of scheduled rents.
b. the total of all rents and revenues generated by a property.
c. potential gross income minus debt service and reserves.
d. revenue from all sources minus losses from uncollected rents, vacancies, and evictions.

9.35 The efficiency of marketing activities can be measured in terms of

a. cost per tenant prospect generated per lease.
b. number of ads produced per marketing dollar.
c. dollars expended per square foot of vacant space.
d. percentage of reserves expended on marketing.

9.36 If a property's vacancy rate is significantly lower than market rates, it may be a sign that the manager needs to

a. lower rental rates.
b. raise rental rates.
c. find better tenants.
d. improve management quality.

9.37 What are the three kinds of maintenance a manager has to carry out for a managed property?

a. Constructive, deconstructive, and reconstructive
b. Routine, preventive, and corrective
c. Scheduled, planned, and improvised
d. Emergency, elective, and optional

9.38 The Americans with Disabilities Act requires property managers to

a. ensure that disabled employees have the same level of access to facilities that all employees have.
b. hire the disabled whenever possible.
c. remove all existing barriers to the free movement of disabled persons within the property, regardless of the cost.
d. remodel the ground floor of the property in accordance with ADA standards if it was built before 1978.

9.39 Commercial fire and hazard insurance policies usually require coverage to equal at least 80 percent of the property's

a. replacement value.
b. reproduction value.
c. original cost.
d. depreciated basis.

9.40 Trust funds to be handled by a property manager are likely to include all of the following except

a. rents collected from tenants.
b. cash for the management firm's operating expenses.
c. security deposits.
d. capital contributions from the property owner.

9.41 What kind of agency is commonly created by a management agreement?

a. Universal
b. Specific
c. General
d. Vicarious

9.42 Which of the following describes a gross lease?

a. The tenant pays a base rent plus some or all of the operating expenses.
b. The tenant pays a fixed rent, and the landlord pays all operating expenses.
c. The tenant pays a base rent plus an amount based on income generated in the leased space.
d. The tenant pays a rent that increases at specified times over the lease term.

9.43 If an apartment contains a refrigerator that is not included in the lease,

a. the lessee is required to buy it from the landlord.
b. the landlord is required to remove it.
c. the lease is invalidated because of an incomplete property description.
d. the property manager does not have to maintain it.

9.44 A basic responsibility of a landlord is to

a. provide leased space at market rental rates.
b. deliver a habitable property.
c. keep the rental space freshly painted.
d. refrain from entering the leased space at any time during the lease term.

9.45   How does a constructive eviction occur?

   a. A landlord obtains a court order to force the tenant to vacate the leased premises.
   b. A court officer forcibly removes the tenant from the premises.
   c. A tenant declares a landlord in default and vacates the leased premises.
   d. A landlord declares a tenant in default and takes possession of the leased premises.

9.46   Among the essential elements of a management plan is consideration of

   a. the competitive market for the property.
   b. the property manager's career goals.
   c. the property owner's net worth.
   d. the management firm's income goals.

10.1   A licensee sells 5/6 of an acre for $28,000, and receives a 6% commission. If she splits with her broker 50-50, what did she receive per square foot?

    a. $.023 / SF
    b. $.046 / SF
    c. $.037/ SF
    d. $.002 / SF

10.2   Lots in the South Hyde subdivision are selling for approximately $.50 / SF. The Grandersons want to build a 2,500 SF home on a 1.5 acre corner lot. The custom builder can build the home for $135 / SF. What will the completed property cost the Grandersons?

    a. $359,170
    b. $370,170
    c. $32,670
    d. $374,070

10.3   Ivan owned a 1/4 acre lot. He wanted to construct a 120' x 80' tennis court on the lot. What approximate percentage of the lot will be left over, if any, when he has completed the construction?

    a. 12%
    b. 88%
    c. 3%
    d. 15%

10.4   A developer wants to develop a 16-acre subdivision. He figures that the streets and common area will take up about 30% of this overall area. If the minimum lot size is to be 12,000 SF, how many lots can the developer have on this property?

    a. 42
    b. 487
    c. 40
    d. 57

10.5   A homeowner wants to insulate the new recreation room in her basement. She has been told that 3" of insulation would do the job. The walls are all 9' high and respectively measure 13', 13', 18', and 18' in length. How many rolls will she need if each roll measures 3" x 2' x 50'?

    a. 6
    b. 56
    c. 5
    d. 9

10.6   Maria plans to mulch the flower area around her house. The house measures 40' x 30', and she figures she'll mulch an area 8' in width to form a big rectangle all around the perimeter. What is the square footage of the resulting mulched area?

    a. 64 SF
    b. 2,576 SF
    c. 1,824 SF
    d. 1,376 SF

10.7. Calculate how many acres are in the Southeastern ¼ of the Western ½ of the Eastern ½ of Section 9.

a. 20 acres
b. 40 acres
c. 60 acres
d. 5 acres

10.8. Homeowner Savannah owns the Southeastern ¼ of the Southwestern ¼ of the Northwestern ¼ of Section 4. How many acres is that property?

a. 4 acres
b. 40 acres
c. 10 acres
d. 8 acres

10.9 Yard of Pizza has a percentage lease on its 1,800 SF space in Lincoln Shops. The terms are $1.40 / SF / month rent plus 1.75% of the store's gross income. If monthly sales averaged $41,500 last year, how much annual rent did Yard of Pizza pay last year?

a. $38,955
b. $43,420
c. $30,240
d. $21,525

10.10 A home appreciated 2 2/3% one year, then 5 1/5% the next year, then 7 1/4% the third year. What was the average appreciation over the 3-year period expressed as a decimal?

a. 5.04%
b. 15.24%
c. 7.56%
d. 4.8%

10.11 A homeowner paid $185,000 for a house three years ago. The house sells today for $239,000. How much has the property appreciated?

a. 23%
b. 77%
c. 29%
d. 123%

10.12 Seller Frank receives an offer of $290,000 on a property he listed at $308,000. How much is the offer as a percent of the listing price?

a. 87%
b. 91%
c. 94%
d. 106%

10.13 A property is being appraised using the income capitalization approach. Annually, it has potential gross income of $30,000, vacancy and credit losses of $1,500, and operating expenses of $10,000. Using a capitalization rate of 9%, what is the indicated value (to the nearest $1,000)?

a. $206,000
b. $167,000
c. $222,000
d. $180,000

10.14 If gross income on a property is $75,000, net income is $30,000 and the cap rate is 8%, the value of the property using the income capitalization method is

a. $625,000
b. $375,000
c. $3,750,000
d. $937,500

10.15 The roof of a property cost $16,000. The economic life of the roof is 20 years. Assuming the straight-line method of depreciation, what is the depreciated value of the roof after 3 years?

a. $16,000
b. $13,600
c. $18,400
d. $12,000

10.16 Lee had to report his home office depreciation for the tax year. He has a 2,500 SF home and a 500 SF office area. Lee paid $280,000 for his home, and he figures the land portion carries about 25% of that value. If Lee depreciates on a 39-year basis, how much can he write off for his home office depreciation per year?

a. $1,077
b. $1,436
c. $5,384
d. $2,108

10.17 A property is being appraised by the cost approach. The appraiser estimates that the land is worth $80,000 and the replacement cost of the improvements is $350,000. Total depreciation from all causes is $54,000. What is the indicated value of the property?

a. $296,000
b. $456,000
c. $324,000
d. $376,000

10.18 An apartment owner paid $500,000 for her complex 5 years ago. An appraiser at that time valued the land @ $100,000, but land has appreciated 25% over this period. The investor has used a 40-year straight-line depreciation method to depreciate the property. What is its current value using the cost approach?

a. $437,500
b. $462,500
c. $475,000
d. $546,875

10.19 An apartment building that recently sold for $400,000 had monthly gross rent receipts of $3,200. What is its monthly gross rent multiplier?

a. 80
b. .01
c. 110
d. 125

10.20 A rental home has monthly gross income of $3,300. A suitable gross income multiplier derived from market data is 14.7. What estimated sale price (to the nearest $1,000) is indicated?

a. $297,000
b. $486,000
c. $582,000
d. $519,000

10.21 Amy obtains a 75% LTV loan on her new $400,000 home with an annual interest rate of 6%. What is the first month's interest payment?

a. $1,800
b. $500
c. $2,000
d. $1,500

10.22 Emily has an interest-only home equity loan at an annual interest rate of 5.3%. If her monthly payment is $1,580, how much is the loan's principal balance (to the nearest $1,000)?

a. $444,000
b. $358,000
c. $190,000
d. $292,000

10.23 The loan officer at Sixth Fourth Bank tells Amanda she can afford a monthly payment of $1,000 on her new home loan. Assuming this is an interest-only loan, and the principal balance is $249,000, what interest rate is Amanda getting?

a. 4.82%
b. 5.03%
c. 6.25%
d. 3.69%

10.24 The Keegans obtain a fixed-rate amortized 30-year loan for $280,000 @ 6.25% interest. If the monthly payments are $1,724, how much interest do the Keegans pay in the second month of the loan?

a. $1,748.33
b. $1,456.95
c. $1,458.33
d. $1,724.00

10.25 A lender offers the Greys two alternative loan packages for their $60,000 home equity application. One option is an interest-only loan for 5 years @ 6.5% interest with no points, and the second, a 6.25% interest-only loan for 5 years with 1 point to be paid at closing. Which loan will cost the Greys less total interest, and by how much?

a. The first option, by $150.
b. The second option, by 150.
c. The second option, by $750.
d. Both options charge the same amount of interest.

10.26 Jose recently obtained a 90% loan on his $410,000 home, and he had to pay $6,150 for points. How many points did he pay?

a. 1.4 points
b. 1.67 points
c. 2.48 points
d. 1.5 points

10.27 Mack is buying Roy's house for $500,000. Mack's loan amount is $325,000. He has agreed to pay 1.5 points at closing. How much will Mack pay for points?

a. $450
b. $4,500
c. $4,875
d. $7,500

10.28 A lender determines that a homebuyer can afford to borrow $390,000 on a mortgage loan. The lender requires an 80% loan-to-value ratio. How much can the borrower pay for a property and still qualify for this loan amount?

a. $414,000
b. $312,000
c. $487,500
d. $510,000

10.29 Home buyer Janet pays $1,600 / month for the interest-only loan on her new house. The loan's interest rate is 6.75%. If she obtained a 75% loan, what was the purchase price?

a. $313,333
b. $31,604
c. $379,259
d. $256,000

10.30 Loan applicant Taylor has an annual gross income of $76,000. How much will a lender allow Taylor to pay for monthly housing expense to qualify for a loan if the lender uses an income ratio of 30%?

a. $2,160
b. $1,900
c. $1,215
d. $4,433

10.31 An investor paid $80,000 for a lot and $600,000 to have an apartment building constructed on it. He has depreciated the property for the past 10 years on a 39-year straight-line schedule. If he sells the property this year and realizes $780,000, what is his capital gain?

a. $253,846
b. $274,000
c. $100,000
d. $179,000

10.32. A homeowner bought a house five years ago for $250,000. Since then, the homeowner has spent $2,000 to build a screened porch and has added a central air-conditioning system at a cost of $5,000. What is the homeowner's adjusted basis if the house is sold today?

a. $256,000
b. $257,000
c. $244,000
d. $245,000

10.33 A homeowner sold her house and had net proceeds of $265,000. Her adjusted basis in the home was $231,000. She immediately bought another house for $301,000. What was her capital gain?

a. $265,000
b. $36,000
c. $34,000
d. None

10.34 Debra bought a home for $360,000, paying $72,000 down and taking a mortgage loan of $288,000. The following year she had a new roof put on, at a cost of $15,000. What is Debra's adjusted basis in the house if she now sells the house for $450,000?

a. $87,000
b. $288,000
c. $303,000
d. $375,000

10.35 A certain investor wants an 11% return on investment from any real estate investment. A property priced at $360,000 has gross income of $60,000 and expenses of $22,000. Approximately how much too high or too low is the price of this property for the investor to obtain her desired return exactly?

a. $1,000 overpriced.
b. $8,000 underpriced.
c. $15,000 overpriced.
d. $16,000 underpriced.

10.36 An office building investor sees a listing of an office building which is priced at $2 million. He loves the property, but he knows he needs to make a return of at least 8% to satisfy his partners. If the building is 25,000 SF, rents for $10/SF per year, has 5% vacancy, and annual expenses of $70,000, should he buy it? What is his return?

a. No, since he will yield 2.00%.
b. Yes, since he will yield 8.375%.
c. Yes, since he will yield 8%.
d. Yes, since he will yield 9.125%.

10.37 Chad owns a small retail property that he inherited from his father. There are no mortgages or interest expenses connected with the property. Chad takes an annual cost recovery expense of $7,000. The property has a monthly gross income of $1,650 and monthly operating expenses of $600. Chad's taxable income from this property will be taxed at a rate of 30%. What is the tax liability for the year?

a. $1,680
b. $5,940
c. $2,100
d. $7,000

10.38 A property has a net income of $150,000, interest payments of $105,000, principal payments of $30,000, and annual cost recovery of $7,000. The property's tax rate is 28%. What is the property's annual tax on income?

a. $14,550
b. $40,040
c. $10,640
d. $2,240

10.39 An investor bought 4 oversized lots in order to subdivide. He paid $700,000 for the lots. After subdividing, the investor was able to sell each lot for $230,000. Excluding commissions and closing costs, what per cent profit did the investor realize?

a. 0%
b. 45%
c. 23.9%
d. 31.4%

10.40 A school district's tax rate is 10 mills. The school district's required revenue from taxes is $10,000,000. What is the tax base of the area?

a. $10,000,000
b. $100,000,000
c. $1,000,000,000
d. $100,000,000,000

10.41 A homeowner's residence has an assessed valuation of $280,000, and a market value of $340,000. The homestead exemption is $50,000. Tax rates for the property are 7 mills for schools; 3 mills for the city; 2 mills for the county; and 1 mill for the local community college. What is the homeowner's tax bill?

a. $2,990
b. $3,640
c. $2,300
d. $4,420

10.42 The village of Goodsprings has an annual budget requirement of $8,000,000 to be funded by property taxes. Assessed valuations are $400,000,000, and exemptions total $25,000,000. What must the tax rate be to finance the budget?

a. 2.00%
b. 2.13%
c. 1.32%
d. 21.33%

10.43 A property has sold for $508,000. The listing agreement calls for a commission of 7%, and the seller and listing broker have agreed in writing that the selling broker will receive half of this amount. How much will the listing agent receive if the agent is scheduled to get a 40% share from his broker?

a. $17,780
b. $14,224
c. $10,668
d. $7,112

10.44 Kevin, who works for selling broker Paul, sells a house listed by listing broker Adams. The house sells for $325,000. The co-brokerage split between Paul and Adams is 50-50. Kevin is on a 65% commission schedule with Paul. If the total commission rate is 6.5%, what is Kevin's commission?

a. $6,866
b. $5,282
c. $10,563
d. $13,731

10.45. A sale transaction closes on April 1, the ninety-first day of the tax year. The day of closing belongs to the seller. Real estate taxes for the year, not yet billed, are expected to be $3,150. According to the 365-day method, what should appear on the closing statement?

a. A debit to the buyer and credit to the seller for $2,364.62
b. A debit to the buyer and credit to the seller for $785.34
c. A credit to the buyer and debit to the seller for $785.34
d. A credit to the buyer and debit to the seller for $2,364.62

10.46 Alexis is buying Jack's house. The closing date (day belongs to seller) of the sale transaction is September 1 (day 244 of the year). Her loan has a monthly payment of $577.84, with $525 going to interest in the first month. At closing, Alexis must pre-pay interest for the period of Sept. 2-Sept. 30. Use the 365-day method for prorating. What is her prepaid interest amount?

a. $507.50
b. $525.00
c. $543.10
d. $558.58

10.47 A sale transaction on rental property closes on December 16. The landlord received the December rent of $1,380 on December 1. Assuming the closing day is the buyer's, and that the 365-day method is used for prorating, which of the following entries would appear on the settlement statement?

a. Debit seller $667.74.
b. Credit seller $1,380.00.
c. Debit buyer $712.26.
d. Credit buyer $712.26.

10.48 A home sells for $322,600 in Primm County. Here, transfer taxes are set at $1.00 per $500 of the sale price. Title insurance runs $450, and the attorney costs $550. The agent's commission is 7%, and the mortgage balance is $210,000. Annual real estate taxes are estimated to be $4,000, half of which will have to be charged to the seller. If the seller pays all of these expenses, what will she net at closing?

a. $86,873
b. $88,371
c. $81,372
d. $86,372

10.49 A farmer wants to net at least $5,000/acre on the sale of his 300-acre property. If he allows for 10% commissions and closing costs, and to allow for negotiating room, he wants to get 95% of the listing price as the selling price, what should his listing price be per acre?

a. $5,750
b. $5,882
c. $4,250
d. $5,848

10.50. The Wildes have purchased a $740,000 home. The land is worth 25%, and they insure the improvements @ 75% of their replacement value. If the Wildes suffer damage estimated at $500,000, and they have an 80% co-insurance clause, what will their recovery be from the policy?

a. Zero
b. $531,915
c. $500,000
d. $468,750

10.51 The Uptons carry a $280,000 property insurance policy which covers 75% of the replacement cost of their insurable property, valued at $380,000. They have an 80% co-insurance requirement in the policy. If the family incurs a $300,000 loss, what if any amount will the Uptons recover?

a. $319,999
b. $281,250
c. $280,000
d. $375,000

Section V: Alabama State-Level Practice Tests

State Test 11: The Alabama Regulatory Environment

11.1   Which law created the Alabama Real Estate Commission?

    a. Alabama Real Estate Law
    b. US Congressional Act of 1958
    c. Legislative Act 1927
    d. AREC was not created by a law.

11.2   Of the nine members of the AREC, how many must be consumer members with no real experience for the previous 10 years?

    a. 1
    b. 2
    c. 3
    d. None

11.3   All members of the AREC must have been Alabama residents and citizens for

    a. 5 years
    b. 10 years
    c. 7 years
    d. 3 years

11.4   How do individuals become members of the AREC?

    a. Each is appointed by the governor with the consent of the State Senate.
    b. Seven of the nine members are appointed by the governor with the remaining two elected by the General Assembly.
    c. Each member is appointed by the State Senate from a list provided by the governor.
    d. They are all elected by the general public in annual elections.

11.5   AREC members serve _____ year terms.

    a. 2
    b. 7
    c. 3
    d. 5

11.6   Which of the following is NOT a function of the AREC?

    a. Enforce real estate laws
    b. Prosecute complaints
    c. License real estate practitioners
    d. Establish the Revenue Fund

11.7 A real estate license that is no longer valid and may not be renewed is called what?

    a. An expired license
    b. An inactive license
    c. A suspended license
    d. A lapsed license

11.8 Which of the following is required to hold a valid real estate license?

    a. John Brooks who is selling his father's property
    b. Sarah Conners who is an attorney who handles wills and trusts
    c. Shawn O'Leary who manages the condominium building where he lives
    d. Ted Jenkins who sells cemetery lots

11.9 How much of the $30 Recovery Fund fee collected from each license applicant is deposited into the state treasury for the AREC Revenue Fund?

    a. All $30
    b. Half - $15
    c. Two-thirds - $20
    d. None

11.10 What happens to monies remaining in the revenue fund at the end of the fiscal year?

    a. Remaining funds are disbursed to the Research and Education Center.
    b. Remaining funds are transferred to the following year.
    c. Remaining funds are transferred to the Recovery Fund.
    d. Remaining funds are invested in accordance with Alabama law.

11.11 If an individual believes his real estate broker has violated Alabama license law, resulting in monetary damages to the individual, what should he do?

    a. Contact the Attorney General
    b. Demand the qualifying broker terminate the broker
    c. Call the police
    d. File a complaint with the AREC

11.12 When a complaint is filed against a licensee for a law or rule violation, the AREC assigns an investigator who will work with the _____ to determine if probable cause exists to file a formal complaint.

    a. Attorney General
    b. State Attorney
    c. State Treasurer
    d. Commission

11.13 When the Commission schedules a hearing based on a violation complaint, how much notice does the Commission provide to the accused for the hearing?

    a. 30 days
    b. 10 days
    c. 5 days
    d. 15 days

11.14 Charlie is a broker who has had a complaint filed against him by his client Sue. The AREC has scheduled a hearing on the complaint and is including witnesses that Sue has requested be subpoenaed to testified on her behalf. Who is responsible for paying expenses for these witnesses?

a. Charlie
b. AREC
c. Sue
d. Expenses are not paid for witnesses.

11.15 License law violations are

a. Class A felonies.
b. Class B felonies.
c. Class A misdemeanors.
d. Class B misdemeanors.

11.16 A guilty determination for a licensee's violation would NOT result in

a. a licensee reprimand.
b. an order to pay restitution.
c. an order to take continuing education courses.
d. a $7,500 fine.

11.17 Under what conditions would the AREC issue a cease and desist order for a license law violation?

a. If the violation is causing monetary damage to the complainant
b. If the violation is committed by an unlicensed individual
c. If the individual has not yet completed continuing education
d. If the violation is committed by a business entity

11.18 A complaint was filed against licensee Mary, and a hearing was held in which Mary was found guilty of the violation. Mary does not agree with this finding. What can Mary do?

a. Mary can apply to the AREC for a reversal of their finding.
b. Mary can list all of the reasons she feels the finding is wrong and bring the list to her qualifying broker.
c. Mary can file a law suit against the AREC for the unfair guilty finding.
d. Mary can apply for a rehearing within 30 days of the guilty finding.

11.19 When the AREC has granted a rehearing, the hearing must be held

a. as soon as practicable.
b. within 30 days.
c. whenever the AREC's schedule allows.
d. within 60 days of receipt of rehearing application.

11.20 Fred wants to appeal the guilty finding for a license law violation. What must he do?

a. File the appeal within 60 days of the final order
b. Post a $200 bond with the circuit court
c. Notify the AREC of his grounds for the appeal
d. Apply at HUD for a nullification order

11.21 How is the Recovery Fund funded?

a. With fines and other penalty fees collected for license law violations
b. From a proportionate share of the Revenue Fund
c. With the Revenue Fund balance at the end of the fiscal year
d. By the Recovery Fund fee collected from each license applicant

11.22 Total payments from the Recovery Fund for multiple claims on the same transaction are limited to

   a. $25,000.
   b. $50,000.
   c. $75,000.
   d. There is no limit.

11.23 No payment will be made from the Recovery Fund for acts or omissions

   a. of licensees who do not have an interest in the subject property.
   b. of reprimanded licensees.
   c. of licensees when complainant notifies AREC when a judgment is initiated.
   d. of licensees marketing time-share projects.

Test 12: Alabama Licensing Regulation

12.1 Who must hold a valid Alabama real estate license?

    a. Any corporation selling real estate in Alabama
    b. Any person expecting compensation for working in a real estate office
    c. Any person or business receiving fees for practicing real estate in Alabama
    d. Any sole proprietorship, partnership, or corporation leasing real estate in Alabama

12.2 If performed for compensation, which of the following activities does NOT require a real estate license in Alabama?

    a. Leasing or renting real property
    b. Listing property for sale
    c. Negotiating real estate commissions
    d. Writing real estate contracts

12.3 James was a real estate licensee for 5 years when his license was revoked 6 months ago. He would like to legally practice real estate again. How can he do that?

    a. He must meet all the requirements for an original license and obtain AREC approval.
    b. He must apply to the AREC for his license to be reactivated.
    c. He must retake the state license examination and pay a revocation penalty fee.
    d. He must complete 15 hours of continuing education and pay the required revocation fee.

12.4 Terry is a resident of Georgia and would like to apply for an Alabama real estate license. Terry must do all of the following EXCEPT

    a. apply for the Alabama license on the AREC designated form for nonresidents.
    b. be bound by all Alabama real estate license laws.
    c. show proof of holding a Georgia real estate license.
    d. specify to which real estate office he will be registered.

12.5 Nonresidents applying for an Alabama original or reciprocal license must sign an affidavit

    a. allowing their state of residence to have jurisdiction over the activities in Alabama.
    b. agreeing their state of residence will have the same investigative and discipline authority as Alabama has over Alabama licensees.
    c. agreeing Alabama can take any applicable civil actions against the nonresident licensee.
    d. designating that the state of residence real estate commission will be served as agent for the Alabama nonresident applicant.

12.6 Joseph wishes to apply for an Alabama salesperson license, but he has a felony criminal history with a guilty plea. What must happen for Joseph to qualify for his license?

    a. The AREC must review the conviction to determine if Joseph is eligible for licensure.
    b. Joseph must use an Application of Criminal History Review to request his eligibility for licensure be determined.
    c. He must agree to a state criminal history check but not a national check.
    d. Nothing must happen because Joseph has pleaded guilty to a felony and is not eligible for an Alabama license.

12.7 Applicants for a salesperson license must submit fingerprints along with the criminal history review application. Which of the following is NOT a good idea when having fingerprints taken?

    a. Have the prints taken by an authorized official at a law enforcement agency.
    b. Have the prints printed on the back of the criminal history review application.
    c. Follow the example of prints provided to assure the quality of prints taken and submitted.
    d. Have the prints signed by both the applicant and the official taking them.

12.8 Which of the following is NOT part of the education requirements for a salesperson license?

    a. High school completion
    b. Pre-license coursework completion
    c. College degree
    d. None of the above

12.9 Which of the following documentation would be used to provide proof of age when applying for a salesperson license in Alabama?

    a. Green card
    b. Voter's registration card
    c. US passport
    d. High school diploma

12.10 Which document could be used as proof of Alabama state residency?

    a. Home telephone bill
    b. Current credit report
    c. Current bank statement
    d. Voter's registration card

12.11 Which documentation could be used as proof of high school completion outside the U.S.?

    a. GED certificate
    b. Notarized transcript and letter of recommendation from high school outside of US
    c. US college transcript showing high school education sufficient for college admittance
    d. Any college transcript with completion of two full terms

12.12 Calvin obtained his Alabama real estate license while he was a resident of Louisiana. He recently moved to Alabama. What must Calvin do to maintain his Alabama license?

    a. He must pay a change of residency fee to the AREC.
    b. He must terminate his affiliation with the Alabama broker under whom he was working.
    c. He must notify the AREC of his change of residency within 10 days.
    d. He must retake the Alabama licensure examination and reapply for his Alabama license.

12.13 Individuals applying for a temporary license in Alabama must

    a. already hold an original license.
    b. pay a $30 Recovery Fund fee.
    c. pass the state exam within 12 months of completing the pre-license course.
    d. complete a 30-hour pre-license course within 1 year of start date.

12.14 Once an individual has obtained a temporary license, he must

    a. complete 20 hours of continuing education coursework within 6 months.
    b. complete 15 hours of post-license coursework within 12 months.
    c. complete all post-license coursework and pass the exam within 6 months or have his license lapse.
    d. complete 30 hours of post-license coursework within 6 months to avoid his license becoming inactive.

12.15 An individual with a temporary license must complete the post-license course and apply for the original license

    a. on or before the temporary license expiration date.
    b. before the temporary license is placed on inactive status.
    c. after the temporary license is placed on inactive status.
    d. within 6 months of temporary license application date.

12.16 Which of the following statements is FALSE?

    a. Applicants for original licensure must complete the post-license course within 12 months of temporary licensure.
    b. Temporary licenses expire on midnight of the last day of the month 1 year from the date of issuance.
    c. Applicants for original licensure must pay the Recovery Fund fee when applying for the original license.
    d. Applicants for original licensure must submit proof of post-license course completion to the AREC prior to temporary license expiration.

12.17 The Alabama real estate license period is

    a. 4 years.
    b. 3 years, always ending in odd numbered years.
    c. 2 years, always ending in even numbered years.
    d. 2 years from date of license issuance, regardless of even or odd numbered years.

12.18 If Sue Ellen's original license was issued on March 5, 2027, when is her license renewal due?

    a. August 31, 2028
    b. March 31, 2029
    c. September 30, 2029
    d. October 1, 2028

12.19 If Sue Ellen's original license was issued on March 5, 2027, what is the absolute deadline to renew her license to prevent it from lapsing?

    a. October 1, 2028
    b. September 30, 2029
    c. August 31, 2029
    d. March 31, 2028

12.20 Continuing education requirements must be completed

    a. by August 31 of renewal year.
    b. every year.
    c. by September 30 of final year of license period.
    d. prior to license lapse date.

12.21 Continuing education requirements include _____ hours of risk management coursework.

    a. 15
    b. 9
    c. 3
    d. 1

12.22 Which of the following is required to successfully complete a continuing education course?

   a. 70% score
   b. 75% score
   c. 80% attendance
   d. 100% attendance

12.23 Which of the following can substitute for 15 hours of continuing education?

   a. 30 hours of active duty in the US military
   b. 10 years of licensure
   c. Service as a member of the state legislature during the license period
   d. 1 year of inactive license status

12.24 An applicant for an Alabama reciprocal license must hold a license in a qualifying state other than Alabama. What constitutes a "qualifying state"?

   a. One that offers the same opportunities to Alabama licensees
   b. One with similar real estate laws as Alabama
   c. One where the applicant completed pre-license course and passed a national and state law exam
   d. One that uses the same national exam as Alabama uses

12.25 An applicant for an Alabama reciprocal license must provide proof of licensure from the state where he or she is licensed. Such proof must be issued within _____ of application for Alabama license.

   a. 60 days
   b. 120 days
   c. 3 months
   d. 6 months

12.26 An applicant for an Alabama reciprocal license must complete ____ hours of coursework in Alabama.

   a. 15
   b. 60
   c. 6
   d. no

12.27 Phil would like to reactivate his inactive license. Which of the following is he NOT required to do for reactivation?

   a. Complete continuing education requirements for current license period
   b. Pay the reactivation fee
   c. Retake post-license coursework
   d. Apply to AREC

12.28 When a licensee transfers from one qualifying broker to another, what evidence is acceptable of the transfer?

   a. The mail receipt from sending the transfer documents to the AREC
   b. The AREC-provided certificate of transfer
   c. The newly issued license
   d. No evidence is necessary.

12.29 For what reason might Qualifying Broker Chelsea return Broker Fran's license to the AREC?

   a. To have Fran's license suspended
   b. To stop Fran from doing business in Chelsea's name
   c. To transfer Fran to another qualifying broker
   d. For not completing at least three transactions in a 12-month period

13.1   Which of the following is a personal requirement for Alabama broker licensure?

a. At least 18 years old
b. Alabama state resident
c. No licensure revocation in past 2 years
d. No criminal conviction in past 5 years

13.2   Which of the following is a licensure requirement for an Alabama real estate broker?

a. Submit fingerprints on application for licensure
b. Agree to state and national criminal background check
c. Submit application for licensing eligibility if any criminal convictions
d. Apply for fitness determination to be made by registered qualifying broker

13.3   An applicant for broker licensure must

a. complete a 60-hour pre-license course.
b. pass the licensure examination within 12 months of course completion.
c. hold a salesperson license in Alabama for 3 years prior to broker licensure application.
d. terminate his or her salesperson licensure prior to submitting broker licensure application.

13.4   Who is required to apply for a company's real estate license?

a. The corporation's CEO
b. A partnership's managing partner
c. An LLC's qualifying broker
d. The corporation's accounting firm

13.5   Sam owns ABC Property Brokers, and his friend Tom is the qualifying broker at Ace Realty. Sam has asked Tom to be the qualifying broker at his firm. Tom would like to work for Sam, but he would also like to keep his current qualifying broker position at Ace. How can Tom do that?

a. Tom must apply for ABC's company license in his name and be registered under both companies.
b. Tom must become an officer of ABC Property Brokers and report the change to the AREC.
c. Tom must become a partner in both companies and operate out of separate offices for each company.
d. Tom must obtain a written agreement from both companies and perform all business from the same location.

13.6   When does a company license expire?

a. August 31 of even numbered years
b. September 30 of even numbered years
c. 2 years after the date of issuance
d. October 1 every 2 years

13.7   Sarah is Jerry's qualifying broker. Jerry recently violated license law and caused financial damages to his client Dan. Who is responsible for those damages?

a. Jerry
b. Dan
c. Sarah
d. Sarah and Jerry

13.8 If Sarah wants to terminate her status as Jerry's qualifying broker due to Jerry's law violation, what must Sarah do?

    a. Sarah must fire Jerry and return his license to the AREC.
    b. Sarah must notify Jerry in front of two witnesses of the status change.
    c. Sarah must notify both Jerry and the AREC in writing of her intent to terminate her status with Jerry.
    d. Sarah must request that Jerry terminate his status with Sarah and have his license issued under a new qualifying broker.

13.9 If a company's qualifying broker dies, how long does the company have to apply for a temporary qualifying broker license for an officer, member, or salesperson of the company?

    a. 30 days
    b. 60 days
    c. 6 months
    d. 1 year

13.10 How long may a temporary qualifying broker operate?

    a. 30 days
    b. 60 days
    c. 6 months
    d. 1 year

13.11 What happens if the company does not designate a fully licensed qualifying broker to replace the temporary broker within the required timeframe?

    a. The company license and all licenses under it are placed on inactive status.
    b. The company license is suspended.
    c. The temporary qualifying broker automatically becomes the new qualifying broker.
    d. The company is fined by the AREC.

13.12 Licensee Connie is located within Montgomery city limits, but her family owns a farm in rural Boylston where Connie would like to open a home office. The farmhouse has a family room that would be perfect for her office. Clients could enter the office through the farmhouse living room, and Connie could use the existing telephone line for her business calls. She could even put her business sign out by the road to draw in business. What's wrong with Connie's plan?

    a. Because Connie is located within Montgomery city limits, she is required to operate her office from within the city limits.
    b. Her office must have its own space with a separate business phone.
    c. Home offices are required to have their own separate entrance.
    d. Connie's plan violates all of the place of business requirements.

13.13 Trust funds are required to be held in a federally insured banking institution in Alabama. Such funds are insured up to

    a. $200,000.
    b. $500,000.
    c. $150,000.
    d. $250,000.

13.14 Funds deposited into trust accounts typically do NOT include

    a. earnest money.
    b. broker commissions.
    c. security deposits.
    d. advance rental payments.

13.15 When Stan signed the purchase contract for his property, there was more than one qualifying broker involved in the transaction: Stan's listing broker's qualifying broker and Stan's selling broker's qualifying broker. Which of these qualifying brokers should be responsible for depositing and holding the trust funds for Stan's transaction?

    a. Stan's listing broker's qualifying broker
    b. Stan's selling broker's qualifying broker
    c. Either of these qualifying brokers
    d. Neither of these qualifying brokers

13.16 Who is the trustee for a trust account?

    a. The qualifying broker
    b. The client who owns the funds
    c. The bank where the funds are held
    d. The licensee who collected the funds

13.17 The closing on Tania's property sale was held on March 3. What is the deadline for disbursing the funds held in trust for this transaction?

    a. March 3
    b. March 13
    c. March 10
    d. March 31

13.18 The rules of interpleader

    a. assign a mediator to resolve trust fund disbursement disagreements.
    b. designate the qualifying broker as the individual to disburse trust funds.
    c. state that trust fund disbursements must be set in writing prior to transaction closing.
    d. force trust fund disbursement disagreements to be resolved by the courts.

13.19 Under the rules of interpleader, the qualifying broker

    a. determines disbursement of funds.
    b. is released from disagreement liability.
    c. can be sued for failure to disburse funds.
    d. holds the funds until the disagreement is resolved.

13.20 How trust funds are handled is determined by

    a. the qualifying broker.
    b. the client who submitted the funds.
    c. the bank where the trust account is held.
    d. the law.

13.21 Terrance is the qualifying broker at Uptown Realty. He has trust accounts set up to hold funds belonging to his clients. What could happen if Terrance borrowed funds from one of the accounts to use for his office renovation?

    a. Nothing would happen as long as he paid the money back before it needed to be disbursed for the transaction closing.
    b. Nothing would happen because the account belongs to Terrance, so he can use the money at his discretion.
    c. Terrance can lose his license for using the funds for his business expenses.
    d. Terrance could be prosecuted for commingling funds.

13.22 Commingling occurs when

    a. a qualifying broker deposits both his own funds and a client's funds into the same trust account.
    b. a qualifying broker deposits his own money into a client's trust account to cover bank service fees.
    c. a qualifying broker deposits funds from two different clients into the same trust account.
    d. a qualifying broker deposits both his personal funds and his business funds into the same account.

13.23 John commingled funds and was investigated and found guilty by the AREC. Which of the following penalties does John NOT have to worry about?

    a. License suspension
    b. Reprimand
    c. License revocation
    d. $25,000 fine

13.24 The AREC has several suggestions to help with escrow account reconciliation, including which of the following?

    a. Separate rental and sales accounts.
    b. Keep canceled checks together in a separate file for easy access.
    c. Pay commissions prior to deducting bank service charges to assure payment will be covered.
    d. Keep all pending and closed contracts together to have a complete record of all transactions.

13.25 Alabama law requires escrow accounts to be reconciled

    a. monthly.
    b. bi-monthly.
    c. when bank statements are received.
    d. There is no legal requirement for reconciliation.

13.26 When must a licensee provide an estimated closing statement to a seller?

    a. When the listing agreement is signed
    b. When an offer is received
    c. 3 days prior to transaction closing
    d. At closing

13.27 Which law requires a loan estimate to be provided to a borrower within a designated timeframe?

    a. ADA
    b. RESPA
    c. ECOA
    d. TRID

13.28 When does the law require a lender to provide a loan estimate to a borrower?

    a. 3 days prior to closing on the mortgage loan
    b. When the borrower applies for the loan
    c. Within 3 business days of the loan application
    d. When the borrower submits an offer on a property

13.29 Which of the following statements is TRUE?

    a. Estimated closing statements outline transaction closing costs.
    b. Estimated closing statements outline loan costs as part of the transaction closing costs.
    c. Closing disclosures must be provided to the borrower at the time of loan application.
    d. Loan estimates must be provided to the borrower within 3 days of the loan application.

13.30 Under the terms of the seller's listing, payment of the real estate commission is a

a. buyer debit.
b. buyer credit.
c. seller credit.
d. seller debit.

13.31 Property surveys paid by the buyer are a

a. buyer debit.
b. buyer credit.
c. seller credit.
d. seller debit.

13.32 The earnest money deposit is a

a. buyer debit.
b. buyer credit.
c. seller credit.
d. seller debit.

13.33 Prorated prepaid rent is

a. seller debit and buyer debit.
b. seller credit and buyer credit.
c. buyer credit and seller debit.
d. buyer debit and seller credit.

13.34 Which law prohibits lenders from demanding excessive deposits for escrow accounts?

a. TILA
b. RESPA
c. TILA-RECAD
d. TRID

13.35 Lily wants to sell her home. She has decided to handle the sale herself. What type of license does Lily need?

a. A qualifying broker license
b. A real estate broker license
c. A real estate salesperson license
d. None

13.36 Local or county governments within Alabama may NOT

a. impose a tax on real estate signage used to advertise the sale of property.
b. restrict the placement of signage for the sale of property.
c. set rules on the size of signage used to advertise the sale of real estate.
d. restrict the height of signage used to advertise the sale of property.

13.37 Alabama law requires closing statements to be kept in the broker's files for

a. 3 years.
b. 5 years.
c. 2 years.
d. no required time period.

14.1 An agreement between the broker and the client that creates a fiduciary relationship and which must be in writing is a(n)

   a. brokerage agreement.
   b. informed consent.
   c. agency agreement.
   d. deed in trust.

14.2 Which of the following statements is false?

   a. Any person who gets information, advice, or services from a real estate licensee is a consumer.
   b. A consumer's agreement based on full disclosure needed to choose brokerage services is informed consent.
   c. A person being provided brokerage services when there is no agency agreement is a customer.
   d. Property management services that require licensure are often included in available brokerage services.

14.3 Something of significance that may affect a party's decision whether or not to enter into a contract is called a(n)

   a. fiduciary duty.
   b. material fact.
   c. informed consent.
   d. brokerage service.

14.4 Which law sets the roles and duties of real estate brokers?

   a. TILA
   b. RESPA
   c. AREC
   d. RECAD

14.5 According to Alabama law, when must a licensee disclose a non-agency relationship to the consumer?

   a. At first contact
   b. At first property showing
   c. When the consumer asks about available services
   d. Before confidential information is exchanged

14.6 When or how often must qualifying brokers explain the agency disclosure office policy to licensees?

   a. Every year
   b. During the licensee employment interview
   c. Before signing an independent contractor employment contract
   d. Prior to signing any listing agreements

14.7 When is an agency relationship created?

   a. Upon initial contact with customer
   b. When the relationship agreement is signed
   c. After the non-agency relationship has been disclosed
   d. When the listing agreement is recorded

14.8　What is the difference between a customer and a client?

    a. A client pays the commission.
    b. A client is a seller while a customer is a buyer.
    c. A client has signed an agreement for specific services.
    d. A licensee has duties to a client but not to a customer.

14.9　Which of the following is NOT an allowed brokerage relationship in Alabama?

    a. Dual agency
    b. Single agency
    c. Subagency
    d. Transaction facilitator

14.10　In which brokerage relationship is the broker NOT working under a signed agreement?

    a. Single agency
    b. Transaction facilitator
    c. Subagency
    d. Dual agency

14.11　Broker Josiah is representing both the buyer and the seller in the sale of a property in Birmingham. To legally do this, what must Josiah do?

    a. Disclose the non-agency relationship to both the buyer and the seller
    b. Sign an agency agreement with both clients' qualifying broker prior to providing any brokerage services
    c. Obtain written consent from both clients to enter into the relationship agreement
    d. Notify both clients which will receive preferential treatment during the transaction

14.12　What type of brokerage relationship would be of interest to a savvy seller who just needs a bit of help with marketing her property?

    a. Single agency
    b. Transaction facilitator
    c. Buyer agency
    d. Dual agency

14.13　What type of agency relationship is in place if two licensees at the same company represent the seller and the buyer in the same transaction?

    a. Single agency
    b. Transaction facilitator
    c. Undisclosed dual agency
    d. Dual agency

14.14　Alabama mandates a consumer's right to a minimum level of service. This mandate does NOT include which of the following services?

    a. Helping a consumer negotiate price
    b. Presenting and receiving offers
    c. Assisting with financing
    d. Answering questions

14.15 Licensees are required to keep their client's confidential information confidential even if

    a. disclosing the information is required by law.
    b. the information was obtained through public knowledge.
    c. the client authorizes the disclosure in writing.
    d. the information would help the buyer decide whether or not to purchase the property.

14.16 The most common type of lawsuit against licensees concerns

    a. misappropriation.
    b. practicing law without a license.
    c. misrepresentation.
    d. failure to provide services.

14.17 If a seller fails to disclose significant property defects out of ignorance, the seller is most likely guilty of

    a. fraudulent misrepresentation.
    b. negligent misrepresentation.
    c. innocent representation.
    d. misrepresentation by omission.

14.18 When is the rule of caveat emptor allowed to be used in Alabama?

    a. When there are significant defects in a home being sold by the builder
    b. When a seller has a fiduciary relationship with the buyer
    c. When used residential property is being sold
    d. When the property defect poses a safety risk to the buyer

14.19 What is the safest way for a property seller to avoid liability for misrepresentation?

    a. Provide the buyer with a completed property disclosure form
    b. Avoid telling the seller's agent about any property defects
    c. Do not disclose any property defects
    d. Hold the seller's agent responsible for the nondisclosure

14.20 When a seller chooses to receive offers directly from the selling agent and not the listing agent, who is responsible for providing the seller with an estimated closing statement?

    a. The listing agent
    b. The selling agent
    c. The qualifying broker
    d. None of the above

15.1 Pleading nolo contendere means the accused

    a. admits guilt but does not agree to accept punishment.
    b. accepts responsibility for the crime and accepts punishment.
    c. denies responsibility for the crime and does not agree to punishment.
    d. does not admit guilt but accepts punishment.

15.2 Noncompliance with Alabama license law and the AREC administrative rules can result in any of the following punishments EXCEPT

    a. probation.
    b. reprimand.
    c. restitution.
    d. fine.

15.3 Which of the following would be considered a crime involving moral turpitude?

    a. Gross exaggeration
    b. Vandalism
    c. Trespassing
    d. Burglary

15.4 Cheryl sues her agent Carla and is awarded monetary damages as a result of Carla's neglect during Cheryl's real estate transaction. Carla is embarrassed about the suit and scared she could lose her license, so she doesn't want anyone to know about the suit. What violation might Carla be guilty of?

    a. Not spending enough time on the listing
    b. Violating anti-discrimination laws
    c. Marketing real estate without a license
    d. Failure to report the legal action to the AREC

15.5 If John receives an offer on a property he has listed and does not present the offer to the seller because John thinks the offer has too many conditions attached, has John violated the law?

    a. No, John is looking out for the best interest of his client as required by law.
    b. No, as the client's agent, John is acting on his client's behalf by rejecting the offer.
    c. Yes, John is misrepresenting the situation to the customer submitting the offer.
    d. Yes, John is failing to fulfill his obligations to his client.

15.6 Tim has been convicted of forging his client's signature on several documents. As a real estate broker, what license law has Tim violated?

    a. The Uniform Electronic Signature Act
    b. Impersonating the property owner
    c. Pleading guilty or nolo contendere
    d. Dishonest dealings, bad faith, untrustworthiness

15.7   Jessie's client has filed a legal suit against him for mishandling the client's trust funds. Jessie knows he is required to notify the AREC of any legal action being taken against him. Wanting to be sure he meets the 10-day deadline for notifying the AREC, Jessie hand delivers the complaint to the Commission's office. However, Jessie is later notified by the AREC that he has failed to report the legal action in accordance with the law. How has Jessie violated the law?

   a. Jessie did not also notify his qualifying broker of the action.
   b. Jessie did not send the notification to the AREC via certified mail.
   c. Jessie did not include an explanation of his actions along with the complaint.
   d. Jessie did not violate that law; the AREC is in error.

15.8   Sally is ready to schedule her licensure examination, but she's afraid she won't do well. She has an idea that she might do better if she can convince the examination provider that she has a disability and needs special accommodations for taking the exam. She completes the special accommodation form, making up information about a disability and then mails the form. While Sally might actually be provided special accommodations that may or may not help her with the exam, what has she actually done?

   a. Sally has shown ingenuity in assuring she will pass the exam.
   b. She has forged a document required for licensure.
   c. She has failed to meet all licensure requirements.
   d. She has violated the Americans with Disabilities Act.

15.9   Jeremy's brother Paul is getting ready to take the real estate licensure exam. Jeremy, who recently passed his exam with a high score, wants to help Paul, so Jeremy offers to use Paul's identification and take the exam for him. After all, they're brothers and look a lot alike, so no one should question the identification. If Paul goes along with this, he will have violated licensure requirements by being dishonest. What law will Jeremy have violated?

   a. Dishonesty in procuring a license
   b. Failure to show good faith
   c. Making false promises
   d. Unfair trade practices

15.10 Scott represents a buyer who is interested in buying a home that Scott's father owns. To avoid violating the law, what must Scott do?

   a. Scott must have his father list the property with Scott's brokerage.
   b. Scott must tell the buyer that the property belongs to his father.
   c. Scott must have another agent within the brokerage handle the transaction.
   d. Scott must become an undisclosed dual agent.

15.11 Andy is Duane's agent and is handling the sale of Duane's farm. The transaction went smoothly and closed right on time. However, after moving into the farmhouse, the buyer discovered severe structural defects that were not found in the property inspection. The buyer said he would not have bought the property if he'd known about the defects and now wants to sue Andy for not disclosing the defects. What might prevent Andy from being guilty of violating the law?

   a. Andy can point out that Alabama is a caveat emptor state and disclosure was not required.
   b. Andy can fault the property inspector for not discovering the defect.
   c. Andy can offer a rebate to the buyer to help with the cost of repairs.
   d. Andy can point out that he did not personally know about the defect.

15.12 Tony is selling his daughter's home and knows that the stairway to the basement is rather wobbly. He also knows there was once mold in the basement, but his daughter had it professionally removed. Tony does not tell the potential buyer about either issue, but when the buyer finds out, he claims Tony has violated the law by not disclosing the two issues. What might prevent Tony from being guilty of violating the law?

   a. Tony can fault the buyer for not having a property inspection performed.
   b. Tony can say he did not personally know about the issues.
   c. Tony can point out that Alabama is a caveat emptor state and disclosure was not required.
   d. Tony can offer the buyer an under-the-table rebate if he buys the property anyway.

15.13 Matt has promised a potential buyer that the crack house down the street from the subject property will be shut down by the police by the time the buyer has closed on the property. He even explains the steps the police have already taken to shut the place down. The buyer decides he will purchase the house but only because the crack house will no longer be a problem. The truth is that the neighbors have been complaining for more than a year about the crack house, and local police have done nothing about it. Matt has violated not one, but two laws. Which two?

   a. Misrepresentation and failure to disclose
   b. False promises and honesty and good faith in a transaction
   c. Deceitful advertising and misrepresentation
   d. Fulfilling obligations to client and failure to disclose

15.14 Matt is selling a home in a neighborhood that includes a crack house that police have been unsuccessful in shutting down. Matt is determined to sell the house regardless of the crack house. So he places an ad describing the wonderful house, the up-and-coming neighborhood, the proximity to schools and shopping, and the safety of the immediate area. Just in case that ad isn't enough to sell the house, Matt convinces another agent in his company to help market the house under the same pretenses. Matt now has violated two laws. What two in this scenario?

   a. False promises to induce and Misrepresentation through other agents
   b. Misrepresentation and Failure to disclose
   c. Deceitful advertising and Misrepresentation through other agents
   d. Dishonesty and False promises to induce

15.15 When and where must a licensee identify him or herself as a real estate licensee?

   a. In all advertisements
   b. Immediately when selling licensee's own property
   c. Upon initial contact with customer
   d. When answering phone calls to the brokerage company

15.16 Angelo has a listing agreement with client Pete. A couple of weeks after signing the agreement with Pete, Angelo transfers to a different qualifying broker. Can he take Pete's listing with him?

   a. Yes, he signed the agreement with Pete so he is Pete's agent no matter who the qualifying broker is.
   b. No, unless Pete agrees to transfer with him
   c. Yes, he already has advertisement published with his name as the licensee selling the property.
   d. No, because Pete's listing agreement is a contract with the original qualifying broker, not with Angelo personally

15.17 Alabama license law emphasizes honesty, good faith, and trustworthiness. Which of the following violations demonstrates a lack of honesty, good faith, and trustworthiness?

   a. Using fraud to obtain a real estate license
   b. Following rule of caveat emptor
   c. Failing to identify self as licensee in advertisement
   d. All of the above

15.18 Which of the following can be attributed to most law violations?

    a. Failure to disclose
    b. Failure to fulfill obligations
    c. Lack of honesty
    d. Negligence

15.19 Which of the following is a violation of Alabama license law?

    a. Unlicensed person advertising sale of own home
    b. Unlicensed person leasing son's property
    c. Unlicensed person renting homes for compensation
    d. Licensee selling own home

15.20 Which of the following statements is FALSE?

    a. Unlicensed persons may not be compensated for performing acts that require licensure.
    b. Employing an unlicensed person to perform real estate activities is against the law.
    c. Helping an individual circumvent licensing requirements is a law violation.
    d. Simply associating with an unlicensed person who performs real estate activities for compensation is not a violation.

15.21 If a licensee intends to purchase a property, the licensee must disclose his intention

    a. only if the seller's agent is an associate of the licensee.
    b. only if the seller's agent is not an associate of the licensee.
    c. whether the licensee is buying the property indirectly or directly.
    d. only if the licensee is buying the property indirectly.

15.22 Failure to disclose the true terms of a contract is a violation of the law, but the law requires the disclosure to be to whom?

    a. Any interested party to the contract
    b. Only the lender
    c. The AREC
    d. Only any involved guaranteeing agency

15.23 If a licensee holds a purchase agreement in which the property sale price is $450,000 but discloses to the lender that the sale price is $550,000 so the buyer can obtain a higher mortgage loan, what has the licensee done?

    a. Overpriced the listing
    b. Over-financed the buyer
    c. Inflated the commissionable numbers in the transaction to increase the commission.
    d. Misrepresented the facts presented in the transaction documents

15.24 Holly is handling the purchase of a home for her client Reagan. Holly knows she has certain obligations to Reagan, but she thinks some of those obligations are ridiculous. She especially thinks keeping some information confidential is unnecessary. After all, she's not an attorney. So when Holly finds a great home for Reagan to purchase, she lets the seller's agent know Reagan is willing to pay more than the asking price for the home. Consequently, the seller counteroffered with a higher price. Not knowing what Holly had done, Reagan paid the higher price. What did Holly actually do wrong?

    a. She failed to disclose the true terms of a contract.
    b. She misrepresented the facts.
    c. She acted incompetently and negligently.
    d. She entered a dual agency agreement without Reagan's consent.

15.25 License law prohibits a licensee employed by a qualifying broker from mishandling trust funds. Which of the following does NOT constitute this licensee's mishandling of trust funds?

a. Accepting cash as earnest money
b. Transferring earnest money from a trust account into an operating account
c. Depositing cash into qualifying broker's trust account
d. Commingling funds

15.26 Which of the following constitutes illegal commingling?

a. Depositing funds from different transactions into the same trust account
b. Depositing funds from different clients into the same trust account
c. Depositing client funds and business funds for the same transaction into the same trust account
d. Depositing business funds to cover bank charges into a client trust account

15.27 Which of the following statements is TRUE?

a. Funds belonging to others must be deposited into an insured account.
b. Trust fund accounts must insure each deposit for $200,000.
c. Trust fund accounts must be located in any bank whose home office is in Alabama.
d. Trust funds must be deposited into a financial institution located in Alabama.

15.28 Which of the following is NOT a violation of the recordkeeping requirement?

a. Licensees must give copies of all documents to the qualifying broker.
b. Licensees must give copies of all documents to the client.
c. Qualifying brokers must keep records for at least 3 years.
d. Names and dates of funds belonging to others must be included in the records.

15.29 If Dennis owns a business that only collects funds owed in relation to real estate transactions, does Dennis or the business need to be licensed under Alabama real estate license law?

a. No because Dennis and the business are not performing acts that require licensure
b. No because Dennis performs real estate acts under the brokerage for which he collects funds
c. Yes because Dennis is being compensated for collecting the funds
d. Yes because collecting funds in relation to real estate transactions requires licensure

15.30 Judy's sister often helps Judy with her real estate business. Her sister sometimes shows homes, negotiates commissions, and so forth. Judy knows she is not allowed to pay her sister a commission for any property she helps sell, but Judy doesn't feel right not compensating her at all. So Judy decides to set up payments to her sister based on the profits Judy's business is making. Judy is not paying a commission to an unlicensed person, so she's ok, right?

a. Yes, the law prohibits commission payments to unlicensed individuals.
b. No, her sister is not actually selling the properties but is just assisting so she should not be paid.
c. No, paying an unlicensed person any compensation for performing acts that require licensure is a law violation.
d. Yes, Judy is obligated to compensate any individual who performs real estate acts.

15.31 Whether or not a rebate or incentive is a violation of the law depends on

a. why it is given.
b. how much is given.
c. when it is given.
d. who gives it.

15.32 Which of the following violations could result in criminal charges being brought against the licensee?

a. Offering a lottery
b. Compensating an unlicensed individual for performing real estate acts that require licensure
c. Accepting compensation for anyone other than the qualifying broker
d. Failure to provide estimated closing statements

15.33 Failure to provide the AREC with any requested information in the required time frame is a violation. What is the required time frame?

a. 24 hours
b. 5 days
c. 30 days
d. Within a reasonable time

15.34 Qualifying brokers are required to report business address changes to the AREC. To avoid a violation, what must be done?

a. Notify the AREC within 10 days of address change
b. Notify the AREC via certified mail
c. Pay change of address fee for business license only
d. Return all licenses tied to previous address to the AREC

15.35 How does the following advertisement violate Alabama license law?

Older home in beautiful established neighborhood. 3 bedrooms, 2 baths, finished basement, 2-car garage, large front porch. No homeowner association. For more details, contact Sonya Harrington, a licensed real estate broker, at 555-8855.

a. No brokerage name is included in the ad.
b. No location is included in the ad.
c. No asking price included in the ad.
d. Deceptive advertising by calling the neighborhood beautiful.

15.36 When may a licensee place a for sale sign on a property?

a. After the listing agreement is signed
b. After the licensee has viewed the property and taken photos
c. After the property owner has given consent
d. When local laws permit sign placement

15.37 Why is taking a net listing a law violation?

a. The commission is not based on a percent of the sale price.
b. The seller does not agree to the amount of commission paid.
c. The sale price is set with no room for negotiation with the buyer.
d. The listing is prohibited in Alabama.

15.38 The law regarding the listing agreement expiration date

a. requires automatic extensions.
b. requires the agreement to be in writing.
c. prohibits a set expiration date.
d. prohibits agreements lasting less than 60 days.

Section VI: Alabama License Examination Sample Test

Sample Test: Alabama Practice Exam

S 1.   A farmer temporarily installs produce coolers in a leased farm stand in order to prevent spoilage. The coolers would be considered which of the following?

    a.   Trade fixtures that are real property.
    b.   Trade fixtures that are personal property.
    c.   Temporary real property.
    d.   Emblements.

S 2.   Property can be converted from real to personal property and from personal property to real property by means of which processes, respectively?

    a.   Assemblage and plottage.
    b.   Application and dissolution.
    c.   Severance and affixing.
    d.   Planting and harvesting.

S 3.   The highest form of ownership interest one can acquire in real estate is the

    a.   legal life estate.
    b.   conventional life estate.
    c.   defeasible fee simple estate.
    d.   absolute fee simple estate.

S 4.   The distinguishing feature of a defeasible fee simple estate is that

    a.   it can be passed on to heirs.
    b.   it has no restrictions on use.
    c.   the estate may revert to a grantor or heirs if the prescribed use changes.
    d.   it is of unlimited duration.

S 5.   Maria acquires a property from her uncle Alfonso. When Maria dies, the estate will pass to Alfonso's other niece, Serena. The type of estate that Maria has in the property is a

    a.   conventional life estate.
    b.   legal life estate.
    c.   fee simple defeasible estate.
    d.   tenancy by the entireties.

S 6.   One difference between a cooperative estate and a condominium estate is that

    a.   a condominium owner owns a unit of air space whereas the co-op owner owns a proprietary lease.
    b.   a condominium sale adversely affects other unit owners.
    c.   the coop owner owns stock and a freehold real estate interest whereas the condominium owner simply has a proprietary lease.
    d.   the condominium owner owns the common elements and the airspace whereas the coop owner only owns the apartment.

S 7. Who are the essential parties involved in an estate in trust?

    a.   Owner, trustor and lawyer.
    b.   Owner, trustor and trustee.
    c.   Trustee, title company, and beneficiary.
    d.   Trustor, trustee and beneficiary.

S 8. A condominium owner enjoys a

    a.   share in an association that owns one's apartment.
    b.   tenancy in common interest in airspace and common areas of the property.
    c.   fee simple ownership of the airspace in a unit and an undivided share of the entire property's common areas.
    d.   fee simple ownership of a pro rata share of the entire property.

S 9. With various types of junior liens, the order of payment priority is generally established according to

    a.   the date of recordation.
    b.   what form of tax is in question.
    c.   the order of disbursement.
    d.   whether the lien was subordinated.

S 10. What is a lien-theory state in contrast to a title-theory state?

    a.   A state in which liens are given priority over other encumbrances.
    b.   A state in which a mortgagor retains title to the property when a mortgage lien is created.
    c.   A state in which the holder of a mortgage lien receives title to the mortgaged property until the debt is satisfied.
    d.   A state in which liens must be recorded to be enforceable.

S 11. A property owner has an easement appurtenant on her property. One day the property is sold to another party who is opposed to the easement. Following the closing, this particular form of easement

    a.   terminates.
    b.   transfers with the property.
    c.   transfers with the owner to a new property.
    d.   becomes a license on the property.

S 12. What fundamental legal purpose is fulfilled by title records?

    a.   Keeping the county apprised of tax payments.
    b.   Preventing identity theft.
    c.   Giving constructive notice of one's rights and interests in the property.
    d.   Assembling all relevant documents in a single place.

S 13. What is "chain of title?"

    a.   The list of all parties who have ever owned real estate.
    b.   The bundle of rights linked to the recorded title to a parcel.
    c.   A chronology of successive owners of record of a parcel of real estate.
    d.   Involuntary conveyance of title by statutory rules of descent.

S 14. Which of the following provides the strongest evidence of marketable title?

    a.   A general warranty deed.
    b.   A title certificate.
    c.   Title insurance.
    d.   An attorney's opinion.

S 15. A store owner enters into a lease that charges rent per square foot, a common area fee, and a portion of the store owner's gross income from the property. This kind of lease is a

   a. triple charge, or triple net lease.
   b. proprietor's lease.
   c. percentage lease.
   d. retailer's gross lease.

S 16. An owner leases a property to a business in exchange for rent. The tenant is required to pay all operating expenses as well. This is an example of a

   a. proprietary lease.
   b. percentage lease.
   c. gross lease.
   d. net lease.

S 17. A lease automatically terminates under which of the following circumstances?

   a. The tenant fails to pay rent.
   b. The leased property is foreclosed.
   c. The tenant goes out of business.
   d. The landlord cancels the lease.

S 18. A county or municipal authority usually grants a certificate of occupancy for new construction only after

   a. all contractors' work has been inspected.
   b. all work has been completed for at least sixty days.
   c. the construction conforms to building codes.
   d. the tax assessor has valued the improvement.

S 19. A property owner is precluded by deed restriction from developing a thirty foot boat dock. The limitation prompts the owner to sell to another party. The new owner

   a. is free to build the dock since the next door neighbor built a similar dock two weeks later.
   b. takes title subject to the same restriction.
   c. can build the dock with special permission from the zoning board.
   d. may build, since the restriction is extinguished by the sale.

S 20. Emily sells Rycole a property containing a deed condition. The condition stipulates that the forested portion of the property must never be razed for development. Three months later, Rycole proceeds to harvest the trees and turn the area into an executive golf course. What recourse, if any, does Emily have under the deed condition?

   a. She has the right to re-possess the property because the grantee has violated the condition.
   b. The condition has ceased to apply because she allowed the violation to continue for a certain period of time.
   c. She can claim the proceeds from the harvested trees.
   d. She can force Rycole to sell the property to a new owner who agrees to comply with the condition.

S 21. What is the essential purpose of legal descriptions of real property?

   a. To create a consistent, unchanging standard for uniquely locating a property.
   b. To enable courts and attorneys to calculate property size accurately.
   c. To comply with common law for real property.
   d. To eliminate cumbersome metes and bounds descriptions.

S 22. Which of the following characterizes metes and bounds descriptions?

    a.   They use meridians and base lines.
    b.   They identify an enclosed area, beginning and ending at the same point.
    c.   They use lot and block numbers.
    d.   They incorporate elevation into the descriptions.

S 23. A buyer agrees to all terms of a seller's offer except the length of time for a contingency to procure financing. The buyer extends the financing period in the offer by one week, signs the form, and mails it back to the seller. At this point, the seller's offer

    a.   is void.
    b.   becomes an executory contract.
    c.   becomes a counteroffer.
    d.   has been accepted, since the modification was a contingency.

S 24. Real estate contracts that are not personal service contracts

    a.   may be assigned.
    b.   are not assignable.
    c.   must be in writing.
    d.   are exempt from the statute of frauds.

S 25. Which of the following contracts must be in writing to be enforceable?

    a.   A parol contract.
    b.   A six-month lease.
    c.   A two-year lease.
    d.   An executory contract.

S 26. Agent Bob, who works for Broker Bill, obtains an owner listing to lease a building. Bill's other agent, Sue, locates a tenant for Bob's listing. Broker Bill in this instance is

    a.   an implied agent.
    b.   a dual agent.
    c.   a single agent.
    d.   a subagent.

S 27. A transaction broker should disclose his or her agency relationship to prospective buyers and sellers

    a.   upon first substantive communication.
    b.   upon completion of the listing agreement.
    c.   immediately following completion of any offer.
    d.   immediately prior to closing.

S 28. A transaction facilitator in a residential transaction represents

    a.   the seller.
    b.   the buyer.
    c.   both seller and buyer.
    d.   neither seller nor buyer.

S 29. A principal instructs an agent to inform minority buyers that the property for lease was just leased an hour ago and is no longer available. The agent refuses to comply. In this case,

    a.   the agent should exercise caution until the listing expires, then decline to renew it.
    b.   the principal has proposed an illegal act, which should not be obeyed.
    c.   the agent is liable for breaching the listing terms.
    d.   the agent may sue the principal for discrimination and misrepresentation.

S 30. The amount of a real estate broker's commission is established by

    a.   agreement among competing brokers.
    b.   negotiation with clients.
    c.   the local Board of Realtors®.
    d.   state real estate license law.

S 31. A client revokes an exclusive right-to-sell listing two months prior to expiration. The reason stated: the client is too busy to meet with the agent. In this case,

    a.   the client is criminally liable for negligence.
    b.   the client may be liable for a commission and marketing expenses.
    c.   the agent can sue the client for specific performance, even if no customer had been located.
    d.   the agent must accept the revocation without the possibility of damage recovery.

S 32. A protection period clause in an exclusive listing provides that

    a.   the owner is protected from all liabilities arising from the agent's actions performed within the agent's scope of duties.
    b.   the agent has a claim to a commission if the owner sells or leases to a party within a certain time following the listing's expiration.
    c.   agents are entitled to extend a listing agreement's term if a transaction is imminent.
    d.   an owner is not liable for a commission if a prospective customer delays in completing an acceptable offer.

S 33. Real estate advertising must conform to regulatory standards and requirements. One requirement is

    a.   a broker may only place blind ads in social media outlets.
    b.   a broker must have all advertising approved by the local real estate board.
    c.   the advertising must not be deceptive.
    d.   sales agents may only advertise in their own name.

S 34. The three principal brokerage firms in a market agree to pay sales agents 15% more than any other competitor currently in practice. This is an example of

    a.   collusion.
    b.   price fixing.
    c.   allocation of markets.
    d.   steering.

S 35. Two leading agencies jointly agree to raise commissions charged to residential sellers to 7.5% of the sales price. Which of the following is true?

    a.   This is a perfectly legitimate business practice.
    b.   The brokers have illegally fixed prices.
    c.   The brokers have allocated markets.
    d.   The brokers have engaged in legal collusion.

S 36. A sale contract contains an open-ended financing contingency: if the buyer cannot obtain financing within a reasonable time, the deal is off. Six months later, the buyer still cannot secure financing. Which of the following is true?

    a.   The seller may cancel the contract, since it can be ruled invalid.
    b.   The buyer can continue indefinitely to seek financing, and the seller's property must remain off the market, since "reasonable" is not defined.
    c.   The escrow agent is entitled to the buyer's deposit.
    d.   The seller can force a lender to commit to a loan under fair financing laws.

S 37. In the event of a buyer's default, a provision for liquidated damages in a sale contract enables a seller to

    a. sue the buyer for specific performance.
    b. force the buyer to quitclaim equitable title.
    c. sue the buyer for the broker's marketing expenses.
    d. claim the deposit as compensated damages for the buyer's failure to perform.

S 38. Which of the following is true of an option-to-buy agreement?

    a. The potential buyer, the optionee, is obligated to buy the property once the option agreement is completed.
    b. The optionor must perform if the optionee takes the option, but the optionee is under no obligation to do so.
    c. The contract can be executed at no cost to the optionee.
    d. It is a bilateral agreement.

S 39. If a manufacturer that is the major employer in a small city moves its operations to another city, it is reasonable to expect

    a. a fall in housing demand, but no other changes in the real estate market.
    b. a decline in demand for all types of real estate in the real estate market.
    c. an immediate fall in the demand for industrial real estate, but no other changes in the real estate market.
    d. an immediate decline in the prices for industrial and office real estate, but no impact on the residential market.

S 40. If a commercial real estate market is undersupplied, it is likely that

    a. rental prices in that market will fall.
    b. rental prices in that market will rise.
    c. rental prices will remain stable until equilibrium is reached.
    d. construction will increase to the point of equilibrium.

S 41. The amount of available property that becomes occupied over a period of time is called

    a. vacancy.
    b. absorption.
    c. equilibrium.
    d. occupation.

S 42 The roof of a property cost $20,000. The economic life of the roof is 20 years. Assuming the straight-line method of depreciation, what is the depreciated value of the roof after 3 years?

    a. $20,000.
    b. $17,000.
    c. $14,000.
    d. $3,000.

S 43. The income capitalization approach to appraising value is most applicable for which of the following property types?

    a. Single family homes.
    b. Apartment buildings.
    c. Undeveloped land.
    d. Churches.

S 44. In the income capitalization approach, an appraiser

    a.   estimates gross income and multiplies times the gross income multiplier.
    b.   estimates effective income, subtracts tax, and applies a capitalization rate.
    c.   estimates net income and applies a capitalization rate to it.
    d.   estimates potential income and applies a capitalization rate to it.

S 45. Net operating income is equal to

    a.   potential income minus expenses minus debt service.
    b.   effective gross income minus potential income.
    c.   potential gross income minus vacancy and credit loss minus expenses.
    d.   effective gross income minus vacancy and credit loss.

S 46. If net income on a property is $40,000 and the cap rate is 10%, the value of the property using the income capitalization method is

    a. $100,000.
    b. $400,000.
    c. $1,000,000.
    d. $4,000,000.

S 47. The key feature of an adjustable mortgage loan is that

    a.   the interest rate may vary.
    b.   the monthly payment increases over the life of the loan.
    c.   the principal balance does not amortize.
    d.   the loan term can be shortened or lengthened.

S 48. Why is a wraparound mortgage loan potentially interesting to a home seller as an investment?

    a.   It is a senior loan that can be easily subordinated for additional debt.
    b.   A wraparound lender can profit when the interest rate of the wraparound exceeds that of the underlying mortgage.
    c.   The underlying loan is retired early.
    d.   The second mortgage borrower may make payments directly to the first mortgage lender.

S 49. A builder is required to secure a loan with mortgages on three properties. This is an example of

    a.   a participation mortgage loan.
    b.   a blanket mortgage loan.
    c.   a permanent mortgage loan.
    d.   a bridge loan.

S 50. Which of the following is true of a loan with negative amortization?

    a.   The interest rate on the loan increases as the principal balance decreases.
    b.   Payments are not sufficient to retire the loan.
    c.   The loan balance is diminishing, or going negative.
    d.   Additional interest is being added to the monthly payment.

S 51. The loan-to-value ratio is used as an underwriting mechanism because

    a.   the LTV determines the profitability of the loan.
    b.   the loan amount needs to be less than the property's value.
    c.   borrowers tend to inflate the true value of the property.
    d.   a full-price loan overfinances the borrower.

S 52. In the past, borrowers were often surprised by unexpected or undisclosed borrowing fees and expenses at closing. This phenomenon has been largely corrected through disclosure requirements mandated by which of the following laws?

a. Equal Credit Opportunity Act
b. Truth-in-Lending laws
c. National Disclosure Procedures Act
d. Federal Fair Housing Laws

S 53. Which of the following is an important function of the secondary mortgage market?

a. Participants borrow funds from banks so the banks can make more loans.
b. Participants issue tax certificates and sell them to primary lenders.
c. Participants purchase pools of defaulted loans from lenders to keep them solvent.
d. Participants sell mortgage-backed securities in order to buy pools of loans.

S 54. Cash flow is a measure of how much pre-tax or after-tax cash an investment property generates. To derive cash flow it is therefore necessary to exclude

a. cost recovery expense.
b. interest expense.
c. loan principal payments.
d. net operating income.

S 55. The method for deriving an investor's return on investment, or ROI, is by

a. dividing net operating income by cash flow.
b. multiplying the required yield times after-tax cash flow.
c. dividing net income by the price paid for the property.
d. multiplying cash flow times the price paid for the property.

S 56. Which of the following items would affect a homeowner's adjusted basis?

a. Installing a higher capacity air conditioning and purifying system.
b. Replacing a washing machine.
c. Stripping and staining hardwood floors.
d. Replacing a broken picture window.

S 57. Which of the following is true with respect to real property taxation by the federal government?

a. It imposes ad valorem property taxes and capital gain tax.
b. It may not impose property taxes or tax liens.
c. There are no federal ad valorem taxes on real property.
d. It imposes ad valorem tax, but not capital gain tax.

S 58. Ad valorem taxes are based on

a. the replacement value of property.
b. the assessed value of property.
c. the millage value of property.
d. the broker's estimate of value.

S 59. A retirement facility prohibits ownership of any unit by persons under 55 years of age. The association claims it has made the prohibition properly. Which of the following is true?

a. They are violating the Civil Rights Act of 1866.
b. They are violating the Fair Housing Amendments Act of 1988.
c. They are guilty of age discrimination.
d. The prohibition may be legal if performed correctly.

S 60. An agent receives a full-price offer from a minority party. The agent presents the offer to the seller and discloses the buyer's minority status. The seller at that point instructs the agent to inform the buyer that the property has just gone under contract. The agent duly complies, telling the offeror that the home has just been temporarily removed from the market and is unavailable – but may be available soon if the contract falls through. Which party or parties, if any, have violated fair housing laws?

a. The agent only.
b. The owner only.
c. The agent and the owner.
d. Neither agent nor owner.

S 61. Which of the following are examples of closing items not prorated between buyer and seller?

a. Taxes.
b. Inspection fees.
c. Utilities.
d. Condominium assessments.

S 62. Which of the following activities is not allowed under the Real Estate Settlements and Procedures Act?

a. A broker having any business relationship with an insurance company that is involved in the broker's transaction.
b. A broker pre-qualifying a buyer for a mortgage loan.
c. A lender requiring a deposit from a borrower for a tax and insurance escrow account.
d. A lender paying a fee to a broker for referring a borrower to the lender.

S 63. Which of the following communication records must (as opposed to should) be kept?

a. Notes on every conversation.
b. Copies of required communications to principals.
c. Notes from company training sessions.
d. Business cards of licensees one meets at open houses.

S 64. To minimize the risk of violating fair housing laws, a licensee should

a. refuse to use terms that refer to or describe any of the classes of persons protected by the laws.
b. avoid working in neighborhoods that are predominantly occupied by a single ethnic group.
c. make discriminatory or derogatory remarks in conversation only, never in writing.
d. give better service to members of a protected class than is standard for other clients or customers.

S 65. What are "tenant improvements?"

a. Modifications to a rental suite to conform to a tenant's usage specifications
b. Marketing programs that yield a higher quality of tenant
c. Increased revenue resulting from a rise in rental rates
d. Increased occupancy resulting from a population increase in the market area

S 66. For the proper handling of client and owner monies, a property manager is generally required to

a. deposit all funds every month in the management firm's central operating account.
b. employ a notary to witness and record every deposit or payment received.
c. maintain a special trust account in a qualified financial depository.
d. disburse all funds to their legal owners on a weekly basis.

S 67. Jennifer advised her clients they needed to paint their living room before showing the property. The walls of these rooms were all 8' high. The wall lengths were 14', 18', 16', and 18'. If a gallon of paint covers 200 SF, how many whole gallons would the homesellers have to buy?

    a.   1
    b.   2
    c.   3
    d.   6

S 68. An investor just purchased a rectangular 2-acre retail lot for $2,500 a frontage foot. If she paid $1,000,000 total, what was the depth of the lot?

    a.   400'
    b.   250'
    c.   871'
    d.   218'

S 69. Andra can afford to spend $5,000 in closing costs to refinance her home. The lender quotes closing costs of $800 plus 2 points. The house appraised out at $240,000, and she can get an 80% loan. Can Annika afford to refinance?

    a.   No, she is short by $64.
    b.   No, she is short by $1,600.
    c.   Yes, with $360 left over.
    d.   Yes, she in fact breaks even.

S 70. A lender offers an investor a maximum 70% LTV loan on the appraised value of a property. If the investor pays $230,000 for the property, and this is 15% more than the appraised value, how much will the investor have to pay as a down payment?

    a. $93,150
    b. $79,350
    c. $90,000
    d. $69,000

S 71. A house is being appraised using the sales comparison approach. The house has three bedrooms, two bathrooms, and a patio. The appraiser selects a comparable house that has three bedrooms, 2.5 bathrooms, and no patio. The comparable house just sold for $400,000. A half-bath is valued at $20,000, and a patio at $4,000. Assuming all else is equal, what is the adjusted value of the comparable?

    a. $400,000
    b. $416,000
    c. $384,000
    d. $424,000

S 72. A family purchased a $90,000 lot to build a custom home. At the date of closing, the lot was assessed at $84,550 and the tax rate was $1.91 / $100 assessed valuation. When they completed the home, the assessment increased by $235,000 to include the new construction. If the monthly tax escrow is based on the assessed value, what will the monthly tax escrow be?

    a. $517
    b. $6,096
    c. $508
    d. $367

S 73. The James family purchased a home for $360,000 five years ago and obtained an 80% LTV loan. Now the property has appreciated 25%. In addition, the loan has been paid down $22,000. What is the James's current equity in the home?

    a. $94,000
    b. $162,000
    c. $90,000
    d. $184,000

S 74. George and Mary have owned a rental house for 10 years. They bought it for $240,000 and estimated the land value @ 25%. If the property is depreciated on a 39-year schedule, and appreciation totals 50% over the period, what is their gain if they sell the property today?

    a. $159,230
    b. $166,150
    c. $181,538
    d. $120,000

S 75. Adelpha's home is valued at $250,000. She has insurance coverage of $160,000 with an 80% co-insurance clause. If Adelpha has a damage claim amounting to $100,000, how much will she receive from her policy?

    a. $32,000
    b. $60,000
    c. $80,000
    d. $100,000

S 76. The Alabama Real Estate Commission consists of 9 members, 1 of whom is a consumer member who must meet which of the following requirements?

    a.   No criminal convictions of any kind
    b.   At least 19 years old
    c.   Real property owner
    d.   Alabama resident for previous 5 years

S 77. When a real estate license is _____, it can no longer be renewed.

    a.   expired
    b.   lapsed
    c.   suspended
    d.   inactive

S 78. A licensee accused of a violation who disagrees with the initial hearing finding may file an application for a rehearing which will be held only if the final decision

    a.   was based on an error of the law.
    b.   was not unanimous.
    c.   was in compliance with AREC rules.
    d.   was within the statutory authority of the AREC.

S 79. If a complainant has requested payment from the Recovery Fund to recover damages not paid by a licensee, the claimant must show

    a.   he or she is not a blood relative of the licensee.
    b.   any amount already recovered from the licensee was not yet applied to the debt owed.
    c.   there is a balance due on the judgment.
    d.   the judgment has not yet been obtained.

S 80. Regarding criminal background checks, which of the following statements is TRUE?

    a. Felony convictions will result in licensure application rejection.
    b. National criminal history checks performed only on applicants with state criminal conviction.
    c. Cost of criminal history checks is covered by the licensure fee.
    d. Criminal history checks must be current to the date of license issuance.

S 81. Which of the following documents is NOT used as proof of permanent residency in the US?

    a. Driver's license
    b. Birth certificate
    c. US visa
    d. Green card

S 82. To obtain a temporary real estate license, the applicant must

    a. complete a 60-hour pre-license course within 6 months of start date.
    b. first obtain an original license.
    c. pass the state exam within 6 months of completing the pre-license course.
    d. find an Alabama supervising qualifying broker within 60 days of passing the exam.

S 83. Continuing education requirements include

    a. 30 hours of coursework every 3 years.
    b. 9 hours of Risk Management coursework.
    c. 6 hours of AREC- approved electives.
    d. 15 hours of coursework every 2 years.

S 84. Applicants for a reciprocal license must

    a. provide proof of licensure from the state where licensed within 120 days of application date.
    b. prove the other state license is active.
    c. complete 15 hours of Alabama coursework.
    d. pass the state exam within 12 months of completing the coursework.

S 85. Which of the following is an actual step to be taken when transferring a license from one qualifying broker to another?

    a. transferring licensee pays the transfer fee.
    b. current qualifying broker files a request for transfer to the new qualifying broker.
    c. new qualifying broker mails the transferring licensee's license to the AREC.
    d. the AREC issues the new license certificate at the beginning of the next license period.

S 86. When does a company real estate license expire?

    a. at midnight on September 30 of the final year of the license period
    b. when the qualifying broker leaves the company
    c. at midnight on August 31 every 2 years
    d. when the company does not renew the license by August 31 on even numbered years

S 87. A qualifying broker may serve multiple companies unless

    a. all of the multiple companies reject the idea in writing.
    b. the AREC denies the application to do so.
    c. all business performed by the qualifying broker is from the same location.
    d. they sell more than $25,000,000 in real estate each year.

S 88. If the parties to a real estate transaction disagree over who receives the funds held in trust, what happens?

   a. The qualifying broker decides how the funds will be disbursed.
   b. The qualifying broker can disburse the funds based on a court order.
   c. The involved parties can have the court order the qualifying broker to disburse the funds.
   d. The rules of interpleader can be applied for disbursement.

S 89. If a broker is determined guilty of mishandling trust funds, what is the limit of restitution that the broker can be ordered to pay?

   a. $2,500
   b. $5,000
   c. The same amount as the mishandled funds
   d. The law does not designate a restitution limit.

S 90. What is the purpose of an estimated closing statement?

   a. To provide the lender with closing amounts to be included in the mortgage loan
   b. To provide either the seller or the buyer a way out of the purchase agreement if the closing amounts are higher than either anticipated
   c. To allow both the seller and buyer to be informed and prepared for closing payments
   d. To allow the licensee to determine the amount of commission to be paid

S 91. What does RESPA require regarding estimated closing statements?

   a. Lenders are to disclose loan closing costs to borrowers.
   b. Lenders may increase loan closing costs 3 days prior to closing.
   c. Lenders set their own limits for escrow account deposits.
   d. Licensees may modify estimated closing statements to match actual closing statements.

S 92. What is owed to the client by the agency agreement?

   a. A listing agreement
   b. A property inspection
   c. An estimated closing statement
   d. Fiduciary duties

S 93. What constitutes a non-agency relationship?

   a. When the customer signs the non-agency agreement
   b. The first contact between the licensee and the customer
   c. The lack of agreement between the licensee and the customer on which services will be provided
   d. The lack of a signed agency agreement

S 94. Which brokerage relationship(s) allows the broker to work with more than one party to the same transaction?

   a. Transaction facilitator
   b. Transaction facilitator and dual agency
   c. Dual agency
   d. Single agency and dual agency

S 95. Which brokerage relationship has a reduced liability for the licensee?

   a. Single agency
   b. Transaction facilitator
   c. Buyer agency
   d. Dual agency

S 96. How is material misrepresentation defined?

a. A licensee representing one party but assisting another party in the same transaction
b. A licensee being neglectful of his or her client
c. A buyer leading the seller to believe the buyer is financially more prepared for the purchase than he or she really is
d. A seller making false statements about a property that affect the buyer's decision to buy

S 97. Alabama license law and the AREC each mandate specific listing services to consumers. Which service is mandated by the AREC that is not mandated by Alabama license law?

a. Presentation of all offers
b. Assistance in negotiations
c. Answering questions related to the transaction
d. All services are required

S 98. If Jeff does not make himself available to answer his client's questions about the process of selling the client's property, what violation is Jeff committing?

a. Failure to disclose defects
b. Not fulfilling obligations to transaction parties
c. Dishonest dealings
d. Unfair trade practices

S 99. Donna has posted the following advertisement. What violation has she committed with this ad?

Home for sale: Newly built 2-bedroom home in exclusive neighborhood. Close to churches and fitness clubs. Great home for family without children. For details, call Donna Springer at 555-3856. A Better Brokerage listing.

a. Donna has not identified herself as a licensee.
b. Donna's ad is deceitful.
c. Donna has not listed the asking price for the home.
d. Donna has not included the area where the home is located.

S 100. Julie is a broker at Trust Realty and works with Randy who is also a broker. Julie has made friends with one of Randy's clients and is trying to convince her friend to switch to using Julie as her agent. The client already has a listing agreement with Randy, but Julie has told the client that, since both Julie and Randy work for the same brokerage, there will be no problem with changing agents. What violation has Julie committed?

a. Julie is engaging in undisclosed dual agency.
b. Julie is making her associate appear incompetent.
c. Julie is performing functions reserved specifically for the principal broker.
d. Julie is being dishonest with the client

Section VII: Answer Key

NATIONAL TEST 1: Rights; Interests and Estates; Ownership

1.1 (a) Wells, driveways, and signs on a parcel of land.
The legal concept of real estate encompasses land and all man-made structures that are "permanently" attached to the land. The phrase "permanently attached" refers primarily to one's intention in attaching the item. Obviously, very few if any man-made structures can be permanently attached to the land in the literal sense. But if a person constructs a house with the intention of creating a permanent dwelling, the house is considered real estate. By contrast, if a camper affixes a tent to the land with the intention of moving it to another camp in a week, the tent would not be considered real estate.

1.2 (c) A chicken coop permanently attached to land.
Improvements to real estate include such things as fences, streets, buildings, wells, sewers, sidewalks and piers. Modifications to land or a developer's preparations of a parcel of land can include such activities as grading or clearing, neither of which are considered to be "improvements" in this sense of the word.

1.3 (b) The center of the earth and infinite space above the earth.
The legal concept of land encompasses the surface area of the earth; everything beneath the surface of the earth extending downward to its center; all natural things permanently attached to the earth; and the air above the surface of the earth extending outward to infinity. Land, therefore, includes minerals beneath the earth's surface, water on or below the earth's surface, and the air above the surface.

1.4 (a) enjoyed by the owner of a property.
This group of rights includes the right to Possess, Use, Transfer, Encumber, and Exclude others from using the property. (Remember: "PUTEE") Transfer rights include the right to sell, rent, donate, assign, or bequeath. The owner may also encumber the item by mortgaging it as collateral for debt.

1.5 (b) Any item of property that is not definable as real property.
Personal property is any owned item which is not real estate, and the rights associated with owning the personal property item. Items of personal property are also called chattels or personalty.

1.6 (b) pledge the property as collateral for debt.
The right to encumber the property essentially means the right to mortgage the property as collateral for debt. There may be restrictions to this right, such as a spouse's right to limit the degree to which a homestead may be mortgaged.

1.7 (a) transfer of a portion of the bundle of rights.
An ordinary lease is a common example of the transfer of a portion of one's bundle of rights. The owner relinquishes the right to possess portions of the surface, perhaps a building, in return for rent. The tenant enjoys the rights to possess and use the building over the term of the lease, after which these rights revert to the landlord. During the lease term, the tenant has no rights to the property's subsurface or airspace other than what the building occupies. Further, the tenant does not enjoy any of the other rights in the bundle of rights: he or she cannot encumber the property or transfer it. To a limited degree, the tenant may exclude persons other than the legal owner from the property.

1.8 (d) Yes. The drones infringe on his air rights.
Air rights apply to the space above the surface boundaries of the parcel, as delineated by imaginary vertical lines extended to infinity. Since the advent of aviation, property owners' air rights have been curtailed to allow aircraft to fly over one's property provided the overflights do not interfere with the owner's use and enjoyment of the property. The issue of violation of air rights for the benefit of air transportation is an ongoing battle between aircraft owners, airlines, airports, and nearby property owners.

1.9 (c) Navigable lakes, seas, and oceans.
Littoral rights concern properties abutting bodies of water that are not moving, such as lakes and seas. Owners of properties abutting a navigable, non-moving body of water enjoy the littoral right of use, but do not own the water nor the land beneath the water. The legal premise underlying the definition of littoral

rights is that a lake or sea is a navigable body of water, therefore, public property owned by the state. By contrast, a body of water entirely contained within the boundaries of an owner's property is not navigable. In such a case, the owner would own the water as well as unrestricted rights of usage.

1.10 (a) the high water mark of the body of water at the shoreline.
Ownership extends to the high-water mark of the body of water. The low water mark would imply that the owner owned the water itself at times of high water levels!

1.11 (d) They transfer with the property when the property is sold.
Littoral rights attach to the property. When the property is sold, the littoral rights transfer with the property to the new owner.

1.12 (c) Streams and rivers.
Riparian rights concern properties abutting moving water such as streams and rivers. If a property abuts a stream or river, the owner's riparian rights are determined by whether the water is navigable or not navigable. If the property abuts a non-navigable stream, the owner enjoys unrestricted use of the water and owns the land beneath the stream to the stream's midpoint. If the waterway in question is navigable, the waterway is considered to be a public easement. In such a case, the owner's property extends to the water's edge as opposed to the midpoint of the waterway.

1.13 (b) An item of personal property that has been converted to real property.
A personal property item that has been converted to real property by attachment to real estate is called a fixture. Typical examples are chandeliers, toilets, water pumps, septic tanks, and window shutters. The owner of real property inherently owns all fixtures belonging to the real property. When the owner sells the real property, the buyer acquires rights to all fixtures.

1.14 (a) the owner originally intended to remove it after a period of time.
One's original intention can override the test of movability in determining whether an item is a fixture or not. If someone attached an item to real property, yet intended to remove it after a period of time, the article may be deemed personal property. If a person intended an article to be a fixture, even though the item is easily removable, the article may be deemed a fixture. For example, an apartment renter installs an alarm system, fully intending to remove the system upon lease expiration. Here, the alarm system would be considered personal property.

1.15 (c) Fifty percent of the estate consisting of the indivisible whole of the real property.
An undivided interest is an owner's fractional interest in an entire (undivided) estate, but not in a physical portion of the real property itself. An owner who has an undivided equal interest with another cannot exercise exclusive rights over a portion of the real estate, which is an indivisible whole.

1.16 (a) an estate in land.
Interests are principally distinguished by whether they include possession. If the interest-holder enjoys the right of possession, the party is considered to have an estate in land, or, familiarly an estate. Freehold and leasehold estates in land are further distinguished by whether the duration of the owner's rights can be determined.

1.17 (a) a public interest.
Public entities may own or lease real estate, in which case they enjoy an estate in land. However, government entities also have non-possessory interests in real estate which act to control land use for the public good within the entity's jurisdiction. The prime example of public interest is police power, or the right of the local or county government to zone. Another example of public interest is the right to acquire ownership through the power of eminent domain.

1.18 (c) a freehold estate.
In a freehold estate, the duration of the owner's rights cannot be determined: the rights may endure for a lifetime, for less than a lifetime, or for generations beyond the owner's lifetime. By contrast, leasehold estates have expirations.

1.19 (d) that the estate is limited by a lease term.
A leasehold estate is distinguished by its specific duration, as represented by the lease term. Further, leasehold tenants only enjoy limited property rights: use; temporary possession, and limited exclusion.

1.20 (d) Fee simple defeasible.
The defeasible fee estate is perpetual, provided the usage conforms to stated conditions. Essential characteristics are that the property must be used for a certain purpose or under certain conditions, and, if the use changes or if prohibited conditions are present, the estate reverts to the previous grantor of the estate.

1.21 (c) An ordinary life estate.
A life estate is limited in duration to the life of the owner or other named person. Upon the death of the owner (ordinary life estate) or other named individual (pur autre vie life estate), the estate passes to the original owner (a reversionary interest) or another named party (a remainder interest). Thus with the life estate, the owner enjoys full ownership rights during the estate period, and holders of the future interest own either a reversionary or a remainder interest.

1.22 (b) a legal life estate.
Homestead, dower, and curtesy are legal life estates. A legal life estate is created by state law as opposed to being created by a property owner's agreement. The focus of a legal life estate is defining and protecting the property rights of surviving family members upon the death of the husband or wife.

1.23 (b) The boat, house, and motorcycle.
Separate property consists of: property owned by either spouse at the time of the marriage; property acquired by either spouse through inheritance or gift during the marriage; property acquired with separate-property funds; and income from separate property. Community property consists of all other property earned or acquired by either party during the marriage. A spouse owns separate property free and clear of claims by the other spouse. He or she can transfer it without the other spouse's signature. Upon the death of the separate property owner, the property passes to heirs by will or laws of descent. Community property cannot be transferred or encumbered without the signatures of both spouses. Upon the death of either spouse, half of the deceased's community property passes to the surviving spouse, and the other half passes to the decedent's heirs.

1.24 (d) The right to possess and use the premises.
Leasehold tenants are entitled to possess and use the leased premises during the lease term in the manner prescribed in the lease. They also have restricted rights to exclusion.

1.25 (a) the tenant makes, and landlord accepts, regular rent payments.
In an estate from period-to-period, also called a periodic tenancy, the tenancy period automatically renews as long as the tenant pays rent in a timely manner and the landlord accepts it. At the end of a tenancy period, if the landlord accepts another regular payment of rent, the leasehold is considered to be renewed for another period. A conveyance of leased property does not cancel a leasehold interest.

1.26 (c) terminates on the death of lessor or lessee.
The estate at will, also called a tenancy at will, has no definite expiration date and hence no "renewal" cycle. The landlord and tenant agree that the tenancy will have no specified termination date, provided rent is paid on time and other lease conditions are met. For example, a son leases a house to his father and mother "forever," or until they want to move. The estate at will is terminated by proper notice, or by the death of either party.

1.27 (a) an estate at sufferance.
In an estate at sufferance, a tenant occupies the premises without consent of the landlord or other legal agreement with the landlord. Usually such an estate involves a tenant who fails to vacate at the expiration of the lease, continuing occupancy without any right to do so. For example, a tenant violates the provisions of a lease and is evicted. The tenant protests and refuses to leave despite the eviction order.

1.28 (b) Estate from period to period.
In an estate from period-to-period, also called a periodic tenancy, the tenancy period automatically renews for an indefinite period of time, subject to timely payment of rent. At the end of a tenancy period, if the landlord accepts another regular payment of rent, the leasehold is considered to be renewed for another period.

1.29 (a) tenancy in severalty.
If a single party owns the fee or life estate, the ownership is a tenancy in severalty. Synonyms are sole ownership, ownership in severalty, and estate in severalty.

1.30 (c) tenancy in common.
The tenancy in common, also known as the estate in common, is the most common form of co-ownership when the owners are not married (though tenants in common can be married). The defining characteristics are: two or more owners; identical rights; interests individually owned; electable ownership shares; no survivorship; and no unity of time. With "identical rights", co-tenants share an indivisible interest in the estate, i.e., all have equal rights to possess and use the property subject to the rights of the other co-tenants.

1.31 (a) Parties must acquire respective interests at the same time.
To create a joint tenancy, all owners must acquire the property at the same time, use the same deed, acquire equal interests, and share in equal rights of possession. These are referred to as the four unities.

1.32 (b) cannot will their interest to a party outside the tenancy. The survivorship feature of joint tenancy presents an advantage to tenancy in common, in that interests pass without probate proceedings. On the other hand, joint tenants relinquish any ability to will their interest to parties outside of the tenancy.

1.33 (c) Legal life estate.
A legal life estate is created by state law as opposed to being created by a property owner's agreement. The focus of a legal life estate is defining and protecting the property rights of surviving family members upon the death of the husband or wife.

1.34 (a) A homestead interest cannot be conveyed by one spouse.
A homestead is one's principal residence. Homestead laws protect family members against losing their homes to general creditors attempting to collect on debts. Homestead laws generally provide that: the homestead interest cannot be conveyed by one spouse; both spouses must sign the deed conveying homestead property.

1.35 (a) sell or transfer his interest without the consent of the other tenants in common.
All tenants in common have distinct and separable ownership of their respective interests. Co-tenants may sell, encumber, or transfer their interests without obstruction or consent from the other owners. A co-tenant may not, however, encumber the entire property.

1.36 (c) Income derived from community property
If an income-producing property has been defined as community property, the revenue accruing from the investment is likewise community property.

1.37 (c) The beneficiary
A land trust allows the trustor to convey the fee estate to the trustee and to name himself or herself the beneficiary. The land trust applies only to real property, not to personal property. The agreement, or deed in trust, grants the beneficiary the rights to possess and use the property, and to exercise control over the actions of the trustee.

1.38 (c) The Buick and the second property
Community property laws define property rights of legal spouses before, during, and after their marriage, as well as after the death of either spouse. Community property law distinguishes real and personal property into categories of separate and community property. Separate property belongs to one spouse; community property belongs to both spouses equally. Separate property is that property which is acquired prior to the marriage, by gift or inheritance during the marriage, property acquired by separate-property funds, or income from separate property.

1.39 (a) A cooperative may hold an owner liable for the unpaid operating expenses of other tenants.
Since the corporation owns an undivided interest in the cooperative property, debts and financial obligations apply to the property as a whole, not to individual units as in a condominium.

1.40 (b) The owners enjoy an indivisible interest.
The tenancy in common, also known as the estate in common, is the most common form of co-ownership when the owners are not married (though tenants in common can be married). The defining characteristics

are: two or more owners; identical rights; interests individually owned; electable ownership shares; no survivorship; and no unity of time. With "identical rights," co-tenants share an indivisible interest in the estate, i.e., all have equal rights to possess and use the property subject to the rights of the other co-tenants.

1.41 (a) sell her interest to a third party without the consent of Robert

All tenants in common have distinct and separable ownership of their respective interests. Co-tenants may sell, encumber, or transfer their interests without obstruction or consent from the other owners. A co-tenant may not, however, encumber the entire property.

1.42 (d) It passes by probate to the deceased tenant's heirs.

A deceased co-tenant's estate passes by probate to the decedent's heirs and devisees rather than to the other tenants in common. Any number of heirs can share in the ownership of the willed tenancy.

1.43 (c) The tenants have an equal and indivisible ownership interest.

In a joint tenancy, two or more people collectively own a property as if they were a single person. Rights and interests are indivisible and equal: each has a shared interest in the whole property which cannot be divided up. Joint tenants may only convey their interests to outside parties as tenant-in-common interests. One cannot convey a joint tenant interest.

1.44 (a) there is a single title to the property.

Whereas tenants in common hold separate title to their individual interests, joint tenants together hold a single title to the property. This is referred to as unity of ownership.

1.45 (a) the new owner becomes a tenant in common with the other owners, who continue to hold a joint tenancy with each other and a tenancy in common with the new owner.

A joint tenant may transfer his or her interest in the property to an outside party, but only as a tenancy in common interest. Whoever acquires the interest co-owns the property as a tenant in common with the other joint tenants. The remaining joint tenants continue to own an undivided interest in the property, less the new co-tenant's share.

1.46 (d) It passes to the surviving joint tenants.

In most states, joint tenants enjoy rights of survivorship: if a joint tenant dies, all interests and rights pass to the surviving joint tenants free from any claims of creditors or heirs. When only one joint tenant survives, the survivor's interest becomes an estate in severalty, and the joint tenancy is terminated.

1.47 (c) If they are married.

Tenancy by the entireties is a form of ownership reserved exclusively for husband and wife. It features survivorship, equal interests, and limited exposure to foreclosure. In some states it now applies to same-sex couples.

1.48 (c) The trustee.

In an estate in trust, a fee owner-- the grantor or trustor-- transfers legal title to a fiduciary-- the trustee-- who holds and manages the estate for the benefit of another party, the beneficiary. The trust may be created by a deed, will, or trust agreement.

1.49 (a) sell or mortgage the unit without impediment from individual owners of neighboring units.

Condominium units can be individually sold, mortgaged, or otherwise encumbered without interference from other unit owners. An owner may not sell interests in the apartment separately from the interest in the common elements. Unit owners exclusively possess their apartment space, but must share common areas with other owners.

1.50 (b) the unit's pro rata share of the property value as defined in the declaration.

The unit's pro rata share of the property's ownership as defined in the declaration determines the amount of a unit owner's assessment. For example, if a unit represents a 2% share of the property value, that unit owner's assessment will be 2% of the property's common area expenses.

1.51 (a) shares in a corporation or association and a proprietary lease in a physical unit.

In a cooperative, or co-op, one owns shares in a non-profit corporation or cooperative association, which in turn acquires and owns an apartment building as its principal asset. Along with this stock, the shareholder acquires a proprietary lease to occupy one of the apartment units.

1.52 (d) the corporate entity of the cooperative association.
The corporate entity of the cooperative association is the only party in the cooperative with a real property interest. The association's interest is an undivided interest in the entire property. There is no ownership interest in individual units, as with a condominium.

1.53 (a) undivided interests in the property as tenants in common.
In a freehold time-share, or interval ownership estate, tenants in common own undivided interests in the property. Expense prorations and rules governing interval usage are established by separate agreement when the estate is acquired.

1.54 (c) As soon as it is affixed to the ground.
Mobile home units and manufactured homes are personal property until they are secured to the foundation of the lot in whatever form. Prior to affixing these items are personal property.

1.55 (b) The estate becomes a holdover tenancy, a periodic leasehold estate.
If a tenant with a leasehold estate for years remains in possession of the leased premises after lease expiration, a holdover lease is created. In the absence of a new lease agreement stating otherwise, the holdover tenancy becomes a periodic tenancy.

NATIONAL TEST 2: Encumbrances; Liens; Title Transfer and Recording; Leases

2.1 (c) A third party's interest in a real property that limits the interests of the freehold property owner.
An encumbrance is an interest in and right to real property that limits the legal owner's freehold interest. In effect, an encumbrance is another's right to use or take possession of a legal owner's property, or to prevent the legal owner from enjoying the full bundle of rights in the estate.

2.2 (a) They involve the property that contains the easement and a non-owning party. An easement is an interest in real property that gives the holder the right to use portions of the legal owner's real property in a defined way. One cannot own an easement over one's own property. Easement rights may apply to a property's surface, subsurface, or airspace, but the affected area must be defined. An easement may be affirmative, allowing a use, such as a right-of-way, or negative, prohibiting a use, such as an airspace easement that prohibits one property owner from obstructing another's ocean view.

2.3 (d) An easement appurtenant.
An easement appurtenant gives a property owner a right of usage to portions of an adjoining property owned by another party. The property enjoying the usage right is called the dominant tenement, or dominant estate. The property containing the physical easement itself is the servient tenement, since it must serve the easement use.

2.4 (c) easement by necessity.
An easement by necessity is an easement appurtenant granted by a court of law to a property owner because of a circumstance of necessity, most commonly the need for access to a property. Since property cannot be legally landlocked, or without legal access to a public thoroughfare, a court will grant an owner of a landlocked property an easement by necessity over an adjoining property that has access to a thoroughfare.

2.5 (b) an unauthorized physical intrusion of one property into another.
An encroachment is the unauthorized, physical intrusion of one owner's real property into that of another. Examples of encroachments are: a tree limb extending into the neighbor's property, violating his or her airspace; a driveway extending beyond the lot line onto the neighbor's land; and a fence built beyond the property line.

2.6 (c) a trespasser has been using an owner's property for a certain period with the owner's knowledge but without permission.
If someone uses another's property as an easement without permission for a statutory period of time and under certain conditions, a court order may give the user the easement right by prescription, regardless of

the owner's desires. For a prescriptive easement order to be granted, the following circumstances must be true: the use has been occurring without permission or license; the owner knows or is presumed to have known of the use; and the use has been generally uninterrupted over the statutory prescriptive period.

2.7 (d) how a property may be used and what improvements may be built on it.
A deed restriction is a limitation imposed on a buyer's use of a property by stipulation in the deed of conveyance or recorded subdivision plat. A deed restriction may apply to a single property or to an entire subdivision. A developer may place restrictions on all properties within a recorded subdivision plat. Subsequent re-sales of properties within the subdivision are thereby subject to the plat's covenants and conditions.

2.8 (c) the creditor's claim against the property as collateral security for the loan.
A lien is a creditor's claim against personal or real property as security for a debt of the property owner. If the owner defaults, the lien gives the creditor the right to force the sale of the property to satisfy the debt. For example, a homeowner borrows $5,000 to pay for a new roof. The lender funds the loan in exchange for the borrower's promissory note to repay the loan. At the same time, the lender places a lien on the property for $5,000 as security for the debt. If the borrower defaults, the lien allows the lender to force the sale of the house to satisfy the debt.

2.9 (d) An equitable interest.
A lienor generally has an equitable interest in the property, but not legal ownership. The exception is a mortgage lien on a property in a title-theory state. In these states, the mortgage transaction conveys legal title to the lender, who holds it until the mortgage obligations are satisfied. During the mortgage loan period, the borrower has equitable title to the property.

2.10 (a) Payment of the debt that is the subject of the lien and recording of the satisfaction.
A lien terminates on payment of the debt and recording of documents. Payment of the debt and recording of the appropriate satisfaction documents ordinarily terminate a lien. If a default occurs, a suit for judgment or foreclosure enforces the lien. These actions force the sale of the property.

2.11 (d) involuntary general lien.
A general lien is one placed against any and all real and personal property owned by a particular debtor. An example is an inheritance tax lien placed against all property owned by the heir. A specific lien attaches to a single item of real or personal property and does not affect other property owned by the debtor. In addition, judgment liens are junior, involuntary liens.

2.12 (a) Real estate tax lien.
The category of superior, or senior, liens ranks above the category of inferior, or junior, liens, meaning that superior liens receive first payment from the proceeds of a foreclosure. The superior category includes liens for real estate tax, special assessments, and inheritance tax. Other liens, including income tax liens, mortgage liens and judgment liens, are inferior.

2.13 (d) subordinate the lien.
A lienor can change the priority of a junior lien by voluntarily agreeing to subordinate, or lower, the lien's position in the hierarchy. This change is often necessary when working with a mortgage lender who will not originate a mortgage loan unless it is senior to all other junior liens on the property. The lender may require the borrower to obtain agreements from other lien holders to subordinate their liens to the new mortgage.

2.14 (c) A proceeding to enforce a lien by forcing the sale or transfer of a secured property.
All liens can be enforced by the sale or other transfer of title of the secured property, whether by court action, operation of law, or through powers granted in the original loan agreement. The enforcement proceedings are referred to as foreclosure. Note that lienors already possess equitable title, so they do not need to undertake a legal proceeding to establish this.

2.15 (b) file a foreclosure suit.
Judicial foreclosure occurs in states that use a two-party mortgage document (borrower and lender) that does not contain a "power of sale" provision. Lacking this provision, a lender must file a foreclosure suit and undertake a court proceeding to enforce the lien.

2.16 (a) strict foreclosure. Strict foreclosure is a court proceeding that gives the lender title directly, by court order, instead of giving cash proceeds from a public sale. On default, the lender gives the borrower official notice. After a prescribed period, the lender files suit in court, whereupon the court establishes a period within which the defaulting party must repay the amounts owed. If the defaulter does not repay the funds, the court orders transfer of full, legal title to the lender.

2.17 (d) A license, which terminates upon the owner's death.
A license is a personal right that a property owner grants to another to use the property for a specific purpose (to reach the kindergarten school bus). Unlike a personal easement in gross, which terminates only on the death of the grantee (Betty Luanne, in this instance), a license is revocable at any moment, is not transferable and does not attach to the land. It ceases on the death of either party, or on the sale of the property.

2.18 (d) Dominant tenement.
An easement appurtenant gives a property owner a right of usage to portions of an adjoining property owned by another party. The property enjoying the usage right is called the dominant tenement, or dominant estate. The property containing the physical easement itself is the servient tenement, since it must serve the easement use.

2.19 (b) a deed restriction.
A private party who wants to control the quality and standards of a property can establish a deed restriction. Deed restrictions take precedence over zoning ordinances if they are more restrictive.

2.20 (a) It involves a monetary claim against the value of a property.
A lien is a creditor's claim against personal or real property as security for a debt of the property owner. If the owner defaults, the lien gives the creditor the right to force the sale of the property to satisfy the debt. Liens do not necessarily alter the property value. Liens can be involuntary as well as voluntary. Finally, liens attach to the property, but so do other encumbrances.

2.21 (d) It is knowledge received or imparted through direct experience.
The term "notice" is synonymous with "knowledge." A person who has received actual notice has actual knowledge of something. Receiving actual notice means learning of something through direct experience or communication. Thus, a document in itself cannot be actual notice. It is the seeing of the document that makes it actual notice.

2.22 (b) It is knowledge one could have or should have obtained. Constructive notice, or legal notice, is knowledge of a fact that a person could have or should have obtained. The foremost method of imparting constructive notice is by recordation of ownership documents in public records, specifically, title records. Since public records are open to everyone, the law generally presumes that when evidence of ownership is recorded, the public at large has received constructive notice of ownership.

2.23 (a) grant, deed, and will.
Voluntary transfer, or voluntary alienation, is an unforced transfer of title by sale or gift from an owner to another party. If the transferor is a government entity and the recipient is a private party, the conveyance is a public grant. If the transferor is a private party, the conveyance is a private grant. A living owner makes a private grant by means of a deed of conveyance, or deed. A private grant that occurs when the owner dies is a transfer by will.

2.24 (c) It gives constructive notice of ownership.
Recording is not necessary to make a deed valid. However, it is in the grantee's best interests to do so. Recording the deed gives the public constructive notice of the grantee's ownership.

2.25 (b) granting clause.
The granting, or premises, clause is the only required clause. It contains the conveyance intentions; names the parties; describes the property; and indicates a nominal consideration.

2.26 (a) general warranty deed.
The general warranty deed, or warranty deed for short, contains the fullest possible assurances of good title and protection for the grantee. The deed is technically a bargain and sale deed in which the grantor promises to defend against any and all claims to the title. The overall general warranty covenant is: "I own

and will defend."

2.27 (d) To have an encumbrance removed if the lienholder cannot prove its validity.
Where there is a possibility that prior errors in deeds or other recorded documents might cloud (encumber) the title, the relevant parties execute a quitclaim deed to convey "any and all" interest to the grantee. If a party responsible for encumbering title refuses to quitclaim the interest, the owner may file a quiet title suit. This requires the lienor to prove the validity of an interest. If the defendant is unable to do so, the court removes the cloud by decree.

2.28 (a) A transfer tax based on the price of the property being conveyed.
State law usually requires payment of a documentary stamp tax on a conveyance of real property. The tax is based on the actual price of the property conveyed, thus enabling taxing authorities to ascertain current market value for ad valorem tax purposes. Payment of the tax is evidenced on the deed.

2.29 (b) probate.
A court proceeding called probate generally settles a decedent's estate, whether the person has died testate (having left a valid will) or intestate (having failed to do so).

2.30 (a) It will escheat to the state or county.
If an intestate decedent has no heirs, the estate escheats, or reverts, to the state or county after all claims and debts have been validated and settled.

2.31 (d) Eminent domain.
Various government and public entities can transfer private property to the public sphere by the power of eminent domain. The transfer is involuntary, even though the owner receives compensation. For example, a city government wants to widen a highway to accommodate growth. The government uses eminent domain to condemn and purchase all properties abutting the thoroughfare in order to complete the construction project.

2.32 (a) openly possessing and claiming the property without the owner's consent.
To claim legal title, the adverse possessor must be able to show a claim of right or color of title as reason for the possession; have notorious possession, which is possession without concealment; maintain a consistent claim of hostile possession, which is a claim to ownership and possession regardless of the owner's claims or consent; occupy the property continuously for a statutory period of time; in some states, pay taxes.

2.33 (c) The buyer.
Title records protect the buyer by revealing whether a property has marketable title, one free of undesirable encumbrances. The buyer is legally responsible for knowing the condition of title, since it is a matter of public record.

2.34 (a) a clouded title.
Chain of title refers to the succession of property owners of record dating back to the original grant of title from the state to a private party. If there is a missing link in the chronology of owners, or if there was a defective conveyance, the chain is said to be broken, resulting in a clouded title to the property.

2.35 (b) standard owner's title insurance policy.
An owner's policy may have standard coverage or extended coverage. Standard coverage protects against title defects such as incompetent grantors, invalid deeds, fraudulent transaction documents, and defects in the chain of title. Extended coverage protects against liabilities that may not be of public record, including fraud, unrecorded ownership claims, unintentional recording errors, and unrecorded liens.

2.36 (a) voluntary alienation.
Voluntary alienation is an unforced transfer of title by sale or gift from an owner to another party.

2.37 (d) A quitclaim deed.
A quitclaim deed transfers real and potential interests in a property, whether an interest is known to exist or not. The grantor makes no claim to any interest in the property being conveyed and offers no warrants to protect the grantee. Where there is a possibility that prior errors in deeds or other recorded documents might cloud (encumber) the title, the relevant parties execute a quitclaim deed to convey "any and all"

interest to the grantee.

2.38 (a) pass to the heirs by the laws of descent and distribution.
In this circumstance, the estate, including real property, will pass to lawful heirs according to the state's laws of descent and succession or distribution. These laws apportion the estate without regard to the wishes of the heirs or the intentions of the decedent. Escheat, by which the state takes the property, applies only if there are no legal heirs.

2.39 (d) declined because possession was secretive.
One of the preconditions for a claim of ownership based on adverse possession is notorious possession, or possession without concealment. Even if the length of possession in this case meets the statutory requirement, the drifter's secretiveness would invalidate the claim.

2.40 (b) free of undisclosed defects and encumbrances.
Marketable title is, by definition, one that is free and clear of undesirable and unknown encumbrances, claims, clouds, or other defects. Attorney's abstracts and title certificates do not guarantee that a title is marketable.

2.41 (c) Estate at will.
Three of the four principal types of leasehold estate are: the estate for years, which has a specific lease term; the estate from period-to-period, where the lease term of a specific period automatically renews; and the estate at will, which has no specified lease term. The fourth principal type, the estate at sufferance, is a tenancy without consent that therefore also has no specific term.

2.42 (b) for specified reasonable purposes.
A tenant has the sole right to occupy and use the premises without interference from outside parties, including the landlord. The landlord may enter the premises for specified purposes such as inspections, but the interference must be reasonable and limited. In addition, the landlord can do nothing outside of the lease's express provisions that would impair the tenant's enjoyment of income deriving from use of the premises.

2.43 (a) compliance with the rules and regulations of the building.
The lease defines the tenant's obligations, which principally are to pay the rent on time; maintain the property's condition; and comply with the rules and regulations of the building.

2.44 (b) providing required building support and services.
The lease defines the landlord's obligations, which principally are to provide the necessary building support and services, and maintain the condition of the property. It is the tenant's responsibility to obtain insurance and to determine the fairness of the rent.

2.45 (d) the tenant's estate is still obligated under the lease.
A valid lease creates obligations that survive the death of the landlord or tenant, with certain exceptions. A tenant's estate remains liable for payment of rent if the tenant dies; the landlord's estate remains bound to provide occupancy despite the landlord's death.

2.46 (a) The remaining tenant is responsible for the full rent obligation.
Multiple tenants who sign a single lease are jointly and severally responsible for fulfilling lease obligations. Thus, if one renter abandons an apartment, the other renters remain liable for rent.

2.47 (c) sublease.
Subletting (subleasing) is the transfer by a tenant, the sublessor, of a portion of the leasehold interest to another party, the sublessee, through the execution of a sublease. The sublease spells out all of the rights and obligations of the sublessor and sublessee, including the payment of rent to the sublessor. The sublessor remains primarily liable for the original lease with the landlord. The subtenant is liable only to the sublessor.

2.48 (d) net lease.
A net lease requires a tenant to pay for utilities, internal repairs, and a proportionate share of taxes, insurance, and operating expenses in addition to rent. In effect, the landlord "passes through" actual property expenses to the tenant rather than charging a higher rent level. Net leases vary as to exactly what

expenses the tenant is responsible for. The purest form of net lease requires tenants to cover all expenses, including major repairs and property taxes.

2.49 (a) gross lease.
A gross lease, or full service lease, requires the landlord to pay the property's operating expenses, including utilities, repairs, and maintenance, while the tenant pays only rent. Rent levels under a gross lease are higher than under a net lease, since the landlord recoups expense outlays in the form of added rent.

2.50 (b) An owner-developer wants to retain ownership of the land portion of the improved real property.
Ground leases are primarily used when an owner wishes to lease raw land to an agricultural or mining interest; when unimproved property is to be developed and the owner wants to retain ownership of the land; when the developer or future users of the property do not want to own the land; or when the owner of an improved property wishes to sell an interest in the improvements while retaining ownership of the underlying land.

2.51 (a) either party giving proper notice.
In the absence of an explicit term with a beginning and ending date, a court will generally construe the lease to be a tenancy at will, cancelable upon proper notice.

2.52 (b) a tenancy from period-to-period.
URLTA sets standards for improving oral, vague, or unbalanced lease agreements. In the case of an unclear lease expiration date, the lease is generally deemed to be a periodic tenancy.

2.53 (a) a hotel.
State laws based on URLTA generally do not apply to transient occupancies, such as hotel and motel rentals, proprietary leases in cooperatives, or to occupancy in a residence that is under a contract for deed.

2.54 (c) a temporary possessory interest.
A lease is both an instrument of conveyance and a contract between principal parties to uphold certain covenants and obligations. As a conveyance, a lease conveys an interest, called the leasehold estate, but does not convey legal title to the property. For this reason, a leasehold is also called a less-than-freehold estate.

2.55 (d) A leased fee estate.
In conveying the leasehold estate, the landlord acquires a leased fee estate, which entails the rights to: receive rent; re-possess the property following the lease term; and monitor the tenant's obligations to maintain the premises.

2.56 (c) occupy the property.
The legal essence of a valid lease is that it conveys an exclusive right to use and occupy a property for a limited period of time in exchange for rent and the return of the property after the lease term is over.

2.57 (a) The buyer acquires title subject to the lease, which remains in effect.
The landlord may sell, assign, or mortgage the leased fee interest. However, transferring and encumbering the leased property do not extinguish the obligations and covenants of a lease. Buyers and creditors, therefore, must take their respective interests subject to the terms of the lease.

2.58 (c) When either party gives proper notice.
In the absence of an explicit term with a beginning and ending date, a court will generally construe the lease to be a tenancy at will, cancelable upon proper notice.

2.59 (c) a five-year lease must be in writing to be enforceable.
Generally, a lease for a period exceeding one year cannot be oral but must be in writing to be enforceable because of the statute of frauds.

2.60 (b) The original tenant retains primary responsibility for performance of the original lease contract.
In a sublease-- a transfer of a portion of the leasehold-- the sublessor (original tenant) remains primarily liable for the original lease with the landlord. The subtenant is liable only to the sublessor.

2.61 (d) deficiency judgment.
Whenever there are insufficient funds to retire a defaulted and foreclosed mortgage loan, a deficiency judgment may be ordered – if allowed by law – to make up the difference. To comply with the judgment, the borrower must raise additional funds from other sources to make up the difference between the outstanding loan balance and the proceeds from the foreclosure sale.

2.62 (b) The possession must have been unconcealed, for the necessary length of time, and without permission
Adverse possession is only possible if the possession is open, continuous for the statutory period, and the possessor claims ownership.

2.63 (a) Recording instruments establishes the title's marketability.
When deeds, tax stamps, and liens are recorded, the public is given notice of the property's indebtedness and encumbrances. In turn, any future buyer can visualize what must be done to clear title and convey marketable title.

2.64 (c) A broker's lien
Many states allow a broker in specified circumstances to file a broker's lien against a property following the closing of a transaction. Here, the party who is obligated to pay the broker a commission refuses to pay. The broker's lien, once filed, attaches to the real estate interest owned by the obligated party.

2.65 (a) The lender must approve of the modified loan and selling terms.
The conventional transaction principles are the buyer and the seller. In a short sale, the loan must typically be modified so that the parties can feasibly proceed with the sale. Any time the loan must be modified, the lender assumes a primary role in the negotiations, and must in turn approve of the loan modifications made.

NATIONAL TEST 3: Land Use Regulation & Control; Legal Descriptions; Contract Law

3.1 (d) Zoning ordinances are a primary means of keeping land use in harmony with the master plan.
The master plan fuses state and regional land use laws with local land use objectives that correspond to the municipality's social and economic conditions. The completed plan becomes the overall guideline for creating and enforcing zones, building codes, and development requirements.

3.2 (c) specify usage for every parcel within the zoning authority's jurisdiction.
The intent of zoning ordinances is to specify land usage for every parcel within the jurisdiction. In some areas, state laws permit zoning ordinances to apply to areas immediately beyond the legal boundaries of the city or county.

3.3 (b) To separate land uses so that they do not interfere with each other.
One of the primary applications of zoning power is the separation of residential properties from commercial and industrial uses. Proper design of land use in this manner preserves the aesthetics and value of neighborhoods and promotes the success of commercial enterprises through intelligently located zones. Six common types of zone are: residential; commercial; industrial; agricultural; public; and planned unit development (PUD).

3.4 (c) The public interest
The principal forms of exceptions to a conforming use is legal nonconforming use (grandfathered in); variance based on hardship; and special exception based on the public interest.

3.5 (d) The area of a commercial or industrial facility in relation to the size of the site.
Commercial zoning regulates intensity of usage by limiting the area of store or office per site area. Intensity regulation is further achieved by minimum parking requirements, setbacks, and building height restrictions.

3.6 (c) It requires that multiple tracts of land be developed according to a single design.
Planned unit development zoning restricts use to development of whole tracts that are designed to use space efficiently and maximize open space. A PUD zone may be for residential, commercial, or industrial uses,

or combinations thereof.

3.7 (a) A homeowner in a residential zone converts her residence to a private school.
A legal nonconforming use can be illustrated as follows. A motel is situated in a residential area that no longer allows commercial activity. The zoning board rules that the motel may continue to operate until it is sold, destroyed or used for any other commercial purpose. An illegal nonconforming use is one that conflicts with ordinances that were in place before the use commenced. For instance, if the motel in the previous example is sold, and the new owner continues to operate the property as a motel, the motel is now an illegal, nonconforming use.

3.8 (b) A variance is granted by the zoning board if the owner has a justifiable reason.
A nonconforming use is one that clearly differs from current zoning and is subject to change upon conveyance. A zoning variance allows a use that differs from the applicable ordinance for a variety of justifiable reasons.

3.9 (c) certificate of occupancy.
Building inspectors inspect a new development or improvement for code compliance. If the work complies, the municipality or county issues a certificate of occupancy which officially clears the property for occupation and use.

3.10 (c) It conveys legal title to the acquiring entity.
Eminent domain allows a government entity to purchase a fee, leasehold, or easement interest in privately owned real property for the public good, regardless of the owner's desire to sell or otherwise transfer any interest. In exchange for the interest, the government pays the owner a "just" compensation. To acquire a property, the public entity initiates a condemnation suit. Transfer of title extinguishes all existing leases, liens, and other encumbrances on the property.

3.11 (d) parties responsible for improper disposal of hazardous waste could be charged for the cleanup costs.
Under CERCLA and the Superfund Amendment of 1986, current landowners as well as previous owners of a property may be held liable for environmental violations, even if "innocent" of a violation. Sellers often carry the greatest exposure, and real estate licensees may be held liable for improper disclosure.

3.12 (a) Individual property rights and the public's interest.
The optimum management of real property usage must take into account both the interests of the individual and the interests of the surrounding community. While maintaining the value of an individual estate is important, the owner of an estate must realize that unregulated use and development can jeopardize the value not only of the owner's estate but of neighboring properties.

3.13 (c) police power.
At the local level, county and city governments control land use through the authority known as police power. The most common expressions of police power are county and municipal zoning.

3.14 (d) The owner must sell the property in exchange for market-value compensation.
Eminent domain allows a government entity to purchase a fee, leasehold, or easement interest in privately owned real property for the public good, regardless of the owner's desire to sell or otherwise transfer any interest. In exchange for the interest, the government pays the owner a "just" compensation.

3.15 (a) reasonably promote community health, safety and welfare.
Local planners do not have unlimited authority to do whatever they want. Their zoning ordinances must be clear in import, apply to all parties equally, and promote health, safety, and welfare of the community in a reasonable manner.

3.16 (d) To ensure that improvements comply with codes.
Local governments enforce zoning ordinances by issuing building permits to those who want to improve, repair, or refurbish a property. To receive a permit, the project must comply with all relevant ordinances and codes.

3.17 (b) To regulate the density of dwellings in the residential zone.
Residential zoning regulates density, by limiting the number and size of dwelling units and lots in an area.

3.18 (a) a special exception.
A special exception grant authorizes a use that is not consistent with the zoning ordinance in a literal sense, yet is clearly beneficial or essential to the public welfare and does not materially impair other uses in the zone.

3.19 (c) a legal nonconforming use.
An illegal nonconforming use is one that conflicts with ordinances that were in place before the use commenced. For instance, if a motel that was allowed as a legal nonconforming use is sold, and the new owner continues to operate the property as a motel, the motel is now an illegal, nonconforming use.

3.20 (b) a plat of subdivision.
In addition to complying with zoning ordinances, a developer of multiple properties in a subdivision must meet requirements for subdivisions, including submission of a plat of subdivision.

3.21 (a) accurately identifies the boundaries of the property as distinct from all other properties.
A legal description of real property is one which accurately locates and identifies the boundaries of the subject parcel to a degree acceptable by courts of law in the state where the property is located. The general criterion for a legal description is that it alone provides sufficient data for a surveyor to locate the parcel. A legal description identifies the property as unique and distinct from all other properties.

3.22 (c) reference points, angles, and distances.
A metes and bounds description identifies the boundaries of a parcel of real estate using reference points, distances, and angles. The description always identifies an enclosed area by starting at an origination point, called point of beginning, or POB, and returning to the POB at the end of the description.

3.23 (b) two consecutive common meridians.
The "vertical" area between consecutive meridians is called a range. A range is identified by its relationship to the principal meridian. All ranges are six miles wide.

3.24 (c) two consecutive parallels.
The "horizontal" area between two parallels is called a tier, or a township strip. A tier is identified by its relationship to the base parallel. All tiers are six miles wide.

3.25 (b) Six miles by six miles, or 6 miles square.
A township is the area enclosed by the intersection of two consecutive meridians and two consecutive parallels. Since the parallels and meridians are six miles apart, a township is a square with six miles on each side. Its area is therefore 36 square miles. Remember to differentiate square miles from miles square: 4 square miles is a measure of area (2 miles x 2 miles); 4 miles square is a representation of the sides of a square (4 miles by 4 miles).

3.26 (d) 1/64.
The size in acres of a subsection of a township is a fraction of 640 acres, since there are 640 acres in a section. Thus ten acres is 10/640, or 1/64th of a section.

3.27 (d) properties in a subdivision.
The recorded plat method, also called the lot and block system, is used to describe properties in residential, commercial, and industrial subdivisions. Under this system, tracts of land are subdivided into lots. The entire group of lots comprises the subdivision. In a large subdivision, lots may be grouped together into blocks for ease of reference.

3.28 (c) Metes and bounds.
A metes and bounds description identifies the point of beginning and describes the distance and direction from that point to the first monument, and thence to subsequent monuments and back to the beginning to define the property's enclosed perimeter.

3.29 (d) Thirty-six.
The rectangular survey system divides a township into thirty-six sections.

3.30 (a) 640.
Each side of a section is one mile in length. Thus the area of a section is one square mile, or 640 acres.

3.31 (c) something of value traded in exchange for something of value.
A contract must contain a two-way exchange of valuable consideration as compensation for performance by the other party. The contract is not valid or enforceable if just one party provides consideration. Valuable consideration may be something of tangible value, such as money, or something the party promises to do. It may also be something intangible that a party must give up.

3.32 (a) contain a legal description of the property.
In addition to satisfying the requirements of a valid contract in general, a contract that conveys an interest in real estate must be in writing, contain a legal description of the property, and be signed by one or more of the parties.

3.33 (d) A reasonable time, or until the expiration date on the offer.
If an offer contains an expiration date and the phrase "time is of the essence," the offer expires at exactly the time specified. In the absence of a stated time period, the offeree has a "reasonable" time to accept an offer.

3.34 (b) The buyer's death terminated the offer.
Any of the following actions or circumstances can terminate an offer: acceptance; rejection; revocation; lapse of time; counteroffer; or death or insanity of either party.

3.35 (c) A contract for the sale of undeveloped land.
A real estate contract that is not a personal contract for services can be assigned to another party unless the terms of the agreement specifically prohibit assignment. Listing agreements, for example, are not assignable, since they are personal service agreements between agent and principal. Sales contracts, however, are assignable, because they involve the purchase of real property rather than a personal service.

3.36 (b) the parties act is if there is a contract.
An implied contract is an unstated or unintentional agreement that may be deemed to exist when the actions of any of the parties suggest the existence of an agreement.

3.37 (b) A sale contract before closing.
An executory contract is one in which performance is yet to be completed. A sales contract prior to closing is executory: while the parties have agreed to buy and sell, the buyer has yet to pay the seller and the seller has yet to deed the property to the buyer.

3.38 (a) both parties promise to do something in exchange for the other party's performance.
A bilateral contract is one in which both parties promise to perform their respective parts of an agreement in exchange for performance by the other party. An example of a bilateral contract is an exclusive listing: the broker promises to exercise due diligence in the efforts to sell a property, and the seller promises to compensate the broker when and if the property sells.

3.39 (c) The broker may have a claim for marketing expenses expended during the listing term.
The damaged party may elect the following legal remedies: rescission; forfeiture; suit for damages; or suit for specific performance. However, the broker must show that the seller has breached the contract.

3.40 (d) the failure of a party to perform according to the terms of the contract.
A breach of contract is a failure to perform according to the terms of the agreement.

3.41 (b) The act of declaring that a contract is no longer in effect for a given party.
Parties to a contract may rescind a contract by mutual consent, or a damaged party may rescind the contract unilaterally. This act of rescission cancels the contract and returns the parties to their pre-contract condition, including the refunding of any monies already transferred.

3.42 (a) reflect a mutual understanding or agreement.
Mutual consent, also known as offer and acceptance and meeting of the minds, requires that a contract involve a clear and definite offer and an intentional, unqualified acceptance of the offer.

3.43 (c) unenforceable.

A valid contract that is in writing is enforceable within a statutory time period. A valid contract that is made orally is also generally enforceable within a statutory period, with the exception that some contracts are enforceable only if they are in writing. These laws apply in particular to the transfer of interests in real estate. A void or voidable contract was not a truly valid contract.

3.44 (b) is possibly valid and enforceable.

Incompetent parties, or parties of "unsound mind," may not enter into enforceable contracts. However, during the period of one's incompetency, a court may appoint a guardian who may act on the incompetent party's behalf with court approval.

3.45 (c) a counteroffer.

By changing any of the terms of an offer, the offeree creates a counteroffer, and the original offer is void. At this point, the offeree becomes the offeror, and the new offeree gains the right of acceptance. If accepted, the counteroffer becomes a valid contract provided all other requirements are met.

3.46 (d) valuable consideration.

Valuable consideration can be something of tangible value, such as money, or something a party promises to do or not do. For example, a home builder may promise to build a house for a party as consideration for receiving money from the home buyer.

3.47 (c) is void.

The content, promise, or intent of a contract must be lawful. A contract that proposes an illegal act is void.

3.48 (a) must act within a statutory period.

The statute of limitations restricts the time period for which an injured party in a contract has the right to rescind or disaffirm the contract. A party to a voidable contract must act within the statutory period.

3.49 (b) require certain conveyance-related contracts to be in writing.

The statute of frauds requires that certain contracts must be in writing to be enforceable. Real estate contracts that convey an interest in real property fall in this category, with the exception that a lease of one year's duration or less may be oral.

3.50 (b) The buyer has no obligations to the seller whatsoever.

The mutual consent required for a valid contract is reached through the process of offer and acceptance. If the offeree accepts all terms without amendment, the offer becomes a contract. The exact point at which the offer becomes a contract is when the offeree gives the offeror notice of the acceptance. If an offer contains an expiration date and the phrase "time is of the essence," the offer expires at exactly the time specified.

3.51 (c) may not be discriminatory.

HOA's must use caution in developing restrictions for a new subdivision's land use regulations. In particular no restriction may be discriminatory -- such as an improper resident age requirement -- nor can the restriction violate fair trade laws.

NATIONAL TEST 4: Agency; Listing Agreements

4.1 (b) the laws of agency, or in some states, by statute.

In every state, a body of law, generally called the law of agency, defines and regulates the legal roles of this relationship. While the relationship is subject to contract law, agency law dictates how the relationship will achieve its purposes, regardless of what the listing contract states.

4.2 (c) The relationship is independent of any compensation arrangement.

It is important to understand that the agency relationship does not require compensation or any form of consideration. Nor does compensation define an agency relationship: a party other than the principal may compensate the agent.

4.3 (c) The defaulting party may have a financial consequence.

Involuntary termination of the relationship may create legal and financial liability for a party who defaults or cancels. For example, a client may renounce an agreement but then be held liable for the agent's expenses or commission.

4.4 (b) present all offers to the principal regardless of their amount.
A conventional listing agreement does not authorize an agent to obligate the client to contracts, and it does not allow the agent to conceal offers to buy, sell, or lease coming from a customer or another agent. Further, since a client relies on a broker's representations, a broker must exercise care not to offer advice outside of his or her field of expertise.

4.5 (c) confidentiality.
The confidentiality standard is one of the duties that extends beyond the termination of the listing: at no time in the future may the agent disclose confidential information.

4.6 (d) comparable to that of other practitioners in the area.
The agent is hired to do a job, and is therefore expected to do it with diligence and reasonable competence. Competence is generally defined as a "standard of practice" equal to the level of real estate marketing skills and knowledge of other practitioners in the area.

4.7 (c) disclose the information to the seller.
An agent has the duty to inform the client of all material facts, reports, and rumors that might affect the client's interests in the property transaction. This includes: the agent's opinion of the property's condition; information about the buyer's motivations and financial qualifications; discussions between agent and buyer regarding the possibility of the agent's representing the buyer in another transaction.

4.8 (a) the Andersons.
Since Gerry executed an agency agreement with the Andersons, they become the client and the Lincolns the customer, regardless of who pays the commission.

4.9 (c) a broker who has an agency relationship with a client.
In a subagency, a broker or licensed salesperson works as the agent of a broker who is the agent of a client. Subagents might include a cooperating licensed broker, that broker's licensed salespeople, and the listing broker's licensed salespeople, all of whom agree to work for the listing broker on behalf of the client.

4.10 (b) One agent represents both sides in a transaction.
Dual agency means representing both principal parties to a transaction. The agent represents both buyer and seller or tenant and owner.

4.11 (c) disclosing material facts that affect the value of the property to both parties.
In the role of facilitator, the broker's only fiduciary duties and standards of conduct are those of accounting; skill, care, and diligence; honesty and fair dealing; and disclosure to both parties of all material facts in residential sale transactions affecting the property's value. Some states do not allow for this form of relationship in a real estate transaction.

4.12 (a) The agent is showing the client's property to a prospective buyer.
Agency disclosure must occur upon "substantive contact" between the listing agent and a customer. Examples of substantive contact include: showing the prospect a property; eliciting confidential information from a prospect regarding needs, motivation, or financial qualification; and executing a contractual offer to sell or lease.

4.13 (d) good faith, trust and confidence.
The essence of the agency relationship is trust, confidence, and mutual good faith. The principal trusts the agent to exercise the utmost skill and care in fulfilling the authorized activity, and to promote the principal's best interests.   The agent undertakes to strive in good faith to achieve the desired objective, and to fulfill the fiduciary duties.

4.14 (b) general.
In a general agency, the principal delegates to the agent ongoing tasks and duties within a particular business or enterprise. Such delegation may include the authority to enter into contracts.

4.15 (b) special.
Under a special agency agreement, the principal delegates authority to conduct a specific activity, after which the agency relationship terminates. In most cases, the special agent may not bind the principal to a contract. Real estate brokerage is commonly based on a special agency.

4.16 (c) a party creates an agency relationship outside of an express agreement.
An agency relationship can arise by implication, intentionally or unintentionally. Implication means that the parties act as if there were an agreement. For example, if an agent promises a buyer to do everything possible to find a property at the lowest possible price, and the buyer accepts the proposition, there may be an implied agency relationship even though there is no specific agreement.

4.17 (a) Condemnation of the property
An agency relationship may terminate contrary to the wishes of the parties by reason of: death or incapacity of either party; abandonment by the agent; condemnation or destruction of the property; renunciation; breach; bankruptcy; or revocation of the agent's license.

4.18 (a) The agent has violated the duty of confidentiality.
An agent may not disclose any information that would harm the client's interests or bargaining position, or anything else the client wishes to keep secret. The confidentiality standard is one of the duties that extends beyond the termination of the listing: at no time in the future may the agent disclose confidential information.

4.19 (b) the agent has not violated fiduciary duty.
Since it is illegal to refuse to show buyers the property based on where the buyers live, the agent has not violated fiduciary duty. The duty of obedience only applies to legal activities.

4.20 (d) inform the seller.
An agent has the duty to inform the client of all material facts, reports, and rumors that might affect the client's interests in the property transaction.

4.21 (a) prior to completing a listing agreement.
An agent who intends to represent a seller or owner must disclose the import of the proposed agency relationship in writing before the listing agreement is executed.

4.22 (c) Whenever substantive communication is made beyond casual conversation.
A listing agent must disclose in writing to a buyer or tenant that the agent represents the owner in the transaction. This disclosure must occur before or at the first "substantive contact" with the customer prospect. In some states, buyer representatives must disclose the agency relationship to sellers or their agents upon initial contact.

4.23 (b) upon initial contact.
A buyer agent must disclose the agency relationship to the seller or seller's agent on first contact. Substantive contact is assumed to occur immediately in this circumstance.

4.24 (a) may not represent one party's interests to the detriment of the other.
A dual agent's first duty is to disclose the agency relationship to both principal parties or to withdraw from one side of the duality. After disclosing, the agent must obtain the written consent of both parties. If both parties accept the dual agency, the agent owes all the fiduciary duties to both parties except full disclosure, undivided loyalty, and exclusive representation of one principal's interests.

4.25 (d) practicing law without a license.
An agent should not act or speak outside the agent's area of expertise. A customer may rely on anything an agent says, and the agent will be held accountable. For example, an agent represents that a property will appreciate. The buyer interprets this as expert investment advice and buys the property. If the property does not appreciate, the buyer may hold the agent liable.

4.26 (a) Fiduciary and contractual obligations with the client.
A listing agreement establishes an agency relationship between agent and client that commits the agent to the full complement of fiduciary duties to the client in fulfilling the agreement.

4.27 (d) market, sell and show the property.
Special agency limits the scope of the broker's authority to specific activities, generally those which generate customers and catalyze the transaction. A special agency agreement usually does not authorize a broker to obligate the client to a contract as a principal party. Normally, principals do not delegate the authority to negotiate price to an agent in a residential transaction.

4.28 (b) An implied agency may have been created, with obligations to perform for both seller and agent.
Clients and agents may also create an implied agency listing based on substantive actions rather than on an express agreement. For example, if a seller allows a broker to undertake certain activities toward effecting a transaction without a specific authorization, but with full knowledge and consent, an implied agency may have been created.

4.29 (a) The agent cannot assign the listing agreement.
Since a listing agreement is a personal service contract, it is not assignable. In particular, a broker cannot assign a listing to another broker.

4.30 (b) exclusive right to sell.
The exclusive right to sell listing, or "exclusive," gives the agent the most control over the property and the greatest likelihood of being compensated for his or her marketing efforts.

4.31 (c) A listing that is entered in a multiple listing service.
Though not a distinct type of listing agreement, multiple listing is a significant feature of brokerage practice. Multiple listing is an authorization to enter a listing in a multiple listing service.

4.32 (b) The customer must be legally competent to undertake the transaction.
Effecting a completed transaction means finding a customer who is not only ready, willing, and able, but one who makes an acceptable offer. A ready, willing, and able customer is one who is: amenable to the terms of the transaction (ready and willing), and is financially capable of paying the price and legally capable of completing the transaction (able).

4.33 (a) obtain and distribute compensation.
In the normal course of business, a listing broker delegates marketing responsibilities to salespeople. A salesperson may not, however, seek compensation directly from a client. Only the broker can obtain and disburse the compensation.

4.34 (c) Perry, since he found the customer.
The two principal determinants of procuring cause are being first to find the customer, and being the one who induces the customer to complete the transaction.

4.35 (d) It may be terminated against the agent's will.
A listing may terminate on grounds of: performance; infeasibility; mutual agreement; revocation; abandonment; breach; lapse of time; invalidity of the contract; incapacitation of either party; destruction of the property; or, in this case; involuntary title transfer.

4.36 (b) Sue the broker for money damages.
If the broker cancels the listing or otherwise defaults, the client may sue the broker for money damages.

4.37 (b) exclusive agency agreement.
An exclusive agency listing authorizes a single broker to sell the property and earn a commission, but leaves the owner the right to sell the property without the broker's assistance, in which case no commission is owed.

4.38 (c) open listing.
An open listing is a non-exclusive authorization to sell or lease a property. The owner may offer such agreements to any number of brokers in the marketplace. With an open listing, the broker who is the first to perform under the terms of the listing is the sole party entitled to a commission.

4.39 (d) net listing.
A net listing is one in which an owner sets a minimum acceptable amount to be received from the

transaction and allows the broker to have any amount received in excess as a commission, assuming the broker has earned a commission according to the other terms of the agreement.

4.40 (a) the client.
Generally, buyer and tenant representation agreements are subject to the same laws and regulations as those applying to owner listings. The only difference is the client and his or her transaction expectations.

4.41 (a) To list the owner's property in a multiple listing service.
A multiple listing is not a distinct listing contract but rather a provision in an exclusive listing authorizing the broker to place the listing into a multiple listing service. A multiple listing service is a database of available properties.

4.42 (d) The broker assigns who is to represent the buyer and seller.
The designated agency agreement allows a broker to select a salesperson and associate brokers to act as the client's agent. A designated agency agreement must contain the name of all associate brokers who are authorized to act as supervisory brokers.

NATIONAL TEST 5: Brokerage Business; Sale Contracts

5.1 (d) Non-profit corporation.
A non-profit corporation is a corporate entity which is not legally entitled to generate profit. A non-profit organization may not broker real estate.

5.2 (c) are properly licensed.
A joint venture is a partnership formed to complete a specific business endeavor, such as a real estate development. Individuals, general and limited partnerships, and corporations may participate. A joint venture may broker real estate, provided the co-venturers are duly licensed.

5.3 (b) a single employing broker who has an active broker's license.
Only a broker with an active broker's license can hire and employ a licensed salesperson. A licensed salesperson may work only for the employing broker and may not work for or receive direct compensation from any other broker.

5.4 (c) Offer a property for lease on behalf of the employing broker.
A sales agent is only authorized to represent a broker and carry out such duties as the broker may legitimately delegate. Thus a sales agent does not directly represent the client in a transaction but is rather the agent of the broker and subagent of the client.

5.5 (d) The employing broker.
Agents can only receive compensation from their employing brokers. Co-op commissions, referral fees, and other compensations always flow through the broker to the sales agent.

5.6 (d) $4,940.
First calculate the total commission, then the co-brokerage splits, then the agent-broker split. Thus: $380,000 x 6.5% = $24,700 total commission. ($24,700 x 50%) = $12,350 total listing broker share. ($12,350 x 40% = $4,940 agent's share.

5.7 (c) $4,278.
The total commission is ($245,000 x 3%) = $7,350. The agent gets (65% x $7,350) - $500, which equals $4,278.

5.8 (c) complete the signing of the listing.
Once the seller signs the listing, the next critical task is to get it signed by the appropriate licensee, thereby making the listing a contract. Some states allow a salesperson to do this and in other states, the listing must be given to the broker for signing. This result will set in motion the process of marketing the property. The agency disclosures must take place prior to the execution of the agreement.

5.9 (b) Present the offer to the seller at the earliest possible moment.
When a buyer or tenant makes an offer, the agent must present it to the seller or landlord at the earliest

possible moment. If the terms of the offer are unacceptable, the agent may assist the seller in developing a counteroffer.

5.10 (c) The broker has illegally converted security funds for business use.
Conversion is the act of misappropriating escrow funds for the broker's business or personal use. Conversion carries serious consequences, including license revocation.

5.11 (d) Never.
All advertising must reveal the identity of the broker; licensed brokers and agents may not use blind ads that conceal their identities.

5.12 (a) fair trade and anti-trust laws.
Brokerage companies, like other businesses, are subject to anti-trust laws designed to prevent monopolies and unfair trade practices. In real estate brokerage, the primary manifestations of unfair trade practice are collusion, price fixing and market allocation. In this instance the brokers are price fixing.

5.13 (b) Outside brokers assist a listing agent in procuring a buyer.
A transaction involving a cooperating subagent is called co-brokerage. In a co-brokered transaction, the listing broker may split the commission with the "co-broker," typically on a 50-50 basis.

5.14 (d) Only members of the National Association of Realtors®.
The term Realtor® is a protected trade name of the National Association of Realtors®. Only members of this organization may use the term to refer to themselves.

5.15 (a) represent their employing broker in procuring clients and customers.
Agents may only act on behalf of their broker. They may not assume responsibilities for other listings since listings are not transferable.

5.16 (a) The IC is responsible for his or her own taxes; the broker does not withhold.
Generally, a broker has limited control over the actions of a contractor. Specifically: a broker can require performance results, but is limited in demanding how a contractor performs the work; and the broker does not take responsibility for a contractor's income and social security taxes.

5.17 (b) competitive conditions.
Commission structures are negotiated between the agent and employing broker as a function of competitive market conditions. The amount of commission being paid is negotiated between the brokerage firm and the client.

5.18 (c) avoid disclosing what price the owner will accept.
An agent must be extremely careful at this point to abide by fiduciary obligations to the client, whoever that party may be. Discussions of price are particularly delicate: whether the client is buyer or seller, the agent's duty is to uphold the client's best interests. Thus it is not acceptable to suggest to a customer what price the client will or will not accept.

5.19 (d) mixing escrow funds with the broker's operating funds.
Commingling, a prohibited activity, is the act of mixing the broker's personal or business funds with escrow funds.

5.20 (a) There is insufficient evidence of anything other than a normal business practice.
Charging identical commission rates in itself is legitimate. Price-fixing occurs when competitors have in fact colluded together to set prices.

5.21 (c) all the obligations and promises are performed and the transaction is closed.
An executory contract is one for which the signatories have yet to perform their respective obligations and promises. Upon closing, the sale contract is fully performed and no longer exists as a binding agreement.

5.22 (a) Use a standard contract promulgated by a state agency or a real estate board.
It is advisable, and legally required in most states, for a broker to use a standard contract form promulgated by state agencies or real estate boards, as such forms contain generally accepted language. This relieves the broker of the dangers of creating new contract language, which can be construed as a practice of law for

which the broker is not licensed.

5.23 (b) be written.
A contract for the sale of real estate is enforceable only if it is in writing. A buyer or seller cannot sue to force the other to comply with an oral contract for sale, even if the contract is valid.

5.24 (a) The contract has been legitimately cancelled and is null and void.
To be valid, a contract must meet the criteria of: competent parties, voluntary act of good faith, mutual consent, legal purpose, and valuable consideration. The buyer broke the mutual consent requirement by opting out before being told of the seller's acceptance. Thus, there is no valid contract.

5.25 (c) An offer and acceptance.
A contract of sale is created by full and unequivocal acceptance of an offer. Offer and acceptance satisfy the mutual consent requirement for a valid contract. The offeree must accept the offer without making any changes whatsoever.

5.26 (d) Equitable title.
A sale contract gives the buyer an interest in the property that is called equitable title, or ownership in equity. If the seller defaults and the buyer can show good faith performance, the buyer can sue for specific performance, that is, to compel the seller to transfer legal title upon payment of the contract price.

5.27 (b) a condition that, if unmet, renders the contract unenforceable.
A contingency is a condition that must be met before the contract is enforceable. If one party cannot meet a contingency condition by a specified deadline, the other party may cancel the contract.

5.28 (c) The buyer may be able to have the contract canceled.
The termite inspection clause is a contingency clause. If one party cannot meet a contingency condition by a specified deadline, the other party may cancel the contract. Did the clause state that the inspector had to be properly licensed? If so, the buyer has a good case for cancellation.

5.29 (a) Until the seller communicates acceptance of the offer.
An offeror may revoke an offer for any reason prior to communication of acceptance by the offeree.

5.30 (b) Fred has entered into contracts with both Jack and Sally to sell the same property.
Jack's acceptance of Fred's offer creates a valid contract, just as Fred's acceptance of Sally's offer creates a valid contract. Fred should have revoked his offer to Jack before accepting Sally's offer.

5.31 (d) agency relationships and property condition.
It is common for the seller to disclose the property condition requiring the buyer to acknowledge receipt of the disclosure. The broker discloses the applicable agency relationships in the transaction and names the party who must pay the brokerage commission.

5.32 (b) valuable consideration and a right to buy.
An option-to-buy is an enforceable contract in which a potential seller, the optionor, grants a potential buyer, the optionee, the right to purchase a property before a stated time for a stated price and terms. In exchange for the right of option, the optionee pays the optionor valuable consideration.

5.33 (a) Schmidt must sell to Carboy for $10,000.
Mary's option-to-buy contract is enforceable, assuming she paid a consideration for it.

5.34 (d) It is always assignable unless the contract prohibits assignment.
A real estate contract that is not a personal service contract can be assigned to another party unless the terms of the agreement specifically prohibit assignment. An option-to-buy is therefore assignable in the absence of such a prohibiting clause.

5.35 (c) At the end of the contract period, the vendor conveys legal title, provided the vendee has fulfilled all obligations.
A contract for deed is a bilateral agreement between a seller, the vendor, and a buyer, the vendee, in which the vendor defers receipt of some or all of the purchase price of a property over a specified period of time. At the end of the period, the buyer completes payment to the vendor of the full purchase price and the

vendor deeds legal title to the vendee.

5.36 (b) the parties have completed a verbal, executory contract.
As a sale contract created by an offer and acceptance, the parties have an executory contract: the parties have yet to perform their respective obligations and promises. However, as a contract for the sale of real estate, this verbal contract is not enforceable. An enforceable real estate sale contract must be in writing.

5.37 (c) The assignor has completed a legal action.
Either party to a sale transaction can assign the sale contract to another party, subject to the provisions and conditions contained in the agreement.

5.38 (d) any conveyance may trigger an acceleration of any loans secured by the property.
The mortgage agreement may or may not state that the seller's loan will be accelerated by the lender and called due on sale. The due-on-sale clause in the sale contract merely stipulates that the buyer and seller recognize the possibility that loans that survive the closing may be called due.

5.39 (d) The option is expired, and the tenant has no rightful claim to money paid for the option.
The option automatically expires at the end of the option period. The landlord has no obligation, either to sell the property or to return the consideration, after the expiration date.

5.40 (c) the seller retains legal title while the buyer makes partial payments until the contract is fully executed.
In a contract for deed, the seller, or vendor, defers receipt of some or all of the purchase price of a property over a specified period of time. During the period, the vendor retains legal title and the vendee acquires equitable title. At the end of the period, the buyer pays the vendor the full purchase price and the vendor deeds legal title to the vendee.

5.41 (d) Telephone Consumer Protection Act
The TCPA was enacted to rein in invasive telemarketing practices by requiring certain identification procedures, compliance with do-not-call requests, and a Do-Not-Call list registry.

5.42 (a) the CAN-SPAM Act.
The CAN-SPAM Act bans unwanted commercial messages sent to wireless devices, requires prior authorization to transmit certain messages, and requires an opt-out provision where the receiver can shut off the advertiser from sending future messages.

5.43 (b) Keeping enough operating funds in a trust account to cover bank fees.
Brokers may maintain an amount of operating funds in the trust account in order to pay monthly banking fees.

5.44 (a) fair trade practices.
The activity is called group boycotting and is a violation of fair trade laws. It is an illegal activity for a number of competitors in a given market to "gang up" on a competitor in that market so as to limit the boycotted party's access to customers and patrons.

NATIONAL TEST 6: Economics; Appraisal

6.1 (b) demand for the item is increasing in relation to supply of the item.
In a market economy, the primary interactions between supply, demand and price are: if supply increases relative to demand, price decreases; if supply decreases relative to demand, price increases; if demand increases relative to supply, price increases; and if demand decreases relative to supply, price decreases.

6.2 (d) Supply and demand are equal, and price and value are equal.
A market tends toward a state of equilibrium in which supply equals demand, and price, cost, and value are identical. According to this principle, market demand moves to meet supply, and supply moves to meet demand. If there is an extreme shortage of an item for which there is normally a strong demand, suppliers will rush to increase production to close the gap. If inventories of an item are very high, suppliers will stop production until the oversupply has been depleted.

6.3 (c) the uniqueness of every parcel.
In comparison with other economic products and services, real estate has certain unique traits. Traits of real estate include: inherent product value; uniqueness of every property; demand must come to the supply; illiquidity; slow to respond to changes; and a decentralized local market.

6.4 (d) Prices rise.
If demand is increasing and a moratorium slows supply, demand will begin to outpace supply, forcing prices to rise as the product becomes scarcer in relation to demand.

6.5 (b) an increase in demand for all types of real estate.
New businesses will arise to support the new company. They will hire new employees, some from out of town. The new employees will need housing. Hence the demand for residential real estate, as well as for commercial and industrial, will intensify, and it will also stimulate new construction.

6.6 (d) The number of available units that become occupied over a period of time.
Absorption is the amount of available property that becomes occupied over a period of time.

6.7 (a) rising prices.
Within the business cycle of real estate, declining vacancy indicates a combination of increasing demand which "fills up" supply which in turn decreases. As space becomes scarcer, rents for available space increase.

6.8 (b) desire, utility, scarcity, and purchasing power.
The value of something is based on the answers to four questions: how much do I desire it; how useful is it; how scarce is it; and am I able to pay for it.

6.9 (b) will increase.
If there is no longer a supply to meet the increasing demand of a growing population, prices for existing supply will rise.

6.10 (d) the market tending toward equilibrium.
A market tends toward a state of equilibrium in which supply equals demand, and price, cost, and value are identical. Thus if supply is scarce, construction will increase to stabilize the imbalance.

6.11 (c) the market is over-supplied.
Falling prices indicate an oversupply of commercial properties in relation to demand. In this case, construction of new supply will also slow down.

6.12 (a) have been increasing.
A rise in prices is a market signal that there is an undersupply of product in relation to demand. As the market moves toward equilibrium, builders construct more buildings to meet the unmet demand.

6.13 (c) It is often difficult to convert to cash.
Since real estate is often a large, long-term investment that has no exact duplicate, the process of a buyer's evaluating and choosing the right property is long and complex; hence, finding a buyer at a desired price can take a long time.

6.14 (b) The number of persons employed in base industries in an area
Base employment is the number of persons employed in the base industries that represent the economic foundation of an area. It is the driving component of total employment, which includes secondary and support industries, and which creates demand for all types of real estate.

6.15 (d) The total existing space of a certain type that is unoccupied at a given time
Vacancy is the amount of total real estate inventory of a certain type that is unoccupied at a given time. It is often stated as a percentage of total inventory, the vacancy rate for that property type.

6.16 (a) local government influencing the real estate market, regardless of demand.
Local governments sometimes declare a moratorium on new construction because of present or projected inadequacies of the infrastructure—water, sewer, power, roads, etc.—or because of the desire to conform to a master plan. The result may be to drive up prices, as supply cannot freely increase to meet demand.

6.17 (c) In- and out-migrations of major employers
Changes in employment numbers in a local market area, especially in major industries, have a direct impact on real estate demand in the area. Money supply, interest rates, and trade imbalances also have an impact, but they are regional or national factors rather than strictly local.

6.18 (b) Vacancy rises and prices fall.
New construction generally occurs to meet an excess of demand. By adding supply, it tends to increase vacancy and lower prices until supply-demand equilibrium is achieved.

6.19 (d) Residential
While all types of users may have these needs, they are most prominent for residential users because of concerns for family comfort and safety. Retail users are more concerned with competitive features of the trade area; office users care more about occupancy costs and suitability for the business; industrial users care more about such features as functionality, accessibility, and the labor pool.

6.20 (c) its susceptibility to swings in the local economy.
Because a real property cannot be transferred to a large, central real estate marketplace, its marketability is closely tied to local conditions. Investors and users must come to the product, unlike other types of economic product that can be moved to a place in search of greater demand.

6.21 (b) anticipation.
Anticipation is the value principle that a buyer will pay a price based on the benefits the buyer expects to derive from a property over a holding period. For example, if an investor anticipates an annual rental income from a leased property to be one million dollars, this expected sum has a direct bearing on what the investor will pay for the property.

6.22 (b) A homeowner adds a third bathroom to a house and thereby increases the appraised value by $10,000.
The principle of contribution focuses on the degree to which a particular improvement affects market value of the overall property. In essence, the contribution of the improvement is equal to the change in market value that the addition of the improvement causes. For example, adding a bathroom to a house may contribute an additional $15,000 to the appraised value. Thus the contribution of the bathroom is $15,000.

6.23 (a) assemblage.
Assemblage, or the conjoining of adjacent properties, sometimes creates a combined value that is greater than the values of the unassembled properties. The excess value created by assemblage is called plottage value.

6.24 (d) Market value is an estimate; market price is the price at which a property sold.
Market value is an estimate of the price at which a property will sell at a particular time. The market price, as opposed to market value, is what a property actually sells for. Market price should theoretically be the same as market value if all the conditions essential for market value are present. Market price, however, may not reflect the analysis of comparables and of investment value that an estimate of market value includes.

6.25 (a) Countable living area must be attached to the main house.
Generally, one cannot count an outbuilding that is not attached to the main house, i.e., a barn or shed.

6.26 (b) From the exterior walls, above grade, excluding open areas
Gross living area is measured from the outside and includes all attached and enclosed areas, minus rooms below grade and portions of area above grade.

6.27 (b) Make dollar adjustments to the sale prices of comparable properties to account for competitive differences with the subject.
The sales comparison approach consists of comparing sale prices of recently sold properties that are comparable with the subject, and making dollar adjustments to the price of each comparable to account for competitive differences with the subject. After identifying the adjusted value of each comparable, the appraiser weights the reliability of each comparable and the factors underlying how the adjustments were made. The weighting yields a final value range based on the most reliable factors in the analysis.

252

6.28 (d) takes into account the competitive value of specific amenities of the subject property.
The sales comparison approach is widely used because it takes into account the subject property's specific amenities in relation to competing properties. In addition, because of the currency of its data, the approach incorporates present market realities.

6.29 (a) adds value to a comparable that is inferior to the subject property.
If the comparable is inferior to the subject in some characteristic, an amount is added to the price of the comparable. If the comparable is better than the subject in some characteristic, an amount is deducted from the sale price of the comparable. This neutralizes the comparable's competitive advantage or disadvantage in an adjustment category. For example, a comparable has a swimming pool and the subject does not. To equalize the difference, the appraiser deducts an amount, say $6,000, from the sale price of the comparable.

6.30 (b) requires the fewest and smallest adjustments.
As a rule, the fewer the total number of adjustments, the smaller the adjustment amounts, and the less the total adjustment amount, the more reliable the comparable.

6.31 (c) $395,000.
Since the comparable has an extra bath, it is adjusted downward to equalize with the subject. Conversely, since it has no patio, the appraiser adds value to the comparable. Thus, $400,000 minus $7,000 plus $2,000 equals $395,000.

6.32 (d) Add the estimated land value and cost of improvements and subtract the accrued depreciation of the improvements.
The cost approach consists of estimating the value of the land "as if vacant;" estimating the cost of improvements; estimating and deducting accrued depreciation; and adding the estimated land value to the estimated depreciated cost of the improvements.

6.33 (b) is very accurate for a property with new improvements that represent the highest and best use.
The strengths of the cost approach are that it: provides an upper limit for the subject's value based on the undepreciated cost of reproducing the improvements. It is also very accurate for valuing a property with new improvements which are the highest and best use of the property.

6.34 (c) a property loses the same increment of value each year over the economic life of the property.
All property improvements have an economic life, which becomes incrementally shorter year after year as physical deterioration takes its toll. The property as a whole does not lose value, since land itself does not depreciate. Similarly, an improvement can regain value if it is repaired or updated. Finally, not all properties lose value from economic obsolescence.

6.35 (d) $575,000.
To appraise value using the cost approach, add the land value to the value of the depreciated improvement. Thus you have $150,000 + ($475,000 - 50,000), or $575,000.

6.36 (b) Divide the income a property generates by a rate of return.
An appraiser obtains an indication of value from the income capitalization method by dividing the estimated net operating income for the subject by the rate of return, or capitalization rate. The formula is: NOI / Cap rate = Value.

6.37 (c) uses a method that is also used by investors to determine how much they should pay for an investment property.
The strength of the income approach is that it is used by investors themselves to determine how much they should pay for a property. Thus, in the right circumstances, it provides a good basis for estimating market value. The approach, however, does not project what an income property's future income will be. Moreover, it is not an applicable method for estimating value if the subject is a non-income producing property.

6.38 (a) $370,000.
First, identify net income by subtracting out vacancy and expenses. Then divide by the capitalization rate. Thus, ($60,000 –3,000 – 20,000) ÷ 10% = $370,000.

6.39 (d) 150.
The monthly gross rent multiplier for a property is equal to the price divided by the monthly rent. Thus, ($450,000 ÷ $3,000) = 150.

6.40 (c) $406,000.
Multiply the monthly gross income times 12 to derive annual income. Multiply annual income times the gross income multiplier to derive the estimate of price. Thus, $2,400 times 12 equals $28,800. This times 14.1 equals $406,080, or $406,000 rounded.

6.41 (c) the state in which the appraiser operates.
A state-certified appraiser is one who has passed the necessary examinations and competency standards as established by each state in conformance with the federal standards.

6.42 (a) The Financial Institutions Reform, Recovery and Enforcement Act (FIRREA).
Title XI of FIRREA requires that competent individuals whose professional conduct is properly supervised perform all appraisals used in federally-related transactions. As of January 1, 1993, such federally-related appraisals must be performed only by state-certified appraisers.

6.43 (a) if two similar properties are for sale, a buyer will purchase the cheaper of the two.
According to the principle of substitution, a buyer will pay no more for a property than the buyer would have to pay for an equally desirable and available substitute property. For example, if three houses for sale are essentially similar in size, quality and location, a potential buyer is unlikely to choose the one that is priced significantly higher than the other two.

6.44 (a) is physically and financially feasible, legal, and the most productive.
This valuation principle holds that there is, theoretically, a single use for a property that produces the greatest income and return. A property achieves its maximum value when it is put to this use. The use must, however, be legal.

6.45 (d) $400,000.
Market value is an opinion of the price that a willing seller and willing buyer would probably agree on for a property at a given time if: the transaction is for cash; the property is exposed on the open market for a reasonable period; buyer and seller have full information about market conditions ; there is no abnormal pressure on either party; it is an "arm's length" transaction; title is marketable; and the price does not include hidden influences such as special financing deals. The amount Lynne actually paid is the market price. The previous listing price and Ken's offer might be interesting data for the appraiser, but the appraisal must also consider other market data, such as comparable sales.

6.46 (a) there may be no recent sale price data in the market.
The sales comparison approach is limited in that every property is unique. As a result, it is difficult to find good comparables, especially for special-purpose properties. In addition, the market must be active; otherwise, sale prices lack currency and reliability.

6.47 (c) selects comparable properties, adjusts the comparables, and estimates the value.
The steps are to first identify comparable sales; then compare comparables to the subject and make adjustments to comparables; then, finally, weigh values indicated by adjusted comparables for the final value estimate of the subject.

6.48 (b) the seller offers below-market seller financing.
The principal factors for comparison and adjustment are time of sale, location, physical characteristics, and transaction characteristics. An adjustment may be made for such differences as mortgage loan terms, mortgage assumability, and owner financing.

6.49 (b) weights the comparables.
The last step in the approach is to perform a weighted analysis of the indicated values of each comparable. The appraiser, in other words, must identify which comparable values are more indicative of the subject and which are less indicative. However, all comparables are taken into account, not simply the nearest comparable.

6.50 (b) market value is not always the same as what the property cost.
The limitations of the cost approach are that: the cost to create improvements is not necessarily the same as market value; and depreciation is difficult to measure, especially for older buildings.

6.51 (b) replacement cost.
Reproduction cost is the cost of constructing, at current prices, a precise duplicate of the subject improvements. Replacement cost is the cost of constructing, at current prices and using current materials and methods, a functional equivalent of the subject improvements.

6.52 (d) functional obsolescence.
Functional obsolescence occurs when a property has outmoded physical or design features which are no longer desirable or acceptable to current users.

6.53 (b) incurable economic obsolescence.
Economic (or external) obsolescence is the loss of value due to adverse changes in the surroundings of the subject property that make the subject less desirable. Since such changes are usually beyond the control of the property owner, economic obsolescence is considered an incurable value loss.

6.54 (c) depreciation.
Depreciation is the loss of value in an improvement over time. The loss of an improvement's value can come from any cause, such as deterioration, obsolescence, or changes in the neighborhood.

6.55 (a) estimates depreciation, subtracts depreciation from cost, and adds back the land value.
The steps in the costs approach are: (1) estimate land value; (2) estimate reproduction or replacement cost of improvements; (3) estimate accrued depreciation; (4) subtract accrued depreciation from reproduction or replacement cost; and (5) add land value to depreciated reproduction or replacement cost.

6.56 (b) Uniform Standards of Professional Appraisal Practice (USPAP)
USPAP is the professional code of conduct established by the Appraisal Qualifications Board that regulates appraisal practice in the USA. Standards relate to reporting requirements, methodologies, and proper disclosures to clients and the public.

NATIONAL TEST 7: Finance

7.1 (b) A state in which a mortgagee has equitable title to a secured property.
States differ in their interpretation of who owns mortgaged property. Those that regard the mortgage as a lien held by the mortgagee (lender) against the property owned by the mortgagor (borrower) are called lien-theory states. Those that regard the mortgage document as a conveyance of ownership from the mortgagor to the mortgagee are called title-theory states.

7.2 (d) It is evidence of the borrower's debt to the lender.
A valid mortgage or trust deed financing arrangement requires a note as evidence of the debt.

7.3 (a) trust deed or mortgage.
The mortgage or trust deed is evidence of the collateral pledge of the purchased property as security for the loan.

7.4 (b) mortgagor.
The mortgagor is the borrower and the mortgagee is the lender. As a memory aid, notice that "lender" and "mortgagee" both have two "e"s. "Mortgagor" and "borrower" both have two "o"s.

7.5 (d) $1,000.
Multiply the rate times the loan amount and divide by 12 to calculate monthly interest. Thus, ($200,000 x 6%) ÷ 12 = $1,000.

7.6 (b) $1,000,000.
The equation for the loan amount is (annual interest divided by the interest rate) = loan amount. Thus, ($5,000 x 12) ÷ .06 = $1,000,000.

7.7 (a) 7.5%.
The equation for the interest rate is (annual payment / loan amount) = interest rate. Thus ($18,750 / $250,000) = 7.5%.

7.8 (b) $12,000.
A discount point is one percent of the loan amount. Thus, one point on a $600,000 loan equals ($600,000 x 2%) or ($600,000 x .02), or $12,000.

7.9 (b) Part of each periodic payment is applied to repayment of the loan balance in advance and part is applied to payment of interest in arrears.
In an amortizing loan, part of the principal is repaid periodically along with interest, so that the principal balance decreases over the life of the loan. The annual interest is never the same, since the principal balance to which the interest rate applies changes every year. Interest on a loan is always paid in arrears, not in advance.

7.10 (b) private mortgage insurance.
Mortgage insurance protects the lender against loss of a portion of the loan (typically 20-25%) in case of borrower default. Private mortgage insurance generally applies to loans that are not backed by the Federal Housing Administration (FHA) or Veterans Administration (VA) and that have a down payment of less than 20% of the property value. The FHA has its own insurance requirement for loans with a down payment of less than 20%.

7.11 (d) The fraction of the appraised value of the property offered as collateral which the lender is willing to lend.
The relationship of the loan amount to the property value, expressed as a percentage, is called the loan-to-value ratio, or LTV. If the lender's loan to value ratio is 80%, the lender will lend only $80,000 on a home appraised at $100,000. The difference between what the lender will lend and what the borrower must pay for the property is the amount the borrower must provide in cash as a down payment.

7.12 (c) buyer's down payment.
Price less loan is the down payment. This is also the buyer's initial equity.

7.13 (a) refusing a loan because the borrower does not match the lender's target market.
The Equal Credit Opportunity Act (ECOA) requires a lender to evaluate a loan applicant on the basis of that applicant's own income and credit rating, unless the applicant requests the inclusion of another's income and credit rating in the application. In addition, ECOA has prohibited a number of practices in mortgage loan underwriting, including refusing a loan based on an applicant's demographic characteristics.

7.14 (b) $1,680.
Monthly income qualification is derived by multiplying monthly income by the income ratio. Thus (72,000 / 12) x .28 = $1,680. Remember to first derive the monthly income.

7.15 (b) adjust the applicant's debt ratio calculation and lower the loan amount.
Since a lender lends only part of the purchase price of a property according to the lender's loan-to-value ratio, a lender will verify that a borrower has the cash resources to make the required down payment. If someone is lending an applicant a portion of the down payment with a provision for repayment, a lender will consider this another debt obligation and adjust the debt ratio accordingly. This can lower the amount a lender is willing to lend.

7.16 (c) All loans secured by a residence.
Regulation Z applies to all loans secured by a residence. It does not apply to commercial loans or to agricultural loans over $25,000. Its provisions cover the disclosure of costs, the right to rescind the credit transaction, advertising credit offers, and penalties for non-compliance with the act.

7.17 (d) the borrower has a limited right to cancel the transaction within a certain period.
A borrower has a limited right to cancel the credit transaction, usually within three days of completion of the transaction. The right of rescission does not apply to "residential mortgage transactions," that is, to mortgage loans used to finance the purchase or construction of the borrower's primary residence. It does, however, apply to refinancing of mortgage loans, and to home equity loans. State law may require a

rescission period and notice on first mortgage loan transactions as well.

7.18 (b) ask the buyer/borrower about his/her religion or national origin.
ECOA prohibits discrimination in extending credit based on race, color, religion, national origin, sex, marital status, age, or dependency upon public assistance. A creditor may not make any statements to discourage an applicant on the basis of such discrimination or ask any questions of an applicant concerning these discriminatory items. A real estate licensee who assists a seller in qualifying a potential buyer may fall within the reach of this prohibition.

7.19 (d) not FHA-insured or VA-guaranteed.
A conventional mortgage loan is a permanent long-term loan that is not FHA-insured or VA-guaranteed. FNMA does not "back" loans; FHA only insures FHA loans; and the VA, not GNMA guarantees loans.

7.20 (b) limited by when the loan was originated.
Rules for assumability vary according to when the FHA-insured loan was originated and whether the original loan was for an investment property or an owner-occupied principal residence. Loans originated before December 1, 1986, are generally assumable without restriction. Loans originated after December 1, 1986, require that the assumer show creditworthiness. Some mortgages executed from 1986 through 1989 contain language that is not enforced as a result of later Congressional action. Mortgages from that period are now freely assumable, despite any restrictions stated in the mortgage.

7.21 (c) how much of a loan the VA will guarantee.
A veteran must apply for a Certificate of Eligibility to find out how much the VA will guarantee in a particular situation.

7.22 (d) Zero.
If a loan is fully amortizing, its loan balance is zero at the end of the loan term.

7.23 (b) The buyer gives the seller a mortgage and note as part of the purchase price of the property.
With a purchase money mortgage, the borrower gives a mortgage and note to the seller to finance some or all of the purchase price of the property. The seller in this case is said to "take back" a note, or to "carry paper," on the property.

7.24 (c) hypothecation.
The process of securing a loan by pledging a property without giving up ownership of the property is called hypothecation.

7.25 (a) The borrower gives the lender a note and a mortgage in exchange for loan funds.
When a borrower gives a note promising to repay the borrowed money and executes a mortgage on the real estate for which the money is being borrowed as security, the financing method is called mortgage financing.

7.26 (c) The trustor conveys title to a trustee in exchange for loan funds from the beneficiary.
A deed of trust conveys title to the property in question from the borrower (trustor) to a trustee as security for the loan. The trustee is a third party fiduciary to the trust. While the loan is in place, the trustee holds the title on behalf of the lender, who is the beneficiary of the trust.

7.27 (a) title-theory state.
States that regard the mortgage document as a conveyance of ownership from the mortgagor to the mortgagee are called title-theory states.

7.28 (b) usury.
Many states have laws against usury, which is the charging of excessive interest rates on loans. Such states have a maximum rate that is either a flat rate or a variable rate tied to an index such as the prime lending rate.

7.29 (c) $7,500.
A point is one percentage point of a loan amount. Thus, 2.5 points on a $300,000 loan equal (.025 x $300,000), or $7,500.

7.30 (a) an amortized loan is paid off over the loan period.
Amortized loans retire the principal balance over the loan period. If a loan does not do this, one must make a balloon payment at the end of the loan term to complete the loan payoff.

7.31 (c) it is a negotiable instrument.
A promissory note is a negotiable instrument, which means the payee may assign it to a third party. The assignee would then have the right to receive the borrower's periodic payments.

7.32 (d) may be required to execute a release of mortgage document.
Lenders may be required to release the mortgage or trust document to the borrower when the borrower has paid off the loan and all other sums secured by the document. The release clause, also known as a defeasance clause, may specify that the mortgagee will execute a satisfaction of mortgage (also known as release of mortgage and mortgage discharge) to the mortgagor.

7.33 (a) an appraisal report.
Loan underwriting is the process of assessing the lender's risk in giving a loan. Mortgage underwriting includes: evaluating the borrower's ability to repay the loan; appraising the value of the property offered as security; and determining the terms of the loan.

7.34 (c) the ability to re-pay, the value of the collateral, and the profitability of the loan.
A lender assesses risks by examining, or qualifying, both borrower and property. In qualifying a borrower, an underwriter weighs the ability of the borrower to repay the loan. In qualifying a property, an underwriter assesses the ability of the property value to cover potential losses. In this evaluation, a lender requires that the appraised value of the property be more than adequate to cover the contemplated loan and costs. Finally, the loan must make money for the lending organization as a basic business precept.

7.35 (b) they want to ensure there is more than enough collateral to cover the loan amount.
Without an ample difference between the property value and the loan amount, a drop in property values could cause the loan balance to exceed the collateral itself. This greatly increases the risk of a loan loss should the borrower default since the balance could not be completely recovered in a foreclosure sale.

7.36 (b) consider the income of a spouse in evaluating a family's creditworthiness.
The Equal Credit Opportunity Act (ECOA) requires a lender to evaluate a loan applicant on the basis of that applicant's own income and credit rating, unless the applicant requests the inclusion of another's income and credit rating in the application. In such a case, a lender may not discount or disregard income from part-time work, a spouse, child support, alimony, or separate maintenance.

7.37 (a) insure the buyer has the earning power to make the loan payments.
Both the income and debt ratios in borrower qualification quantify how much a borrower can safely afford to pay on a mortgage loan. The income ratio focuses on the borrower's earning power.

7.38 (d) debt payments divided by gross income.
The debt ratio formula is (debt obligations) ÷ (income).

7.39 (c) the parties complete all loan origination documents and the loan is funded.
Closing of a mortgage loan normally occurs with the closing of the real estate transaction. At the real estate closing, the lender typically has deposited the funded amount with an escrow agent, along with instructions for disbursing the funds. The borrower deposits necessary funds with the escrow agent, executes final documents, and receives signed copies of all relevant documents.

7.40 (b) Truth-in-Lending laws and Regulation Z.
Regulation Z, which implements the Truth-in-Lending Act, applies to all loans secured by a residence. It does not apply to commercial loans or to agricultural loans over $25,000. It prescribes requirements to lenders regarding the disclosure of costs, the right to rescind the credit transaction, advertising credit offers, and penalties for non-compliance with the Truth-in-Lending Act.

7.41 (a) The Equal Credit Opportunity Act.
ECOA prohibits discrimination in extending credit based on race, color, religion, national origin, sex, marital status, age, or dependency upon public assistance.

7.42 (c) the Real Estate Settlement and Procedures Act.
RESPA is a federal law which aims to standardize settlement practices and ensure that buyers understand settlement costs. RESPA applies to purchases of residential real estate (one- to four-family homes) to be financed by "federally related" first mortgage loans. In addition to imposing settlement procedures, RESPA provisions prohibit lenders from paying kickbacks and unearned fees to parties who may have helped the lender obtain the borrower's business.

7.43 (b) Buying securities, changing the discount rate, and controlling banking reserves.
The Federal Reserve System regulates the money supply by means of three methods: selling or re-purchasing government securities, primarily Treasury bills, changing the reserve requirement for member banks; changing the interest rate, or discount rate, the system charges member institutions for borrowing funds from the Federal Reserve System.

7.44 (a) It cycles funds back to primary lenders so they can make more loans.
Secondary mortgage market organizations buy pools of mortgages from primary lenders and sell securities backed by these pooled mortgages to investors. By purchasing loans from primary lenders, the secondary market returns funds to the primary lenders, thereby enabling the primary lender to originate more mortgage loans.

7.45 (a) Fannie Mae, Freddie Mac, and Ginnie Mae.
As major players in the secondary market, the Federal National Mortgage Association (FNMA, "Fannie Mae"), Government National Mortgage Association (GNMA, "Ginnie Mae), and Federal Home Loan Mortgage Corporation (FHLMC, "Freddie Mac") tend to set the standards for the primary market. FHA, VA, and the Federal Reserve are not organizations in the secondary mortgage market.

7.46 (c) It purchases FHA-backed and VA-backed loans.
Fannie Mae buys conventional, FHA-backed and VA-backed loans; gives banks mortgage-backed securities in exchange for blocks of mortgages; and sells bonds and mortgage-backed securities. It does not guarantee, insure, or originate loans.

7.47 (b) It insures loans made by approved lenders.
The Federal Housing Administration (FHA) does not lend money, but insures permanent long-term loans made by others. The lender must be approved by the FHA, and the borrower must meet certain FHA qualifications.

7.48 (a) It guarantees loans made by approved lenders.
The Veterans Administration (VA) offers loan guarantees to qualified veterans. The VA partially guarantees permanent long-term loans originated by VA-approved lenders on properties that meet VA standards. The VA's guarantee enables lenders to issue loans with higher loan-to-value ratios than would otherwise be possible.

7.49 (c) the loan payments gradually increase.
Graduated payment mortgages allow for smaller initial monthly payments which gradually increase. The interest rate remains fixed as does the loan term.

7.50 (b) the borrower pays additional interest at the onset in order to obtain a lower interest rate.
A buydown loan entails a prepayment of interest on a loan. The prepayment effectively lowers the interest rate and the periodic payments for the borrower. Buydowns typically occur in a circumstance where a builder wants to market a new development to a buyer who cannot quite qualify for the necessary loan at market rates.

7.51 (c) Private mortgage insurance
If a loan's LTV ratio is too high, a lender may require that the borrower purchase private mortgage insurance, commonly called PMI. This insurance secures whatever portion of the loan amount takes the LTV ratio above the typical ratio limit – which is usually 80% of the property's value. This protects the lender from the borrower's default – which can become more likely if the borrower has very little equity in the property.

7.52 (d) Agribusinesses
The Federal Agricultural Mortgage Corporation, or Farmer Mac. Farmer Mac (FAMC) is a federal agency

whose central function is to increase the availability and affordability of credit for American agriculture and American rural communities.

NATIONAL TEST 8: Investments; Taxation; Professional Practices

8.1 (b) negative leverage.
Leveraging is borrowing funds in order to make an investment that is larger than your own resource permits you to do directly. In negative leverage situations, your cost of borrowing funds to make the investment becomes greater than the income the investment returns to you.

8.2 (b) income properties.
Cost recovery, or depreciation, allows the owner of income property to deduct a portion of the property's value from gross income each year over the life of the asset. Principal residences cannot be depreciated (unless portions are treated as a home office.) Further, land cannot be depreciated.

8.3 (c) 19.5 %.
Appreciation amount is the current value of the property minus the original cost. The total appreciation rate is derived by dividing the appreciation amount by the original cost. Subtract the estimated current market value from the price originally paid (239,000 - 200,000 = 39,000) and then divide the result by the original price (39,000 / 200,000 = . 195 or 19.5%).

8.4 (d) a deduction for mortgage interest.
Deducting mortgage interest is a significant tax advantage of owning one's residence. Depreciation and cost-deductions do not apply to a non-income producing residence. Appreciation is a benefit, but not a tax benefit.

8.5 (d) $232,900.
The figure for net proceeds from sale is expressed by the formula: sale price - costs of sale = net proceeds. Thus $250,000 - (6% x 250,000) – 600 – 1,500 = $232,900.

8.6 (b) $471,000.
The beginning basis is the cost of acquiring a property. Basis is increased by capital improvements and decreased by depreciation. The basic formula for adjusted basis is Beginning basis ($450,000) + capital improvements ($9,000 + $12,000) - depreciation ($0) = adjusted basis ($471,000).

8.7 (c) $68,000.
The gain on sale (capital gain) of a primary residence is represented by the basic formula: amount realized (net sales proceeds, $420,000) - adjusted basis ($352,000) = gain on sale ($68,000). Note the purchase price of the second house is irrelevant.

8.8 (a) There is no taxable gain.
There is no taxable gain because the gain falls under the exclusion limit of $250,000. As of August 5, 1997, tax law provides an exclusion of $250,000 for an individual taxpayer and $500,000 for married taxpayers filing jointly on the gain from sale of a principal residence. The seller must have owned the property for at least two years during the five years preceding the date of sale; used the property as principal residence for a total of two years during that five-year period; and have waited two years since the last use of the exclusion for any sale.

8.9 (c) direct investment.
Individuals, corporations, or other investor entities may invest as active investors in a property by buying it directly and taking responsibility for managing and operating the property. This investment mode is called direct investment.

8.10 (a) $2,100.
Annual gross operating income ($1,500 x 12 = $18,000) - annual operating expenses ($500 x 12 = $6,000) = annual net operating income ($12,000); annual net operating income ($12,000) - cost recovery expense ($5,000) = taxable income ($7,000); taxable income ($7,000) x tax rate (30%) = tax liability ($2,100).

8.11 (b) the more the investor stands to gain, the greater the risk that the investor may lose.
The general rule in investments is that the safer the investment, the more slowly it gains in value. The more you want it to gain, and the more quickly, the more you must risk losing it. Reward in investing corresponds directly to the degree of risk.

8.12 (a) income and tax benefits.
The basic financial rewards of an investment include income, appreciation in asset value, positive borrowing leverage, and tax benefits.

8.13 (d) relatively illiquid.
Real estate is by nature more difficult to convert to cash than many other types of investment. Compare the selling of a home with the ease of drawing money out of a bank account or selling a stock.

8.14 (b) a more management-intensive investment.
Real estate tends to require a high degree of investor involvement in management of the investment. Even raw land requires some degree of maintenance to preserve its value. Improved properties often require extensive management, including repairs, maintenance, onsite leasing, tenant relations, security, and fiscal management.

8.15 (a) a general partnership.
A general partnership is a syndicate in which all members participate equally in managing the investment and in the profits or losses it generates.

8.16 (d) gross income minus expenses minus building depreciation.
Taxable income from investment real estate is the gross income received minus any expenses, deductions or exclusions that current tax law allows. Depreciation of land is not allowed.

8.17 (c) deduct interest payments from income.
Taxable income is net operating income minus all allowable deductions. The interest portion of debt service is allowed and is deducted from Net Operating Income as interest expense. Principal repayment is not an allowable deduction on investment properties. Capital gain derivation does not involve interest or principal payments.

8.18 (d) The owner may be able to avoid capital gain tax when the property is sold.
Provided the owner meets certain ownership and use tests, there is no capital gain tax on sale of the property unless the gain exceeds $250,000 for a single taxpayer or $500,000 for married taxpayers who file jointly. Since the property is not used for business, deductions for expenses against income are not allowed.

8.19 (c) may be deducted from the sale price for gains tax purposes.
Selling costs include such expenses as brokerage commissions, relevant advertising, legal fees, seller-paid points and other closing costs. These costs are deducted from the selling price to get the amount realized, which is reduced by the adjusted basis to calculate gain on sale for gains tax purposes.

8.20 (b) the difference between amount realized and adjusted basis.
The formula for gain tax is Taxable Gain on Sale x the owner's marginal tax bracket. The formula for gain on sale is: Amount Realized - Adjusted Basis = Gain on Sale. The formula for Amount Realized is: Selling Price - Selling costs = Amount Realized. Therefore, the gain tax = (Amount Realized - Adjusted Basis) x tax rate.

8.21 (c) A tax district.
Real estate property taxes are imposed by "taxing entities" or "taxing districts" at county and local levels of government. States may legally levy taxes on real property, but most delegate this power to counties, cities, townships and local taxing districts. The federal government does, however, tax income derived from real property and gains realized on the sale of real property.

8.22 (b) properties owned by a government agency.
Certain types of property are exempt from property taxes. Certain classes of property owner may also be exempted or have a reduced liability. Exemptions include government-owned properties, real properties owned by churches, and properties owned by other non-profit organizations.

8.23 (c) It adjusts assessments in a locality to make them more consistent with an average level for the state or other higher level jurisdiction.
Equalization factors level out the unevenness of valuations for groups of properties. For instance, if assessed values of properties in one county are consistently ten percent below the average for other counties, an equalization board may multiply each assessed value in that county by a factor of 110% to raise them to the average level for the state.

8.24 (c) $2,000,000,000.
The mill rate = (tax requirement / the tax base). A mill is one one-thousandth of a dollar ($.001). To solve for the tax base, reconfigure this formula to be: Base = Tax Requirement / Mill Rate. Thus the Base = $20,000,000 / .010, or $2,000,000,000.

8.25 (d) $1,323.
The library tax is ($1.00 x 441) and the fire district tax is ($2.00 x 441). Thus the tax is 441 x $3 = $1,323.

8.26 (b) $5,700.
Special assessments are based on the cost of the improvement and apportioned on a pro rata basis among benefiting properties according to the value that each parcel will receive from the improvement. Here, Mary's share is 38 / 200, or 19%. 19% x $30,000 = $5,700.

8.27 (a) A conveyance instrument for a property that is sold to enforce a tax lien.
A tax deed is a legal instrument for conveying title when a property is sold for non-payment of taxes. The application for a tax deed causes the taxing agency to institute a tax sale or tax foreclosure.

8.28 (d) a statutory right of redemption.
If the taxpayer can redeem the property after the tax sale, this right is known as a statutory right of redemption. In this case, the taxpayer must pay the amount paid by the winning bidder at the tax sale, plus any charges, additional taxes, or interest that may have accumulated.

8.29 (b) the total of all assessed values of properties minus exemptions.
The tax base of an area is the total of the appraised or assessed values of all real property within the area's boundaries, excluding partially or totally exempt properties such as those owned by the government or non-profit organizations.

8.30 (c) multiplying each district's tax rate times the taxable value of the property.
Each property owner's tax bill is determined by multiplying the tax rate for each taxing district times the taxable value of the property. Taxable value is the assessed value after all exemptions and adjustments have been taken into account.

8.31 (a) Civil Rights Act of 1866.
The original fair housing statute, the Civil Rights Act of 1866, prohibits discrimination in housing based on race. The prohibition relates to selling, renting, inheriting, and conveying real estate.

8.32 (c) race, color, religion, and national origin.
Title VIII of the Civil Rights Act of 1968, known today as the Fair Housing Act, prohibits discrimination in housing based on race, color, religion, or national origin.

8.33 (c) Advertising a property as available to·individuals of a particular race.
The prohibition against discriminatory advertising states that an agent may not advertise residential properties in such a way as to restrict their availability to any prospective buyer or tenant.

8.34 (c) An agent persuades a family to put their house on the market because ethnic minority families are beginning to move into the neighborhood.
Blockbusting, a prohibited activity, is the practice of inducing owners in an area to sell or rent to avoid an impending change in the ethnic or social makeup of the neighborhood that will cause values to go down.

8.35 (a) The Home Mortgage Disclosure Act.
The Home Mortgage Disclosure Act requires lenders involved with federally guaranteed or insured loans to exercise impartiality and non-discrimination in the geographical distribution of their loan portfolio. In

other words, the act is designed to prohibit redlining, the practice of restricting loans by geographical are(a)

8.36 (c) privately owned single-family residences listed with a broker.
Among the circumstances where the Fair Housing Act might allow for an exemption is: a privately owned single-family home where no broker is used, with certain additional conditions. In other words, as soon as a broker is used in the sale, the law applies.

8.37 (a) illegal, because the agent changed the terms of the sale to discourage this particular couple.
The Fair Housing Act prohibition against discriminatory misrepresentation states that an agent may not conceal available properties, represent that they are not for sale or rent, or change the sale terms for the purpose of discriminating.

8.38 (d) The owner of a duplex who resides in one of the units refuses to rent the other unit to a non-Christian.
The Fair Housing Act would exempt the owner in this situation because it involves rental of an apartment in a 1-4 unit building where the owner is also an occupant and there is no discriminatory advertising.

8.39 (b) File a complaint with HUD and/or file suit against the offending parties in a state or federal court within the prescribed time period.
The Fair Housing Amendments Act of 1988 prohibits discrimination based on sex. If May feels she has been discriminated against in this way, she may file a complaint with the Office of Fair Housing and Equal Opportunity (OFHEO) in HUD within one year or file suit in a federal or state court within two years of the alleged violation.

8.40 (a) Inform Scott that the condition is illegal and that she cannot comply with it.
Scott is not allowed to discriminate based on race, color, religion, national origin, sex, family status, or handicap. If an agent goes along with a client's discriminatory act, the agent is equally liable for violation of fair housing laws. It is thus imperative to avoid complicity with client discrimination. Further, an agent should withdraw from any relationship where client discrimination occurs.

8.41 (c) require families without children to pay the same security deposit that families with children must pay.
Fair housing laws prohibit discriminatory advertising, discrimination on the basis of national origin, discrimination based on age in dwellings of more than four units, and discrimination against families with children. The fact that the owner is requiring the same deposit from tenants with and without children does not discriminate against families with children but actually favors them.

8.42 (d) It is a single-family house, and the owner owns only one other rental home in addition to his own residence.
Federal fair housing laws do not prohibit age and family status discrimination in residential dwellings of four units or less and in single family houses if sold or rented by owners who have no more than three houses.

8.43 (c) the Fair Housing Amendments Act of 1988.
The Fair Housing Amendments Act of 1988 prohibited discrimination based on sex and discrimination against handicapped persons and families with children. Executive Order 11063 concerned racial discrimination in housing where federal funding was involved; the Civil Rights Act of 1968 concerned discrimination based on race, color, religion, and national origin; Jones v Mayer concerned racial discrimination.

8.44 (c) steering.
Steering is the illegal practice of limiting customers' choices by encouraging or discouraging them about the suitability of an area and directing them only to areas the agent deems suitable for them.

8.45 (a) providing unequal services.
The agent may be illegally providing unequal services by altering the nature or quality of brokerage services to a party based on race, color, sex, national origin, or religion.

8.46 (a) discriminatory misrepresentation by omission.
Discriminatory misrepresentation is the concealing of available properties, representing that they are not for

sale or rent, or changing the sale terms for the purpose of discriminating.

8.47 (c) Prior to the sale of an occupied 1-4 unit dwelling
The Seller's Property Condition Disclosure form must be completed by the seller prior to the closing of any resale of a 1-4-unit residential dwelling. New homes are exempted, as are commercial properties. In some jurisdictions, the property disclosure form must be completed when an offer is completed.

8.48 (d) must still be completed according to local requirements
Whether the seller lists or sells by-owner, he or she must still fulfill the obligation to complete the Property Condition form in a timely fashion. Similarly, the licensee is required to disclose all known material facts regardless of the seller's disclosures.

8.49 (c) A previous occupant died in the house
Sellers are not required to disclose fact that do not materially impact the value or condition of the property including suicides, AIDS-related illness, and other property stigmas. Licensees, however, are required to disclose known material facts.

8.50 (d) love letter.
Buyers sometimes try to enhance the attractiveness of a purchase offer by attaching a personal note to the offer. This appeal to the seller, called a "love letter," typically mentions such things as why the buyer particularly likes the home, how the buyer imagines family life in the home, and how well the buyer will care for the home.

8.51 (a) By requiring the wholesaler to have a real estate license
Some states require the wholesaler in such transactions to hold a real estate license.

NATIONAL TEST 9: Closings; Risk Management; Property Management

9.1 (c) returns funds to the buyer.
If for any reason the transaction cannot be completed, the escrow instructions usually provide a mechanism for reconveying title to the seller and funds to the buyer. In such a case, both parties return to their original status as if no sale had occurred.

9.2 (d) disclose in writing any business relationships they have with other parties involved in the transaction.
Business relationships and affiliations among real estate firms, mortgage brokers, title insurance firms and other such companies that are involved in a transaction are permitted, provided the relationships are disclosed in writing to the consumer, the consumer is free to go elsewhere for the relevant service, and the companies do not exchange fees for referrals.

9.3 (a) The item must be prorated and recorded as a debit to one party and a credit to the other party for the same amount.
An income or expense item that affects both parties is apportioned, or prorated, to each party to reflect the proper amount that each owes or should receive. A prorated item is treated as a debit to one party and a credit to the other party for the same amount.

9.4 (b) at some time after the expense is incurred.
Items paid in arrears are paid after the expense has been incurred.

9.5 (d) A debit to the seller and credit to the buyer for $580.
For income the seller received in advance, the buyer receives a credit and the seller receives a debit. In effect, the seller has received some of the buyer's income, and the seller must pay this share to the buyer. Therefore the seller is debited and the buyer is credited the $580 the buyer is entitled to earn as the new owner.

9.6 (b) A debit to the seller and credit to the buyer for $43.
For an item the buyer will pay in arrears, the buyer receives a credit and the seller receives a debit. In effect, the seller has incurred some of the expenses that the buyer will be paying for after closing. Thus the seller must pay the buyer the used portion of the expense, or $43.

9.7 (b) $546.00.
The daily tax expense, first, is ($2,190 ÷ 365) or $6.00. Since the buyer will pay the taxes after closing, the seller will owe the buyer his or her portion of the tax bill, which is the 91 days from the beginning of the year through closing. Therefore, credit the buyer and debit the seller ($6.00 x 91), or $546.00.

9.8 (d) $1,916.67.
This method assumes all months are 30 days and the year is 360 days. The daily proration is therefore $3,750 ÷ 360, or $10.42. The closing occurs on the 184th day of the year. Thus, ($10.42 x 184) = $1,916.67. Note that if the day of closing is the buyer's, there would be 183 day's worth of prorated expense.

9.9 (d) $735.34.
Assuming a 365 day year, the daily tax expense is ($1,100 ÷ 365), or $3.013. As taxes are paid in arrears, the buyer will be paying the annual bill. Thus, he will be owed a credit for the seller's share of the bill, which is $3.013 x 244 days, or $735.34.

9.10 (a) $116.03.
The buyer's share is the unused portion, or (365 days – 244 days), or 121 days. The daily expense is ($350 ÷ 365), or $.9589. ($.9589 x 121) = $116.03. The seller receives this amount as a credit and the buyer a debit.

9.11 (a) $5,075.00.
If the buyer pays $5,250 interest for 30 days, the daily expense is ($5,250 ÷ 30), or $175.00. If there are 29 days of pre-paid expense, the buyer's charge is ($175.00 x 29), or $5,075.00.

9.12 (c) $17,750.
$887,500 x .02 = $17,750. Remember, one point = 1% of the loan amount.

9.13 (d) $22,500.
$375,000 x 6% = $375,000 x .06 = $22,500.

9.14 (d) the buyer must pay the expense.
Explicit agreements in the sale contract supersede traditional expense-payment responsibilities which can vary from state to state.

9.15 (a) the excess of the buyer's debits over the buyer's credits.
To determine how much money the buyer owes at closing, the buyer's debits are totaled and compared with the total of the buyer's credits. The excess of debits over credits is the amount the buyer must bring to the closing.

9.16 (d) negligence, error or omission in carrying out professional services.
A standard E&O policy provides coverage for "damages resulting from any negligent act, error or omission arising out of Professional Services." It does not cover dishonest or illegal acts, including environmental violations and mishandling of funds.

9.17 (a) Failing to inform and disclose properly.
Agency risks commonly concern the requirement to inform and disclose. Most states require agency relationships to be in writing and to be disclosed to all parties to a transaction. In states that do not use agency, there is still the obligation to explain and disclose the nature of the relationship.

9.18 (b) failing to disclose known adverse facts.
Depending on the state, the licensee may have no further duty to disclose property condition after properly informing parties of their rights and obligations. However, the licensee may still be subject to legal action for failing to disclose adverse facts the licensee knew about or should have known about.

9.19 (d) avoid creating a false impression that the licensee is a certified appraiser.
Misuse of such terms as "appraisal" and "value" could lead to a charge of misrepresenting oneself as an appraiser.

9.20 (b) exceeding the authority of the agreement.
Licensees must stay within the bounds of the authority granted by the agency agreement and avoid doing anything requiring permission without first getting that permission in writing.

9.21 (a) use a checklist of all items, contingencies, dates and responsibilities that must be met.
One way to reduce risk in the contracting process is to use a checklist that covers all the contract items, such as inclusions and exclusions, contingency periods, documents, forms, data checking, and milestone dates.

9.22 (d) the principals may make changes as long as they sign or initial each change.
Real estate professionals who are not attorneys are usually limited to filling in blanks or making deletions on a preprinted contract form prepared by a lawyer. While a licensee may make deletions, additions to a form should be drafted by an attorney. The principals themselves can make changes as long as each change is signed or initialed by all signers.

9.23 (b) obtain education in the content and intent of the laws.
The risk of violating fair housing laws can be minimized through ongoing education that addresses both the intent of the laws and their current content.

9.24 (a) being present at a conversation where the setting of commission rates is discussed.
Antitrust laws forbid brokers to band together to set a price on their services in listing and selling property. Even being overheard discussing commission rates or being present at such a conversation can lead to charges of *price fixing*.

9.25 (a) License discipline, fines, and possible incarceration.
Intentional misrepresentation, as a type of fraud, is a criminal act that may result in fines and incarceration, in addition to discipline from state regulators and professional organizations.

9.26 (c) stating that a client should seek legal counsel.
Unintentional misrepresentation occurs when a licensee *unknowingly* gives a consumer inaccurate information concerning a property, financing or agency service. Information that the licensee, as a professional, should have known to be false or inaccurate may be included in the definition. Telling a client that legal counsel would be advisable is not misrepresentation and, in fact, is often an important risk management technique.

9.27 (d) avoid speculative statements in all reports.
Progress reports should be accurate, timely, in writing, and free of speculation. Speculation may encourage the consumer to believe the agent has expertise that in fact is non-existent. If a consumer has a question about the meaning of something in an inspection report, the licensee should refer the consumer to the person who wrote the report rather than trying to explain it.

9.28 (b) It reduces the chance of presenting an offer from an unqualified buyer.
Using a lender to qualify the buyer protects the agent against leading a seller to believe a purchaser is fully qualified when this may not be the case. Also, lenders and loan agents are better able to look into the buyer's qualifications than a real estate licensee is. If it is necessary to show a property to a potential buyer who has not been qualified by a lender, the licensee can gain some protection by performing an informal qualification and documenting the fact that it was based on the information provided by the buyer.

9.29 (c) the agency relationship.
Maintaining the confidentiality of any information that would harm the client's interests or bargaining position or anything else the client wishes to keep secret, unless the law requires disclosure, is one of the primary duties of agency. The duty to maintain confidentiality generally survives the termination of a listing agreement into perpetuity.

9.30 (a) performing a comparative market analysis.
In preparing a Comparative Market Analysis, licensees should guard against using the terms "appraisal" and "value," which are reserved for the use of certified appraisers. Misuse of these terms could lead to a charge of misrepresenting oneself as an appraiser.

9.31 (d) make a substantial misrepresentation.
The license laws of most states list as illegal advertising activities subject to discipline such actions as making any substantial and intentional misrepresentation, making false promises, and making misleading or untruthful statements in any advertising.

9.32 (c) fiduciary
The management agreement creates an agency relationship between the manager and the principal. This is a fiduciary relationship and, in general, the agent is charged with producing the greatest possible net return on the owner's investment while safeguarding the value of the investment for the owner/investor.

9.33 (b) financial reporting to the principal.
Financial reporting to the principal is a fundamental responsibility of the property manager. Reports may be required monthly, quarterly, and annually. Required reports typically include operating budget, cash flow, profit and loss, and budget comparison statements.

9.34 (d) revenue from all sources minus losses from uncollected rents, vacancies, and evictions.
The total of scheduled rents plus revenues from such sources as vending services, storage charges, late fees, utilities, and contracts is the potential gross income. Subtracting losses caused by uncollected rents, vacancies and evictions gives effective gross income.

9.35 (a) cost per tenant prospect generated per lease.
The efficiency of marketing activities can be judged in terms of how many prospects per completed lease they generate. The lower the cost per prospect per lease, the more effective and efficient the program.

9.36 (b) raise rental rates.
Vacancy rates are directly related to demand and competitive supply in the market. If vacancy rates in the managed property are too high, the manager may have to lower rates or identify problems in the property or its management that are contributing to vacancy level. On the other hand, if the property's vacancy rate is significantly lower than market rates, the manager may conclude that higher rental rates are called for.

9.37 (b) Routine, preventive, and corrective
The foremost maintenance objective is generally to preserve the value of the physical asset for the owner over the long term. Three general types of maintenance are required to keep a property in serviceable condition: routine (day-to-day), preventive (scheduled), and corrective (repairs and replacements).

9.38 (a) ensure that disabled employees have the same level of access to facilities that all employees have.
Employers with at least fifteen employees must follow nondiscriminatory employment and hiring practices and make reasonable accommodations to enable disabled employees to perform essential functions of their jobs. Modifications to the physical components of the building may be necessary to provide the required access to tenants and their customers. Existing barriers must be removed when the removal is "readily achievable," that is, when cost is not prohibitive.

9.39 (a) replacement value.
The amount of coverage provided by certain types of policies may be based on whether the property is insured at depreciated value or current replacement value. Depreciated value is original value minus the loss in value over time. Current replacement value, which is more expensive, is the amount it would cost to rebuild or replace the property at current rates. Commercial policies include coinsurance clauses requiring the insured to bear a portion of the loss. Fire and hazard policies usually require the coverage to be in an amount equal to at least 80 percent of the replacement value.

9.40 (b) cash for the management firm's operating expenses.
Managers are responsible for proper handling of monies belonging to other parties (trust funds) that come into the manager's hands in the course of doing business. For property managers, such trust funds include

rents collected from tenants, security deposits, and capital contributions from the property owner. Funds belonging to the management firm must not be commingled with those of the client.

9.41 (c) General
Property managers are usually considered to be general agents empowered to perform some or all of the ongoing tasks and duties of operating the property, including the authority to enter into contracts.

9.42 (b) The tenant pays a fixed rent, and the landlord pays all operating expenses.
In a gross lease, the tenant pays an established, fixed rent, and the landlord pays all property operating expenses, such as taxes, insurance, utilities, and other services. This is the arrangement commonly used in residential leases. If the tenant pays some of the operating expenses, the lease is a form of net lease.

9.43 (d) the property manager does not have to maintain it.
The lease should set forth items that are excluded or included in the leased property. For instance, a residential lease may include built-in appliances such as dishwashers but exclude freestanding ones, such as refrigerators. At issue for the landlord is the cost of maintenance. If a refrigerator is not included, it does not have to be maintained by the property manager.

9.44 (b) deliver a habitable property.
The landlord (by way of the property manager), is expected to deliver a property that is habitable. This means keeping heating, plumbing, cooling, and electrical systems in good repair as well as maintaining serviceability of floors, stairways, railings, roofs, and windows.

9.45 (c) A tenant declares a landlord in default and vacates the leased premises.
A constructive eviction occurs when a tenant vacates the leased premises and declares the lease void, claiming that the landlord's actions have made the premises unfit for the purpose described in the lease. The tenant must prove that it was the landlord's actions that were responsible and may be able to recover damages.

9.46 (a) the competitive market for the property.
In preparing a management plan, a manager must consider the owner's objectives, including financial goals; the competitive market for the property, both local and regional, depending on the property type; and the features of the particular property. The plan will also include a budget and indications of what the manager intends to do with the property to meet the owner's objectives.

NATIONAL TEST 10: Real Estate Math

10.1 (a) $.023 / SF
5/6ths of an acre = (5 x 43,560 SF) / 6, or 36,300 SF. Her commission was (.06 x $28,000) x .50, or $840. $840 / 36,300 SF = $.023 / SF.

10.2 (b) $370,170
The land costs $.50 x 43,560 SF/ac. x 1.5 ac, or $32,670. The home will cost $135 / SF x 2,500, or $337,500. The total property will cost $370,170.

10.3 (a) 12%
The lot measures 43,560 / 4, or 10,890 SF. The tennis court will take up 9,600 SF, leaving 1,290 SF. This amount is 11.8% of the total lot area.

10.4 (c) 40
The total area available for lots is 11.2 acres (16 acres x 70% for houses), or 487,872 SF (11.2 x 43,560). Dividing this area by 12,000 SF / lot = 40.66. Thus he can have a 40-lot subdivision.

10.5 (a) 6
First, the requirement = 2(13'x 9') +2 (18'x 9') =558 SF. Each roll is 2'x 50', or 100 SF. Thus she will need 6 rolls.

10.6 (d) 1,376 SF
First figure the area to be mulched. If the home is 40 x 30, the flower area adds 8' to each side of the

house. Thus the outside perimeter of the flowered area is (40+8+8) by (30+8+8), or 46' by 56'. The area of the flowered area is (46' x 56') minus the house area of 1,200 SF. This is 1,376 SF.

10.7 (b) 40 acres
First, remember that a section contains 640 acres. The area in question is a forth of a half of a half of the total section. So divide 640 by (4 x 2 x 2). 4 x 2 x 2 is 16 and 640/16= 40 acres.

10.8 (c) 10 acres
The key to this question is to recall that a section has 640 acres. Theresa's property only is a ¼ of a ¼ of a ¼ of the entire section. Multiply 4 x 4 x 4 which equals 64. Savannah owns 1/64 of the section. Divide 640 by 64 and you get the answer of 10 acres.

10.9 (a) $38,955
Their fixed rent is (1,800 SF x $1.40/SF) x 12 months, or $30,240. The percentage rent is ($41,500 x .0175) x 12, or $8,715. Total rent is ($30,240 + 8,715), or $38,955.

10.10 (a) 5.04%
First, convert to decimals: 2 2/3 % = 2.67%; 5 1/5% = 5.2%; 7 1/4% = 7.25%. Thus total appreciation = (2.67% + 5.2% + 7.25%), or 15.12%. Divide by 3 to derive the average: 15.12% / 3 = 5.04%

10.11 (c) 29%.
Appreciation as a per cent can be estimated by (1) subtracting the estimated current market value from the price originally paid (239,000 - 185,000 = 54,000) and (2) dividing the result by the original price (54,000 / 185,000 = . 29 or 29%).

10.12 (c)   94%
To find the percent of listing price the offer is, divide the offer by the listing price. In this question the offer is $290,000 and the listing price is $308,000. $290,000 / $308,000 = .94 or 94%.

10.13 (a) $206,000.
Remember the formula V = I / R where V is value, I is annual income, and R is the cap rate. Variations of this are: R = I / V in solving for the cap rate, and I = V x R in solving for income. Here, first identify net income by subtracting out vacancy and expenses. Then divide by the capitalization rate. Thus, ($30,000 – 1,500 – 10,000) / 9% = $205,555, or $206,000 rounded.

10.14 (b) $375,000.
Value = Income / Cap rate. Thus, V= $30,000 / .08 = $375,000.

10.15 (b) $13,600.
First derive the annual depreciation which is the cost divided by the economic life. Then multiply annual depreciation times the number of years to identify total depreciation. Remember to subtract depreciation from the original cost if the question asks for the ending value. Thus, ($16,000 / 20 years x 3 years) = $2,400 total depreciation. The ending value is $16,000 –2,400, or $13,600.

10.16 (a) $1,077
First, Lee's depreciable basis, without the land, is $280,000 x 75%, or $210,000. The annual depreciation for the entire home is ($210,000 / 39 years), or $5,384.61. Second, his office is 20% of the house (500 sf / 2,500 sf). Therefore Lee can take annual depreciation of ($5,384.61 x 20%), or $1,076.92.

10.17 (d) $376,000.
Cost Approach formula: Land + (Cost of Improvements + Capital Additions – Depreciation) = Value. Thus you have $80,000 + ($350,000 - 54,000), or $376,000.

10.18 (c) $475,000
Use the same Cost Approach formula: Land + (Cost of Improvements + Capital Additions – Depreciation) = Value. The land is worth (100,000 x 125%), or $125,000. Remember, you cannot depreciate the land, only the cost of the improvements. Therefore, annual depreciation is ($400,000 / 40), or $10,000. Total depreciation is ($10,000 x 5 years), or $50,000. Thus the value is ($125,000 + 400,000 – 50,000), or $475,000.

10.19 (d) 125.
Use the formula: GRM = Price / Monthly Rent. Thus, $400,000 / $3,200 = 125.

10.20 (c) $582,000.
Use the formula: GIM = Price / Annual Income. To solve for price convert the formula to Price = GIM x Annual Income. Thus, ($3,300 x 12) equals $39,600 annual income. ($39,600 x 14.7 GIM) = $582,120, or $582,000 rounded.

10.21 (d) $1,500
The loan amount is $400,000 x .75, or $300,000. The first month interest equals ($300,000 x 6%) / 12 months, or $1,500.

10.22 (b) $358,000.
The equation for the loan amount is (annual interest divided by the interest rate) = loan amount. Thus, ($1,580 x 12) / .053 = $357,736 or $358,000 rounded.

10.23 (a) 4.82%.
The equation for the interest rate is (annual payment / loan amount) = interest rate. Thus ($1,000 x 12) / $249,000 = 4.82%.

10.24 (b) $1,456.95
In the first month they pay interest of ($280,000 x 6.25%) / 12, or $1,458. If their fixed payment is $1,724, they paid down the principal by $266 ($1,724 - 1,458). Now they must pay 6.25% interest on the new principal balance of $279,734. This equals (279,734 x .0625) / 12, or $1,456.95.

10.25 (b) The second option, by 150.
The first option's interest total is (6.5% x $60,000) x 5 years, or $19,500. The second option will charge (6.25% x $60,000) x 5 years, plus $600, or a total of $19,350. The 2nd option is $150 cheaper.

10.26 (b) 1.67 points
A discount point is one percent of the loan amount. Jose's loan is ($410,000 x 90%), or $369,000. If he paid $6,150, he paid 1.67% of the loan amount ($6,150 / 369,000), or 1.67 points.

10.27 (c) $4,875.
$325,000 x .015 = $4,875. Remember, one point = 1% of the loan amount.

10.28 (c) $487,500
Use the formula: Price x LTV Ratio = Loan. Then plug in the figures and calculate: Price x .80 = $130,000. Therefore, Price = $390,000 / .80 = $487,500.

10.29 (c) $379,259
First, the annual interest paid is $1,600 x 12, or $19,200. The interest rate is 6.75%. Using the formula (Loan = Interest / Rate), the loan amount is $19,200 / 6.75%, or $284,444. As this is 75% of the price, the price is ($284,444 / .75), or $379,259.

10.30 (b) $1,900.
Monthly income qualification is derived by multiplying monthly income by the income ratio. Thus (76,000 / 12) x .30 = $1,900. Remember to first derive the monthly income.

10.31 (a) $253,846
Total depreciation on this property = ($600,000 / 39 years) x 10 years, or $153,846. His adjusted basis is therefore ($680,000 original price – 153,846 depreciation taken), or $526,154. The gain is then ($780,000 – 526,154), or $253,846.

10.32 (b) $257,000.
Adjusted basis = beginning basis ($250,000) + capital improvements ($2,000 + $5,000) – depreciation (0) = adjusted basis ($257,000).

10.33 (c) $34,000.
Capital gain = amount realized (net sales proceeds, $265,000) - adjusted basis ($231,000) = ($34,000).

10.34 (d) $375,000.
The basic formula for adjusted basis is: Beginning Basis + Capital Improvements - Exclusions and Credits = Adjusted Basis. Debra's adjusted basis is therefore $360,000 + $15,000 = $375,000. The financing terms and subsequent selling price are not relevant.

10.35 (c) $15,000 overpriced.
Use the same formula V = I / R where V is the price and R is the rate of return. Then plug in the numbers to solve for V. The NOI of this property is ($60,000 - $22,000), or $38,000. The return is 11%. Therefore, the value to get this return must be $38,000 / .11, or $345,455. Since the price is $360,000, the price exceeds the amount needed for an 11% return by approximately $15,000 ($360,000 - $345,455 = $14,545).

10.36 (b)   Yes, since he will yield 8.375%
Use the same formula R = I / V where V is the $2 million price, and R is the cap rate or rate of return. To identify income: (25,000 SF x $10/SF) = $250,000 gross income, minus 5% vacancy (.05 x $250,000), or $12,500, minus expenses of $70,000 = $167,500 net income. ($250,000 – 12,500 – 70,000)   Now divide net income of $167,500 by $2,000,000 to derive the return of 8.375%.

10.37 (a) $1,680.
Annual gross operating income ($1,650 x 12 = $19,800) - annual operating expenses ($600 x 12 = $7,200) = annual net operating income ($12,600); annual net operating income ($12,600) - cost recovery expense ($7,000) = taxable income ($5,600); taxable income ($5,600) x tax rate (30%) = tax liability ($1,680).

10.38 (c) $10,640
The basic formula for tax liability is: Taxable Income x Tax Rate = Tax Liability. Taxable Income is Net Operating Income - Interest Expense - Cost Recovery Expense. Therefore, the annual tax is $150,000 (NOI) - $105,000 (Interest Expense) - $7,000 (Cost Recovery Expense) x 28% = $10,640. Note that the principal payment is not deductible in calculating taxable income.

10.39 (d)   31.4%
The formula for profit % is (profit / initial investment). The profit made was ($230,000 x 4) – 700,000 initial investment, or $220,000. Dividing this by the amount invested derives a profit percent of 31.4%.

10.40 (c) $1,000,000,000.
The mill rate = (tax requirement / the tax base). A mill is one one-thousandth of a dollar ($.001). To solve for the tax base, reconfigure this formula to be: Base = Tax Requirement / Mill Rate. Thus the Base = $10,000,000 / .010, or $1,000,000,000.

10.41 (a) $2,990
First, always use the assessed valuation, not the market value. Subtract out the homestead exemption to derive taxable value, or $280,000 – 50,000 = $230,000. As a shortcut to calculating the tax bill, simply add up all the mills, multiply them times .001 to convert mills to decimals, then multiply this number times the taxable value. Thus (7 + 3 + 2 + 1) x .001 x $230,000 = $2,990.

10.42 (b)   2.13%
The rate = budget / tax base. Thus, $8,000,000 / (400,000,000 – 25,000,000) = 2.13%

10.43 (d) $7,112
First calculate the total commission, then the co-brokerage splits, then the agent-broker split. Thus: $508,000 x 7% = $35,560 total commission. ($35,560 x 50%) = $17,780 total listing broker share. $17,780 x 40% = $7,112 agent's share.

10.44 (a) $6,866
Figure the total commission, then the co-brokerage splits, then the broker-agent splits. Thus, ($325,000 x 6.5%) = $21,125. ($21,125 x 50%) = $10,563. ($10,563 x .65) = $6,866.

10.45 (c)   A credit to the buyer and debit to the seller for $785.34.
The daily tax expense, first, is ($3,150 / 365) or $8.63. Since the buyer will pay the taxes after closing, the seller must pay the buyer his or her portion of the tax bill at closing, which is the 91 days from the

beginning of the year through closing. Therefore, credit the buyer and debit the seller ($8.63 x 91), or $785.34.

10.46 (a) $507.50.
If the buyer pays $525 interest for 30 days, the daily expense is ($525 / 30), or $17.50. If there are 29 days of pre-paid expense, the buyer's charge is ($17.50 x 29), or $507.50.

10.47 (d) Credit buyer $712.26.
For the monthly proration using the 365-day method, solve first for the daily rent amount: ($1,380 / 31), or $44.52. Since the landlord received the rent and owes the buyer portions of the rent, the buyer will be credited. The owed amount is for the 16th through the 31st, or 16 days, since the closing day belongs to the buyer. Therefore, credit the buyer and debit the seller ($44.52 x 16),or $712.26.

10.48 (d) $86,372
First calculate the transfer tax: ($322,600 / 500) = 645.2 units of $500. Round this up to 646, then multiply times $1.00 to get $646 transfer tax cost. Next figure the commission @ ($322,600 x .07), or $22,582. Next, the seller's real estate tax proration charge will be $2,000. Then, add up the expenses: ($646 transfer tax + 450 title + 550 attorney + 22,582 commission + 210,000 loan payoff + 2,000 tax proration) = $236,228. Subtracting this from the sale price = $86,372.

10.49 (d) $5,848.
Be careful here. Since the net price is $5,000, the taking price (TP) minus the commission must equal the net price. In other words, the net price is 90% of the taking price. Since TP x 90% = Net, TP = Net / 90%. So the taking price is $5,556 ($5,000 / .9). Apply the same logic to deriving the asking price: the taking price is 95% of the list price, therefore the list price = (taking price / 95%), or $5,848. Now work backwards to prove your answer: (5,848 x 95% margin x .90 net of commission) = $5,000

10.50 (d) $468,750
Use the formula: (Percent of insurable property value carried / 80% replacement cost) x claim = recovery, where the insurable property value variable excludes the land value and is valued at replacement cost. Here, the insurable portion of the property is ($740,000 - 25% land value), or $555,000. The Wildes are carrying insurance to cover 75% of the replacement cost of the entire property. Their recovery amount is therefore (75% / 80%) x $500,000, or $468,750.

10.51 (c) $280,000
Use the formula: (Percent of insurable property value carried / 80% replacement cost) x claim = recovery. Thus, (75% / 80% x $300,000) = $281,250. However, the face value of the policy is the maximum they can receive, which is $280,000.

STATE TEST 11: The Alabama Regulatory Environment

11.1 (c) Legislative Act 1927
The Alabama Real Estate Commission (AREC) was created in 1927 by Legislative Act 1927, No. 344.

11.2 (a) 1
Of the nine members of AREC, the ninth member (one member) must be a consumer who must not have been a licensed real estate broker or salesperson for at least 10 years prior to appointment.

11.3 (b) 10 years
Of the nine members of AREC, all nine are required to be residents and citizens of Alabama for at least 10 years.

11.4 (a) Each is appointed by the governor with the consent of the State Senate.
Individual appointments to the AREC are made from a list of three persons provided to the governor who then appoints each member. The State Senate provides advice and consent on each appointment.

11.5 (d) 5
Members of the AREC serve 5-year staggered terms and may not serve more than two consecutive terms.

11.6 (d) Establish the Revenue Fund
The AREC licenses and regulates the professional practices of real estate, and in doing so, enforces real estate laws, investigates and prosecutes complaints, and establishes the Recovery Fund, not the Revenue Fund.

11.7 (d) A lapsed license
A lapsed license is one that is no longer valid and may not be renewed. Therefore, individuals with lapsed licenses must meet all licensure requirements of first-time applicants.

11.8 (c) Shawn O'Leary who manages the condominium building where he lives
Individuals selling property owned by a spouse, child, or parent to not need to be licensed. Nor do attorneys performing legal work or individuals selling, leasing, or transferring cemetery lots. However, on-site condominium managers do need to be licensed.

11.9 (d) None
The revenue fund is funded with fees, fines, charges, etc. collected from licensees; however, the $30 recovery fund fee is not included in these funds and is not deposited into the revenue fund.

11.10 (b) Remaining funds are transferred to the following year.
Any monies remaining in the Revenue Fund at the end of the fiscal year will transfer over to the following year.

11.11 (d) File a complaint with the AREC
If a real estate broker violates real estate laws or rules, the offended party may file a complaint with the AREC against the violator.

11.12 (a) Attorney General
When a complaint is made about a licensee's conduct or the Commission has reason to believe a licensee has committed a violation, the matter will be assigned to an investigator who will work with the Attorney General to determine if probable cause exists to file a formal complaint.

11.13 (d) 15 days
When a complaint is filed, the AREC serves the accused a copy of the complaint, notifies the qualifying broker, and schedules a hearing, giving the accused a 15-day notice of the time, date, and place of the hearing.

11.14 (c) Sue
The party requesting the subpoenaed witnesses must deposit a cashier's check or certified check with the Commission to cover the witness's fees, mileage, and expenses.

11.15 (c) Class A misdemeanors.
Individuals or corporations who violate Alabama License Law commit a Class A misdemeanor and will be punished accordingly if convicted.

11.16 (d) $7,500 fine.
If a licensee is found guilty of a license law violation, the AREC may discipline the licensee by revoking or suspending the license, fining the licensee $100 to $5,000, and/or reprimanding the licensee. The licensee can also be required to complete continuing education and/or pay restitution.

11.17 (b) If the violation is committed by an unlicensed individual
If the accused individual, firm, corporation, or business entity is unlicensed and engaging in activities which require licensure, the Commission may issue an order to cease and desist the activities.

11.18 (d) Mary can apply for a rehearing within 30 days of the guilty finding.
An accused, applicant, or other party associated with a case heard by the Commission may file an application for rehearing if the individual does not agree with the Commission's findings. The application must specify the grounds for the rehearing and must be filed within 30 days of receiving notice of the Commission's decision.

11.19 (a) as soon as practicable.
If a rehearing is granted, the Commission will schedule the hearing as soon as practicable.

11.20 (b) Post a $200 bond with the circuit court
The AREC's finding is final unless the accused files for an appeal within 30 days of the final order and posts a $200 bond with the circuit court clerk who then notifies the AREC of the appeal.

11.21 (d) By the Recovery Fund fee collected from each license applicant
The Recovery Fund is funded by a fee of $30 paid by each applicant for an original broker or salesperson license.

11.22 (a) $25,000.
Payments for multiple claims associated with the same transaction cannot exceed $25,000 in total, regardless of the number of aggrieved persons or claimants.

11.23 (d) of licensees marketing time-share projects.
No payment will be made for acts or omissions of a broker or salesperson while marketing or developing a time-share project.

STATE TEST 12: Alabama Licensing Regulation

12.1 (c) Any person or business receiving fees for practicing real estate in Alabama
Any person, sole proprietorship, partnership, corporation, branch office, or legal business organization practicing real estate for compensation in Alabama must be licensed as a broker or salesperson. The key is receiving or expecting compensation for real estate acts.

12.2 (d) Writing real estate contracts
Leasing, listing, and negotiating in regard to real property all require a license if done for compensation or the expectation of compensation. However, contracts may only be written or developed by attorneys who are not required to hold real estate licenses.

12.3 (a) He must meet all the requirements for an original license and obtain AREC approval.
Individuals whose license has been revoked must meet all requirements for an original license and must be approved by the AREC.

12.4 (c) show proof of holding a Georgia real estate license.
Nonresidents applying for Alabama real estate licensure must apply on the AREC designated form, specify which office where they will be registered, be bound by Alabama license laws, but must not have a current license in the other state.

12.5 (c) agreeing Alabama can take any applicable civil actions against the nonresident licensee.
Nonresident applicants for an Alabama original or reciprocal license must sign an affidavit agreeing that the AREC has jurisdiction over their real estate activities performed in Alabama, that they will be subject to the same investigations and discipline as Alabama licensees, that the AREC Executive Director or Assistant Director will be served as the nonresident's agent, and that they will be subject to any applicable Alabama civil actions.

12.6 (a) The AREC must review the conviction to determine if Joseph is eligible for licensure.
Applicants with a criminal history may be rejected for licensure in Alabama, but their conviction and eligibility will be reviewed and determined by the AREC. The applicant just use the Application of Determination of Licensing Eligibility and have both a state and national criminal history check performed. If the AREC approves eligibility, the applicant will qualify for licensure.

12.7 (b) Have the prints printed on the back of the criminal history review application.
Fingerprints must be submitted on the approved fingerprint card along with the criminal history review application. The card includes examples of qualify prints and must be signed by both the applicant and the official at the law enforcement agency who takes the prints.

12.8 (c) College degree
Applicants for a salesperson license are required to be high school graduates or the equivalent (GED) and must have completed the pre-license coursework. They are not required to hold a college degree or to have completed any college level coursework.

12.9 (c) US passport
Documentation used for proof of age would include a valid driver's license, a US passport, a birth certificate, or other documentation required by the AREC.

12.10 (d) Voter's registration card
Alabama state residency can be proven by submitting a driver's license, a car tag receipt, a property deed, a residential lease agreement, a property tax bill, or a voter's registration card.

12.11 (c) US college transcript showing high school education sufficient for college admittance
Proof of high school completed outside the US would include a US college transcript showing high school education sufficient for college admittance or a Document-by-Document Evaluation Report verifying foreign education equivalent to US education.

12.12 (c) He must notify the AREC of his change of residency within 10 days.
Nonresidents of Alabama who hold an Alabama real estate license and then become residents of Alabama must submit a change of address to AREC within 10 days of residency.

12.13 (b) pay a $30 Recovery Fund fee.
Applicants for temporary licensure must complete the 60-hour pre-license course within 1 year of start date or start over, must pass the state exam within 6 months of completing the pre-license course or retake the course, and must pay the $30 Recovery Fund fee. The temporary license is to be obtained prior to obtaining the original license.

12.14 (d) complete 30 hours of post-license coursework within 6 months to avoid his license becoming inactive.
Individuals with temporary licenses are required to complete the 30-hour post-license course within the first 6 months of licensure or the temporary license will be placed on inactive status. If the course and application for original license is not completed within 12 months of temporary licensure, the license will expire and lapse.

12.15 (a) on or before the temporary license expiration date.
Individuals with temporary licenses must complete the post-license course and apply for the original license on or before the temporary license expiration, which is midnight on the last day of the month 1 year, or 12 months, from the issuance of the temporary license.

12.16 (c) Applicants for original licensure must pay the Recovery Fund fee when applying for the original license.
If the applicant paid the Recovery Fund fee at the time of temporary license application, he or she does not need to pay it again with the original license application.

12.17 (c) 2 years, always ending in even numbered years.
The license period is 2 years, ending in even numbered years, meaning the license must be renewed in the next even numbered year, regardless of when it was issued.

12.18 (a) August 31, 2028
A license issued in an odd numbered year must be renewed in the next even numbered year, making her license renewal due in 2028. License renewals are due by August 31 of the final year of the license period, making her license renewal due by August 31, 2028. While she has until September 30 to renew the license before it expires, the renewal is actually due by August 31.

12.19 (b) September 30, 2029
A license issued in an odd numbered year must be renewed in the next even numbered year, making her license renewal due in 2028. License renewals are due by August 31 of the final year of the license period, in this case, August 31, 2028. The license does not actually expire until midnight on September 30 if it has not been renewed. However, the licensee still has 12 additional months after expiration to renew the license

without the license lapsing. Therefore, her license would expire on September 30, 2028, but would not lapse until September 30, 2029.

12.20 (c) by September 30 of final year of license period.
Licensees are required to complete 15 hours of continuing education by September 30 of the final year of license period or the license will become inactive on October 1 of that year.

12.21 (c) 3
Of the required 15 hours of continuing education, 3 hours must focus on risk management. The risk management course covers the time period from initial contact to contracting.

12.22 (d) 100% attendance
Completing continuing education courses requires 100% attendance, but students are not required to pass the course with any minimum score.

12.23 (c) Service as a member of the state legislature during the license period
Licensees must complete 15 hours of continuing education each license period. Serving as a member of the state legislature can substitute for 15 hours of education.

12.24 (c) One where the applicant completed pre-license course and passed a national and state law exam
Applicants for an Alabama reciprocal license must hold a license from a state other than Alabama where the applicant completed the required pre-license course and passed the national and state law examination.

12.25 (b) 120 days
An applicant for an Alabama reciprocal license must provide a Certificate of Licensure which was issued within 120 days of application from the state where the applicant is licensed.

12.26 (c) 6
An applicant for an Alabama reciprocal license must complete 6 hours of coursework in Alabama and pass the state exam with a 70% score.

12.27 (c) Retake post-license coursework
To reactivate an inactive license, the licensee must apply to the AREC and pay the reactivation fee, complete continuing education for the current license period prior to application for reactivation, and pay any unpaid Recovery Fund fees. The licensee is not required to retake any coursework.

12.28 (a) The mail receipt from sending the transfer documents to the AREC
When a licensee transfers from one qualifying broker to another, the licensee must mail the license, transfer forms, license certificates, and fee to the AREC by certified or registered mail, return receipt requested. This mail receipt becomes evidence of the license transfer with the mailing date being the effective date of the transfer.

12.29 (b) To stop Fran from doing business in Chelsea's name
A qualifying broker would return a licensee's license to the AREC to stop that licensee from doing business in the qualifying broker's company name. The qualifying broker would notify both the AREC and the licensee and then return the licensee's license to the AREC.

STATE TEST 13: Alabama Brokerage Regulation

13.1 (c) No licensure revocation in past 2 years
The personal requirements for broker licensure include being a US citizen or legal alien, being at least 19 years old, being a high school graduate or the equivalent, being a resident of any US state, having no felony or moral turpitude crime conviction, and having no real estate licensure application rejection or license revocation in the past 2 years.

13.2 (b) Agree to state and national criminal background check
When applying for an Alabama broker license, the applicant must submit fingerprints on the approved

fingerprint card, agree to a state and national criminal background check, submit an Application for Determination of Licensing Eligibility to the AREC if the applicant has any felony or moral turpitude convictions, pay the cost of the criminal history check, and have the AREC determine the applicant's fitness for licensure.

13.3 (a) complete a 60-hour pre-license course.
An applicant for broker licensure must complete a 60-hour pre-license course, pass the examination within 6 months of course completion, hold a salesperson license in any state for 2 or the previous 3 years before broker licensure application. The salesperson license will terminate at the time the broker license is issued.

13.4 (c) An LLC's qualifying broker
Regardless of whether the company is a sole proprietorship, a corporation, a partnership, a branch office, an LLC, or any other lawful business organization, the qualifying broker of that company is the one required to apply for the company real estate license. Unless the CEO or the managing partner is the qualifying broker, he or she is not required to apply for the license.

13.5 (d) Tom must obtain a written agreement from both companies and perform all business from the same location.
As a qualifying broker, Tom may only serve one company unless both companies agree in writing and file the agreement with the AREC. Tom must then perform all business from the same location.

13.6 (b) September 30 of even numbered years
The Alabama license period is 2 years ending on even numbered years. Licenses, including company licenses, expire at midnight on September 30 of the final year of the license period, or every even numbered year.

13.7 (d) Sarah and Jerry
As Jerry's qualifying broker, Sarah is responsible for any violations Jerry commits and any injuries to third parties. However, Jerry too is responsible because he is the one who violated the law and caused the damages.

13.8 (c) Sarah must notify both Jerry and the AREC in writing of her intent to terminate her status with Jerry.
If Sarah want to terminate her status as Jerry's qualifying broker, she must notify both Jerry and the AREC in writing and then return Jerry's license certificate to the AREC. The AREC will then issue a new certificate when Jerry has a new qualifying broker.

13.9 (a) 30 days
Upon the death or disability of a company's qualifying broker, a company officer, member, or salesperson must apply for a temporary qualifying broker license within 30 days of the death or disability of the previous qualifying broker.

13.10 (c) 6 months
Upon the death or disability of a qualifying broker, a company may operate under a temporary qualifying broker for no longer than 6 months, during which time the company must designate a fully licensed broker as the new qualifying broker.

13.11 (a) The company license is placed on inactive status.
If a new fully licensed qualifying broker is not designated to replace the temporary qualifying broker within 6 months of the previous qualifying broker's death or disability, the company license will be placed on inactive status.

13.12 (d) Connie's plan violates all of the place of business requirements.
Place of business requirements state that licensees located within city limits must operate from an office located within the city limits, the office must have its own business telephone and separate entrance, must be a separate space not used for living purposes, and must have a sign on the exterior of the building if allowed. In other words, Connie's entire plan violates the requirements for places of business.

13.13 (d) $250,000.
Each client's funds deposited into federally insured banks are insured up to $250,000 by the Federal

Deposit Insurance Corporation (FDIC).

13.14 (b) broker commissions.
Trust funds typically include earnest money, security deposits, rent payments. While commissions can be paid from the trust funds, there is not typically a deposit made specifically for commission payments.

13.15 (c) Either of these qualifying brokers
When there are multiple qualifying brokers involved in the same transaction, any of the qualifying brokers may deposit and hold the associated funds.

13.16 (a) The qualifying broker
The qualifying broker who opened the trust account and deposited the funds into the account is the trustee for the account.

13.17 (c) March 10
A qualifying broker is to disburse trust funds within 7 days of the transaction completion for which the funds were being held. Therefore, the deadline for disbursing funds related to Tania's closing is March 10.

13.18 (d) force trust fund disbursement disagreements to be resolved by the courts.
The rules of interpleader remove the qualifying broker from the disbursement process and make the disagreeing parties litigate the disbursement so the court decides who is legally entitled to the funds.

13.19 (b) is released from disagreement liability.
Under the rules of interpleader, the qualifying broker deposits the disputed funds with the court who then decides who is legally entitled to the funds. Because it is the court who makes the determination, the qualifying broke is released from any liability regarding the disbursement of the funds.

13.20 (d) the law.
Alabama law defines procedures for how trust funds are to be handled by real estate professionals.

13.21 (c) Terrance can lose his license for using the funds for his business expenses.
Qualifying brokers are not allowed to use funds belonging to others (trust funds) for their own personal or business expenses. To do so could result in the qualifying broker losing his license.

13.22 (a) a qualifying broker deposits both his own funds and a client's funds into the same trust account.
Trust accounts must not hold funds belonging to both the broker and the client. To do so is called commingling. The broker may deposit enough of his own money into the client account to cover bank service charges and may deposit funds belonging to multiple clients into the same account.

13.23 (d) $25,000 fine
If a broker violates trust fund laws and is found guilty of the violation by the AREC, penalties can include suspension or revocation of the broker's license, broker reprimand, a fine of $100 to $5,000, required continuing education, or license suspension/revocation. John would not have to worry about a $25,000 fine because that amount is in excess of what is allowed.

13.24 (a) Separate rental and sales accounts.
The AREC suggests separating rental property accounts from property sales accounts. They also suggest taping canceled checks to the check stub in the checkbook, paying bank service charges before paying commissions, and separating pending and closed contracts.

13.25 (d) There is no legal requirement for reconciliation.
While monthly account reconciliation is recommended, the law has no specific required timeframe for reconciliation.

13.26 (b) When an offer is received
Alabama law requires a licensee to provide an estimated closing statement to a seller at the time an offer or counteroffer on the property is received so the seller will know what to expect at closing.

13.27 (d) TRID
The TILA-RESPA Integrated Disclosure, or TRID, requires a lender to provide the borrower with a loan estimate within 3 business days of the application for the loan.

13.28 (c) Within 3 business days of the loan application
The TILA-RESPA Integrated Disclosure, or TRID, requires a lender to provide the borrower with a loan estimate within 3 business days of the application for the loan.

13.29 (a) Estimated closing statements outline transaction closing costs.
Estimated closing statements outline transaction closing costs and must be provided to the buyer at time of offer and the seller at time of offer presentation. Loan estimates must be provided to the borrower within 3 business days of the loan application, and the closing disclosure must be provided 3 days prior to the transaction closing.

13.30 (d) seller debit.
The real estate commission is typically paid by the seller, making this cost a seller debit.

13.31 (a) buyer debit.
The buyer typically pays for property surveys, making this cost a buyer debit.

13.32 (b) buyer credit.
Earnest money is paid by the buyer and credited towards costs owed by the buyer, making it a buyer credit.

13.33 (c) buyer credit and seller debit.
Rent is typically prepaid by the tenant to the owner-seller. It is then prorated based on the closing date so the buyer receives his/her portion of the tenant's rent for the remainder of the month. Therefore, it is a buyer credit and a seller debit.

13.34 (b) RESPA
The Real Estate Settlement Procedures Act (RESPA) serves to protect the consumer. One way it does so is by prohibiting lenders from demanding excessive deposits for escrow accounts.

13.35 (d) None
Alabama license law exempts property owners from licensing requirements when the owners are managing, leasing, or selling their own property. Therefore, Lily does not need a license to sell her own home.

13.36 (a) impose a tax on real estate signage used to advertise the sale of property.
Local, county, and city governments in Alabama may restrict the size, height, and placement of signs used to advertise real estate for sale or lease, but they may not impose a fee or tax on signage allowed by Alabama law.

13.37 (d) no required time period.
It is recommended to retain closing statements and other related records for 3 years, but there is no retention time period required by law.

STATE TEST 14: Alabama Agency

14.1 (c) agency agreement.
An agency agreement is a written agreement between the broker and the client which creates a fiduciary relationship between the two.

14.2 (d) Property management services that require licensure are often included in available brokerage services.
Brokerage services include real estate activities that require licensure but do not include rental or property management activities.

14.3 (b) material fact.
A material fact is significant information that may affect a party's decision to enter into a contract.

14.4 (d) RECAD
The Alabama Legislature enacted the Real Estate Consumer's Agency and Disclosure Act (RECAD) to set roles and duties of real estate brokers.

14.5 (d) Before confidential information is exchanged
RECAD requires licensees to disclose a non-agency relationship as soon as reasonably possible before any confidential information has been exchanged. Available brokerage services must be disclosed at the same time.

14.6 (a) Every year
RECAD requires qualifying brokers to adopt and maintain an agency disclosure office policy and to explain the policy to licensees at least yearly.

14.7 (b) When the relationship agreement is signed
No agency relationship is assumed, implied, or created until the written agency relationship agreement is signed.

14.8 (c) A client has signed an agreement for specific services.
A client has signed an agreement for specific services while a customer obtains brokerages services without signing an agreement.

14.9 (c) Subagency
The brokerage relationships allowed by RECAD are transaction facilitator, single agency, and dual agency. Subagency is not allowed under state law.

14.10 (b) Transaction facilitator
Transaction facilitators provide third-party services to customers without being required to sign an agreement. All other brokerage relationships require a written agreement with the client (single agency, dual agency).

14.11 (c) Obtain written consent from both clients to enter into the relationship agreement
When representing both the buyer and the seller in a dual agency relationship, the broker must obtain written informed consent from both parties to enter into the relationship agreement. There is no need for a non-agency disclosure if there is a signed relationship agreement, and neither client is to receive preferential treatment or favoritism of any kind.

14.12 (b) Transaction facilitator
A savvy seller who knows what to do would not likely be interested in paying a licensee to help with duties the seller could handle. A transaction facilitator relationship would allow the seller to pay for help with marketing and forego the rest.

14.13 (a) Single agency
While in some states, this would be dual agency, single agents represent the buyer and the seller in Alabama, even if they work at the same company.

14.14 (c) Assisting with financing
Alabama's mandated minimum level of services includes helping consumers negotiate, presenting and receiving offers, and answering questions. While the licensee may offer to provide financing information, that service is not included in a consumer's rights to specific services.

14.15 (d) the information would help the buyer decide whether or not to purchase the property.
Licensees are required to keep their client's information confidential unless the law requires disclosure, the client authorizes the disclosure in writing, or the information becomes public knowledge. Even though the confidential information may encourage or discourage the buyer from purchasing the property, the licensee may not disclose the information unless one of the above conditions exists.

14.16 (c) misrepresentation.
While misappropriation of funds, practicing law without a license, and failure to provide services are all license violations that can lead to a lawsuit, the most common charge is misrepresentation, presumably

because it is tempting and easy for a licensee to misrepresent the features of a property as a means of persuading a buyer to purchase it, and because it is easy for a buyer to misunderstand what the licensee actually represents.

14.17 (b) negligent misrepresentation.
Negligent misrepresentation occurs when significant property defects are not disclosed out of ignorance, as opposed to fraudulent misrepresentation where the defects are purposefully hidden to make the sale.

14.18 (c) When used residential property is being sold
Alabama allows caveat emptor to be used for the sale of used residential property unless the buyer and seller have a fiduciary relationship, or the seller knows the property may pose a health or safety risk to the buyer, or if the buyer asks directly about specific defects. New buildings being sold by the builder fall under implied warranty of habitability and not caveat emptor.

14.19 (a) Provide the buyer with a completed property disclosure form
The best way to disclose defects and avoid misrepresentation is to have the seller honestly complete a property disclosure form and give it to the buyer prior to closing.

14.20 (d) None of the above
When the seller chooses to have offers transmitted directly to him or herself directly from the selling agent, the seller relieves the listing agent from the related duties, such as providing the estimated closing statement. While the selling agent is required to provide the statement to the buyer, that agent is not required to provide it to the seller because the agent is simply transmitting the offer and not presenting it. The qualifying broker is not responsible either because the seller has relieved all agents of that duty by receiving the offers directly.

STATE TEST 15: Alabama License Law Violations

15.1 (d) does not admit guilt but accepts punishment.
Pleading nolo contendere is not an admission of guilt or an acceptance or denial of responsibility for the crime but it is an agreement to accept punishment.

15.2 (a) probation.
Refusing or neglecting to comply with Alabama license law and the AREC administrative rules is a violation punishable by loss of license, fines, reprimands, required coursework, restitution, or any combination of these. Probation is not one of the potential punishments for such a violation.

15.3 (d) Burglary
Crimes involving moral turpitude involve conduct against community standards of justice, honesty, or good morals and shock public conscience with the level of vileness and depravity. They include such crimes as forgery, robbery, burglary, murder, kidnapping, and aggravated assault.

15.4 (d) Failure to report the legal action to the AREC
If Carla lost the suit for neglect, she most likely did not completely fulfill her obligations to her client. Further, if she's scared about losing her license and doesn't want anyone to know about the suit, she most likely did not notify the AREC about the legal action as she's required to do.

15.5 (d) Yes, John is failing to fulfill his obligations to his client.
As an agent, John's obligations to his client require that he present all offers to the client, regardless of whether John thinks the offer is good or bad. By not presenting the offer, John is failing to fulfill his obligations and, thus, violating license law.

15.6 (d) Dishonest dealings, bad faith, untrustworthiness
Being honest and trustworthy in real estate dealings are required by license law, so Tim has violated the law that requires honest dealings, good faith, and trustworthiness.

15.7 (b) Jessie did not send the notification to the AREC via certified mail.
When a licensee has legal action taken against him or her, the licensee is required to notify the AREC

within 10 days of receiving the notice of action. The notification must be in writing, must include a copy of the summons and complaint, and must be sent to the AREC via certified mail. While hand delivering the notice may have seemed like a good idea, doing so did not meet the requirements of the law.

15.8 (c) She has failed to meet all licensure requirements.
Rather than show ingenuity, Sally has shown dishonesty. While she has violated the license law that prohibits dishonesty in procuring a license, she has also failed to meet all licensure requirements, one of the first of which is honesty and trustworthiness.

15.9 (a) Dishonesty in procuring a license
Yes, Jeremy is not showing good faith and is helping his brother be dishonest. However, the law he is actually violating is one that prohibits fraud, misrepresentation, deceit, or material misstatement of fact to help someone else obtain a license.

15.10 (b) Scott must tell the buyer that the property belongs to his father.
To avoid violating the law prohibiting dishonesty in personal real estate transactions, Scott must disclose his interest in the property by telling the buyer the property belongs to Scott's father.

15.11 (d) Andy can point out that he did not personally know about the defect.
Even though Alabama is a caveat emptor state, license law requires that licensees must disclose any latent structural defects, but the licensee must know about the defect and the defect must be a significant factor in the buyer deciding whether or not to buy the property. If Andy did not know about the defect, he did not violate the law.

15.12 (c) Tony can point out that Alabama is a caveat emptor state and disclosure was not required.
Tony is not guilty of violating the law. Under both caveat emptor and Alabama license law, even though Tony knew about both issues, he is not required to disclose defects that are trivial or insignificant. The wobbly staircase is not a structural defect. The mold has been professionally removed so it no longer poses a health or safety risk to the buyer.

15.13 (b) False promises and honesty and good faith in a transaction
Matt has been blatantly dishonest and is not performing in good faith. He has also made false promises to induce the buyer to sign a purchase agreement.

15.14 (c) Deceitful advertising and Misrepresentation through other agents
Matt's ad is deceitful because it describes the area as safe and the neighborhood as up-and-coming; therefore, it violates the law. Further, having another agent continue the deceit is violation of another law.

15.15 (a) In all advertisements
The Alabama license law that prohibits deceptive advertising also requires that advertisements must identify the advertiser as a licensed real estate broker or salesperson. When a licensee is selling his or her own property, the licensee must disclose in a "timely" manner that he or she is a licensee.

15.16 (d) No, because Pete's listing agreement is a contract with the original qualifying broker, not with Angelo personally
A listing agreement is a contract with the qualifying broker or the real estate firm, not the licensee himself. If Angelo convinces Pete to go with him to the new qualifying broker, Angelo will have convinced Pete to breach a contract and substitute a new one that will benefit Angelo, which is a violation of license law.

15.17 (a) Using fraud to obtain a real estate license
While failing to identify self as a licensee in advertising is a law violation, it doesn't necessarily demonstrate a lack of honesty or good faith. It could be an oversight. Since caveat emptor is recognized in Alabama, following that rule is not dishonest or untrustworthy. However, using fraud to obtain a real estate license demonstrates dishonesty, a lack of good faith, and certainly untrustworthiness.

15.18 (c) Lack of honesty
While there are many ways to violate Alabama license law, the overall attribute to most violations is a lack of honesty, a lack of acting in good faith, and a lack of trustworthiness. Often times failing to disclose is an act of dishonesty, and a failure to fulfill obligations is an act of bad faith.

15.19 (c) Unlicensed person renting homes for compensation
Alabama law requires anyone selling, buying, leasing, renting, exchanging real property, or negotiating to perform any of these acts for compensation to be licensed. If an unlicensed person performs any of these acts for compensation, he or she is violating the law. However, unlicensed individuals are allowed to sell their own home or the home belonging to immediate family members.

15.20 (d) Simply associating with an unlicensed person who performs real estate activities for compensation is not a violation.
Unlicensed individuals performing any real estate acts that require licensure and receiving compensation for those acts are violating license laws. A licensee who employs, helps, or even associates with unlicensed individuals performing acts that require licensure is also violating the law.

15.21 (c) whether the licensee is buying the property indirectly or directly.
Alabama license law requires a licensee to disclose his or her interest in a property being sold and when the licensee intends to purchase a property whether directly or indirectly, regardless of who the seller's agent is.

15.22 (a) Any interested party to the contract
Licensees must disclose the true terms of a contract for a real estate sale to any lender, guaranteeing agency, or any other interested party.

15.23 (d) Misrepresented the facts presented in the transaction documents
A licensee misrepresenting the terms of a sale to any lender, guaranteeing agency, or other interested party is a law violation.

15.24 (c) She acted incompetently and negligently.
Alabama law requires a person applying for licensure to be trustworthy and competent. The law also outlines obligations the licensee has to customers and clients. One of those obligations is to keep confidential information, such as a buyer's willingness to pay a higher price, confidential. Not complying with the laws is a violation, but acting as though the laws are ridiculous demonstrates incompetence and negligence.

15.25 (a) Accepting cash as earnest money
A licensee is allowed to accept cash as earnest money, but the licensee must turn the cash over to the qualifying broker for deposit into a trust account and not a business account. The licensee is not allowed to deposit the cash into the trust account him or herself.

15.26 (c) Depositing client funds and business funds for the same transaction into the same trust account
Commingling occurs when money belonging to others is deposited into the same account as money belonging to the broker or broker company. Funds belonging to multiple transactions or multiple clients can be deposited into the same account, just as the broker may deposit enough of his or her own funds to cover bank charges for the trust account.

15.27 (d) Trust funds must be deposited into a financial institution located in Alabama.
Alabama law requires that funds belonging to others be deposited into a separate federally insured account in a financial institution located in Alabama. Each deposit is to be insured by the FDIC for $250,000.

15.28 (b) Licensees must give copies of all documents to the client.
While the licensee must give copies of every document he or she touches or creates to the qualifying broker to be kept for at least 3 years, the licensee is not required to give copies of all documents to the client.

15.29 (a) No because Dennis and the business are not performing acts that require licensure
Individuals and businesses whose sole purpose is to receive payments in relation to real estate transactions do not need a real estate license unless they are also performing real estate acts for compensation. Dennis and his company are not performing real estate acts.

15.30 (c) No, paying an unlicensed person any compensation for performing acts that require licensure is a law violation.
Judy's sister is unlicensed. Consequently, Judy cannot legally compensate her in any way for performing real estate acts that require licensure, like showing properties or negotiating commissions.

15.31 (c) when it is given.
In Alabama, rebates or incentives must be given before or at closing and must be disclosed to all parties involved in the transaction, including the lender. A rebate or incentive given after the transaction closes violates the law. Therefore, when the rebate or incentive is given and whether it is disclosed determines if it is a violation or not.

15.32 (a) Offering a lottery
Lotteries of any kind are illegal in Alabama, so offering a lottery is not only against license law, it is also against criminal statutes and could result in criminal charges against the licensee offering the lottery.

15.33 (d) Within a reasonable time
The AREC allows a "reasonable time" for licenses to provide requested information.

15.34 (d) Return all licenses tied to previous address to the AREC
When the business address changes, the qualifying broker must notify the AREC in writing, return all licenses tied to the previous address, pay a transfer fee for each license returned, include both the new and old address, and do all of the above within 30 days of address change.

15.35 (a) No brokerage name is included in the ad.
Alabama law requires that the qualifying broker or company name be prominently included in all advertising. This ad does not include the brokerage name and, thus, violates the law.

15.36 (c) After the property owner has given consent
Placing a sign on any property without the owner's consent is a violation of the law.

15.37 (d) The listing is prohibited in Alabama.
Alabama is one of many states that prohibit net listings. The risk of conflict of interest is too high and often results in the licensee failing to put the client's interest above his or her own.

15.38 (b) requires the agreement to be in writing.
To avoid a law violation, all listing agreements must be in writing, must include a set expiration date, must not allow automatic extensions, and must have a copy of the agreement provided to the principal.

SAMPLE TEST: Alabama License Examination Sample Test

S 1. (b) Trade fixtures that are personal property.
Trade fixtures are items of a tenant's personal property that the tenant has temporarily affixed to a landlord's real property in order to conduct business. Trade fixtures may be detached and removed before or upon surrender of the leased premises. Should the tenant fail to remove a trade fixture, it may become the property of the landlord through accession. Thereafter, the fixture is considered real property.

S 2. (c) Severance and affixing.
Severance is the conversion of real property to personal property by detaching it from the real estate; affixing, or attachment, is the act of converting personal property to real property by attaching it to the real estate, such as by assembling a pile of bricks into a barbecue pit, or constructing a boat dock from wood planks.

S 3. (d) absolute fee simple estate.
The fee simple freehold estate is the highest form of ownership interest one can acquire in real estate. It includes the complete bundle of rights, and the tenancy is unlimited, with certain exceptions. The fee simple absolute estate is a perpetual estate that is not conditioned by stipulated or restricted uses.

S 4. (c) the estate may revert to a grantor or heirs if the prescribed use changes.
The defeasible fee estate is perpetual, provided the usage conforms to stated conditions. Essential characteristics are: the property must be used for a certain purpose or under certain conditions; and, if the use changes or if prohibited conditions are present, the estate reverts to the previous grantor of the estate.

S 5. (a) conventional life estate.
A conventional life estate is a freehold estate that is limited in duration to the life of the owner or other named person. Upon the death of the owner or other named individual, the estate passes to the original owner or another named party. A legal life estate is created by law as opposed to a property owner's choice.

S 6. (a) a condominium owner owns a unit of air space whereas the co-op owner owns a proprietary lease.
The owner of a condominium has a fee-simple ownership interest in his/her unit and its air space. Whereas, a co-op owner has a leasehold, not fee-simple, interest with the property's corporation. Since the corporation owns an undivided interest in the cooperative property, debts and financial obligations apply to the property as a whole, not to individual units as in a condominium.

S 7. (d) Trustor, trustee and beneficiary.
In an estate in trust, a fee owner-- the grantor or trustor-- transfers legal title to a fiduciary-- the trustee-- who holds and manages the estate for the benefit of another party, the beneficiary.

S 8. (c) fee simple ownership of the airspace in a unit and an undivided share of the entire property's common areas.
A condominium is a hybrid form of ownership of multi-unit residential or commercial properties. It combines ownership of a fee simple interest in the airspace within a unit with ownership of an undivided share, as a tenant in common, of the entire property's common elements, such as lobbies, swimming pools, and hallways.

S 9. (a) the date of recordation.
Among junior liens, date of recording determines priority. The rule is: the earlier the recording date of the lien, the higher its priority. For example, if a judgment lien is recorded against a property on Friday, and a mortgage lien is recorded on the following Tuesday, the judgment lien has priority and must be satisfied in a foreclosure ahead of the mortgage lien.

S 10. (b) A state in which a mortgagor retains title to the property when a mortgage lien is created.
In lien-theory states, laws give a lender on a mortgaged property equitable title rather than legal title. The mortgagor in a lien theory state retains legal title.

S 11. (b) transfers with the property.
The term appurtenant means "attaching to." An easement appurtenant attaches to the estate and transfers with it unless specifically stated otherwise in the transaction documents.

S 12. (c) Giving constructive notice of one's rights and interests in the property.
Recorded instruments may include deeds, mortgages, liens, easements, sale contracts, and marriage, probate and tax records. The primary purpose of recording and maintaining records of these instruments is to provide constructive notice of the conditions of a property's title-- who owns it, who maintains claims against it.

S 13. (c) A chronology of successive owners of record of a parcel of real estate.
Chain of title refers to the succession of owners of record dating back to the original grant of title from the state to a private party. It is thus more than a mere list; it is a chronological list as reflected in title records.

S 14. (c) Title insurance.
A title insurance policy indemnifies the policy holder against losses arising from defects in the title and is thus generally accepted as the best evidence of marketability after a Torrens certificate, which is not available in every jurisdiction. A signed deed is no evidence of marketability, only of an intent to convey title. An attorney's opinion and a title certificate, while forms of evidence of marketability, do not guarantee clear title or offer any protection against a defective title.

S 15. (c) percentage lease A percentage lease allows the landlord to share in the income generated from the use of the property. A tenant pays percentage rent, or an amount of rent equal to a percentage of the tenant's periodic gross sales.

S 16. (d) net lease.
A net lease requires a tenant to pay for utilities, internal repairs, and a proportionate share of taxes, insurance, and operating expenses in addition to rent.

S 17. (b) The leased property is foreclosed.
A foreclosure extinguishes all prior interests in a property, including a leasehold.

S 18. (c) the construction conforms with applicable building codes.
Building inspectors inspect a new development or improvement for code compliance. If the work complies, the municipality or county issues a certificate of occupancy which officially clears the property for occupation and use.

S 19. (b) takes title subject to the same restriction.
Deed restrictions attach to the title of the property. Therefore, the restriction passes to the new buyer.

S 20. (a) She has the right to re-possess the property because the grantee has violated the condition.
A deed condition may restrict certain uses of a property, much like a deed restriction. However, violation of a deed condition gives the grantor the right to re-take possession of the property and file suit for legal title.

S 21. (a) To create a consistent, unchanging standard for identifying a property's unique location.
A legal description of real property is one which accurately locates and identifies the boundaries of the subject parcel to a degree acceptable by courts of law in the state where the property is located. The general criterion for a legal description is that it alone provides sufficient data for a surveyor to locate the parcel. A legal description identifies the property as unique and distinct from all other properties.

S 22. (b) They identify an enclosed area, beginning and ending at the same point.
The metes and bounds description always identifies an enclosed area by starting at an origination point, called point of beginning, or POB, and returning to the POB at the end of the description.

S 23. (a) is void.
By changing any of the terms of an offer, the offeree creates a counteroffer, and the original offer is void. At this point, the offeree becomes the offeror, and the new offeree gains the right of acceptance. If accepted, the counteroffer becomes a valid contract provided all other requirements are met.

S 24. (a) may be assigned.
A real estate contract that is not a personal contract for services can be assigned to another party unless the terms of the agreement specifically prohibit assignment. Listing agreements, for example, are not assignable, since they are personal service agreements between agent and principal. Sales contracts, however, are assignable, because they involve the purchase of real property rather than a personal service.

S 25. (c) A two-year lease.
A contract may be in writing or it may be an oral, or parol, contract. Certain oral contracts are valid and enforceable, others are not enforceable, even if valid. For example, most states require listing agreements, sales contracts, and leases exceeding one year to be in writing to be enforceable.

S 26. (b) a dual agent.
Dual agency occurs whenever a single broker represents both principal parties to a transaction. Here, since Bob and Sue work for Bill, Bill is the dual agent.

S 27. (a) upon first substantive communication.
The agent must provide written notice to all parties or their agents as soon as substantive communication occurs, which can include initial face-to-face contact.

S 28. (d) neither seller nor buyer.
In recent years, the brokerage industry has striven to clear up the question of who works for whom, and who owes fiduciary duties to whom. One solution allows a broker to represent no one in a transaction. That is, the broker acts as a transaction broker, or facilitator, and has no allegiance to buyer or seller.

S 29. (b) the principal has proposed an illegal act, which should not be obeyed.
An agent must comply with the client's directions and instructions, provided they are legal. If the directive is illegal, the agent must also immediately withdraw.

S 30. (b) negotiated with clients.
The amount of a broker's commission is whatever amount the client and broker have agreed to.

S 31. (b) the client may be liable for a commission and marketing expenses.
With an exclusive right-to-sell listing, if the property sells during the term of the revoked listing, the client is liable for the commission. If the property does not sell, the client is liable for the broker's actual costs.

S 32. (b) the agent has a claim to a commission if the owner sells or leases to a party within a certain time following the listing's expiration.
Many listings include a protection clause stating that, for a certain period after expiration, the owner is liable for the commission if the property sells to a party that the broker procured, unless the seller has since listed the property with another broker.

S 33. (c) the advertising must not be deceptive.
Advertising may not be misleading or deceptive in promoting the brokerage or listed properties. Blind ads are also prohibited without exception. Salespersons, moreover, must identify their employer.

S 34. (a) collusion.
Collusion is the illegal practice of two or more businesses joining forces or making joint decisions which have the effect of putting another business at a competitive disadvantage.

S 35. (b) The brokers have illegally fixed prices.
Price fixing is the practice of two or more brokers agreeing to charge certain commission rates or fees for their services, regardless of market conditions or competitors.

S 36. (a) The seller may cancel the contract, since it can be ruled invalid.
A contingency that is too broad, vague, or excessive in duration may invalidate the entire contract on the grounds of insufficiency of mutual agreement. To avoid problems, the statement of a contingency should be explicit and clear, have an expiration date, and expressly require diligence in the effort to fulfill the requirement.

S 37. (d) claim the deposit as compensated damages for the buyer's failure to perform.
If a buyer fails to perform under the terms of a sale contract, the breach entitles the seller to legal recourse for damages. The usual remedy is forfeiture of the buyer's deposit as liquidated damages, provided the deposit is not grossly in excess of the seller's actual damages.

S 38. (b) The optionor must perform if the optionee takes the option, but the optionee is under no obligation to do so.
An option-to-buy places the optionee under no obligation to purchase the property. However, the seller must perform under the terms of the contract if the buyer exercises the option. An option is thus a unilateral agreement. Exercise of the option creates a bilateral sale contract where both parties are bound to perform.

S 39. (b) a decline in demand for all types of real estate in the real estate market.
Businesses that support the departing company will lay off or fire new employees, causing some to leave town in search of work. Some of these businesses may also have to cease operations. Hence the demand for residential real estate, as well as for commercial and industrial, will decline, and new construction will probably also halt until some other factor increases demand again.

S 40. (b). rental prices in that market will rise
An undersupply of commercial properties in relation to demand will most likely increase prices, as renters have fewer choices and less bargaining power.

S 41. (b) absorption.
Absorption is the amount of available property that becomes occupied over a period of time, usually measured in square feet.

S 42. (b) $17,000.
First derive the annual depreciation, which is the cost divided by the economic life. Then multiply annual depreciation times the number of years to identify total depreciation. Remember to subtract depreciation from the original cost if the question asks for the ending value. Thus, ($20,000 ÷ 20 years x 3 years) = $3,000 total depreciation. The ending value is $20,000 – 3,000, or $17,000.

S 43. (b) Apartment buildings.
The income capitalization approach, or income approach, is used for income properties and sometimes for other properties in a rental market where the appraiser can find rental data. The approach is based on the principle of anticipation: the expected future income stream of a property underlies what an investor will pay for the property.

S 44. (c) estimates net income and applies a capitalization rate to it.
The steps are: estimate potential gross income; estimate effective gross income (potential minus vacancy and credit losses); estimate net operating income (effective minus total operating expenses); select a capitalization rate; and apply the capitalization rate. Use the formula: income ÷ cap rate = value.

S 45. (c) potential gross income minus vacancy and credit loss minus expenses.
Net operating income, or NOI, is always income after vacancy, credit loss and expenses. It does not, however, include debt service.

S 46. (b) $400,000.
Value = Income ÷ Cap rate. Thus, V= $40,000 ÷ .10 = $400,000.

S 47. (a) the interest rate may vary.
Adjustable rate mortgages (ARMs) allow the lender to change the interest rate at specified intervals and by a specified amount. Federal regulations place limits on incremental interest rate increases and on the total amount by which the rate may be increased over the loan term.

S 48. (b) A wraparound lender can profit when the interest rate of the wraparound exceeds that of the underlying mortgage.
In a wraparound loan arrangement, the seller receives a junior mortgage from the buyer, and uses the buyer's payments to make the payments on the original first mortgage. This potentially enables the seller to profit from any difference between a lower interest rate on the senior loan and a higher rate on the wraparound loan.

S 49. (b) a blanket mortgage loan.
A blanket mortgage is secured by more than one property, such as multiple parcels of real estate in a development.

S 50. (b) Payments are not sufficient to retire the loan.
Negative amortization causes the loan balance to increase over the term. This occurs if the borrower's periodic payment is insufficient to cover the interest owed for the period. The lender adds the amount of unpaid interest to the borrower's loan balance.

S 51. (b) the loan amount needs to be less than the property's value.
Lenders must have a margin of borrower equity to protect against falling real estate values which increase the risk of the loan. Without this margin, a lender can incur a loan loss in a foreclosure sale since the proceeds may be less than the loan amount.

S 52. (b) Truth-in-Lending laws
Truth-in-Lending Laws, implemented by the Federal Reserve's Regulation Z, regulate the disclosure of costs, the right to rescind the credit transaction, advertising credit offers, and penalties for non-compliance with the act.

S 53. (d) Participants sell mortgage-backed securities in order to buy pools of loans.
Secondary mortgage market organizations buy pools of mortgages from primary lenders and sell securities backed by these pooled mortgages to investors. By selling securities, the secondary market brings investor money into the mortgage market. By purchasing loans from primary lenders, the secondary market returns

funds to the primary lenders, thereby enabling the primary lender to originate more mortgage loans.

S 54. (a) cost recovery expense.
Cash flow is the difference between the amount of actual cash flowing into the investment as revenue and out of the investment for expenses, debt service, and all other items. Cash flow concerns cash items only, and therefore excludes depreciation (cost recovery), which is not a cash expense.

S 55. (c) dividing net income by the price paid for the property.
The investment return measure known as return on investment (ROI) is calculated by dividing net income by the value of the investment. This yields a rate of return on investment.

S 56. (a) Installing a higher capacity air conditioning and purifying system.
Basis is increased by the cost of capital improvements made to the property. Examples of capital improvements are: putting on an addition, paving a driveway, replacing a roof, adding central air conditioning, and rewiring the home. Repairs, maintenance, and redecorating are not generally considered capital improvements.

S 57. (c) There are no federal ad valorem taxes on real property.
There are no federal taxes on real property. The Constitution of the United States specifically prohibits such taxes. The federal government does, however, tax income derived from real property and gains realized on the sale of real property.

S 58. (b) the assessed value of property.
General property taxes are levied on an ad valorem basis, meaning that they are based on the assessed value of the property. Assessed value is determined according to state law, usually by a county or township assessor or appraiser.

S 59. (d) The prohibition may be legal if performed correctly.
The condominium association may be exempt from fair housing prohibitions against age discrimination if it is established as a retirement community in which 80 % of the dwellings have one person who is 55 years of age or older and it has amenities for elderly residents.

S 60. (c) The agent and the owner.
The owner has illegally discriminated, and the agent, by going along with the owner, is equally guilty of violating fair housing laws.

S 61. (b) Inspection fees.
Prorated items are expenses that both parties must share. Non-prorated items are one-time individual charges such as sale commissions, recording fees, and title insurance.

S 62. (d) A lender paying a fee to a broker for referring a borrower to the lender.
RESPA prohibits the payment of fees as part of a real estate settlement when no services are actually rendered. This prohibition includes referral fees for such services as title searches, title insurance, mortgage loans, appraisals, credit reports, inspections, surveys, and legal services.

S 63. (b) Copies of required communications to principals.
Some communications with transaction parties are good and necessary for business. Others are required by law, and records of them must be maintained for a statutory period. Required records typically include listing agreements, offers, contracts, closing statements, agency agreements, disclosure documents, correspondence and other communication records, notes and any other relevant information.

S 64. (a) refuse to use terms that refer to or describe any of the classes of persons protected by the laws.
Before entering into a listing agreement, a licensee should explain that it is necessary to comply with fair housing laws and obtain the potential client's acknowledgment and agreement. The agent should make it clear that the agent will reject the use of terms indicating race, religion, creed, color, national origin, sex, handicap, age or familial status to describe prospective buyers. Such terms should be avoided in conversation as well as in advertising.

S 65. (a) Alterations to a rental space made to fit a particular tenant
Alterations made specifically for certain tenants are called build-outs or tenant improvements. The work may involve merely painting and re-carpeting a rental space, or erecting new walls and installing special electrical or other systems.

S 66. (c) maintain a special trust account in a qualified financial depository.
State laws and real estate commission rules specify how a property manager is to manage trust funds. In general, the agent is to maintain a separate bank account for these funds, with special accounting, in a qualified depository institution. The rules for how long an agent may hold trust funds before depositing them, and how the funds are to be disbursed, are spelled out. The fundamental requirements are that the owners of all funds must be identified, and there must be no commingling or conversion of client funds and agent funds.

S 67. (c) 3
The total area of the living room is (8' x 14' + 8' x 18' + 8' x 16' + 8' x 18') = 528 SF. They will therefore need 528 / 200 SF, or 3 whole gallons.

S 68. (d) 218'
Since the investor paid $1,000,000 total, and that equals $2,500 per frontage foot, there are 400 frontage feet (1,000,000 / 2,500). If the property is two acres, it totals 87,120 SF. Dividing this by 400 produces a lot depth of 217.8

S 69. (c) Yes with $360 left over.
The loan she can get amounts to ($240,000 x 80%), or $192,000. The points charge is ($192,000 x .02), or $3,840. Total closing costs are then $3,840 + 800, or $4640. Thus she has $360 to spare.

S 70. (c) $90,000
First, the sale price is 115% of the appraised value, so the appraised value is $230,000 / 115%, or $200,000. The lender will lend $140,000 (70% of appraised value), so the investor will have to come up with $90,000 ($230,000 – 140,000).

S 71. (c) $384,000.
Since the comparable has an extra half-bath, it is adjusted downward to equalize with the subject. Conversely, since it has no patio, the appraiser adds value to the comparable. Thus, $400,000 minus $20,000 plus $4,000 equals $384,000.

S 72. (c) $508
The total assessed value is ($84,550 + 235,000), or $319,550. The annual tax is based on ($319,550 / 100) = 3195.5 100's. Round up to 3196. To derive the annual tax, multiply 3,196 x 1.91, or $6,104.36. Divide this by 12 for the monthly escrow: ($6,104 / 12) = $508.

S 73. (d) $184,000
The formula for equity is (current value – indebtedness). The current value is ($360,000 + 25% x 360,000), or ($360,000 x 125%), or $450,000. The current debt is ($360,000 x 80%) - $22,000, or $266,000. Their equity is therefore $184,000 ($450,000 - $266,000).

S 74. (b) $166,150
Use the formula: Gain = (Net selling price – adjusted basis) where adjusted basis = (beginning cost – depreciation). The selling price is $240,000 x 5% annual appreciation x 10 years, or ($240,000 + 50% x 240,000), or $360,000. Since land cannot be depreciated, the depreciable basis is ($240,000 total cost – 60,000 land value), or $180,000 (land = 25% total value). Annual depreciation = ($180,000 / 39 years), or $4,615. Thus total depreciation is ($4,615 x 10 years), or $46,150. The adjusted basis is therefore ($240,000 – 46,150), or $193,850. The total gain is therefore ($360,000 – 193,850), or $166,150.

S 75. (c) $80,000
Applying the formula (percent of insurable property value carried / 80% replacement cost) x claim = recovery), divide the amount of coverage carried ($160,000) by 80% of the insurable property value ($250,000) to get the percent of the claim the company will pay (80%). Multiply this percentage by the claim amount to get $80,000, what the company will pay.

S 76. (c) Real property owner
The 1 consumer member of the AREC must be at least 21 years old with no felony convictions, must have been an Alabama resident and citizen for 10 years, and must be a real property owner.

S 77. (b) lapsed
A lapsed license is no longer valid and may not be renewed. If the individual wishes to practice real estate, he or she must again meet all of the licensure requirements of a first-time applicant.

S 78. (a) was based on an error of the law.
A rehearing will only be held if the final decision was based on an error of the law, was in violation of AREC rules, was in excess of the AREC's statutory authority, was made upon an unlawful procedure, was a constitutional or statutory violation, or was clearly wrong based on the evidence.

S 79. (c) there is a balance due on the judgment.
The claimant must show he or she is not the spouse, child, or parent of the licensee, that a judgment has been obtained, that there is a balance due on the judgment, and that any amount already recovered from the licensee has been applied to the damages awarded by the court.

S 80. (d) Criminal history checks must be current to the date of license issuance.
A felony conviction may, but not always, result in a rejection of the licensure application. All applicants must have both a state and national criminal history check with the applicant paying the cost of the history check. Criminal history checks must be current to the date of license issuance.

S 81. (b) Birth certificate
Documents used as proof of permanent residency in the United States include driver's licenses, non-driver identification, green cards, and US visas. Birth certificates are not used for this purpose.

S 82. (c) pass the state exam within 6 months of completing the pre-license course.
To obtain a temporary license, the applicant must complete the pre-license course within 1 year of the start date and pass the state exam within 6 months of completing the course. The applicant must also find an Alabama supervising qualifying broker within 90 days of passing the exam. The original license is obtained after obtaining the temporary license.

S 83. (d) 15 hours of coursework every 2 years.
Continuing education requirements include completing 15 hours of coursework by September 30 of the final year of the 2-year license period, 3 hours of Risk Management courses, and 12 hours of AREC-approved electives.

S 84. (d) pass the state exam within 12 months of completing the coursework.
Applicants for a reciprocal license must provide a certificate of licensure issued within 120 days of the Alabama application from the state where the applicant is licensed, must complete 6 hours of coursework in Alabama, and must pass the state exam within 12 months of completing the coursework. The other state license can be active or inactive.

S 85. (a) Transferring licensee pays the transfer fee.
The licensee is to pay a transfer fee; the new qualifying broker files a request for transfer with the AREC; the licensee mails his or her license by certified or registered mail to the AREC; and the AREC then issues a new license certificate for the remainder of the current license term.

S 86. (a) At midnight on September 30 of the final year of the license period
Just as salesperson and broker licenses, company licenses expire at midnight on September 30 of the final year of the license period which is every even numbered year.

S 87. (c) all business performed by the qualifying broker is from the same location.
Qualifying brokers may serve multiple companies if all companies agree in writing, not written rejection is necessary. The written consent is to be filed with the AREC, but the AREC does not reject the consent. All business must be performed from the same location.

S 88. (b) The qualifying broker can disburse the funds based on a court order.
If the parties disagree over disbursement of the trust funds, the qualifying broker can disburse the funds

only with a court order or written agreement of all the parties. The qualifying broker can deposit the funds with the court under the rules of interpleader to force the disagreeing parties to litigate and have the court decide how the funds will be disbursed.

S 89. (d) The law does not designate a restitution limit.
Mishandling trust funds can result in license suspension or revocation, fines of $100 to $5,000, a combination of both, a licensee reprimand, required continuing education, and/or restitution to be paid. However, the law does not mandate a minimum or maximum restitution amount.

S 90 (c) To allow both the seller and buyer to be informed and prepared for closing payments
The purpose of an estimated closing statement is to show approximate transaction costs so each party can be informed and prepared for closing.

S 91. (a) Lenders are to disclose loan closing costs to borrowers.
Per RESPA, buyers must be informed about closing costs with no inflation of closing costs for the buyer. Lenders must disclose loan closing costs to the borrower and must not demand excessive deposits for escrow accounts. Also both the seller and the buyer are to be provided with estimated closing statements at the time an offer is submitted and presented so there are no surprises at closing.

S 92. (d) Fiduciary duties
Fiduciary duties are owed to the client by the agency agreement and are performed under obligation and trust.

S 93. (d) The lack of a signed agency agreement
Non-agency relationships exist when there is no agency agreement signed.

S 94. (b) Transaction brokerage and limited consensual dual agency
Both transaction facilitator and dual agency allow the broker to work with more than one party to the same transaction. However, in a transaction facilitator, the broker is not an agent representing either party.

S 95. (b) Transaction facilitator
Because there are no fiduciary services in a transaction facilitation, there is reduced liability for the licensee.

S 96. (d) A seller making false statements about a property that affect the buyer's decision to buy
Misrepresentation is when one party makes false statements about a property that affect the other party's decision to enter into a contract. Acts of omission or failure to disclose are also misrepresentation.

S 97. (d) All services are required
Both the AREC and Alabama license law mandate delivery and presentation of all offers, assistance with negotiations, and answering all questions a client may have related to the transaction.

S 98. (b) Not fulfilling obligations to transaction parties
One of the required services that licensees are obligated to provide for their clients is to answer all questions related to the transaction. By not making himself available to answer his client's questions, Jeff is violating his obligations to his client.

S 99. (a) Donna has not identified herself as a licensee.
In addition to violating fair housing laws by noting there should be no children, Donna has not identified herself as a real estate licensee.

S 100. (d) Julie is being dishonest with the client
Julie is being dishonest by telling the client there is no problem in changing agents when the client already has a contract with Randy. This is a violation of Alabama License Law.

Appendix: Performance Programs Company's Test-Taking Tips

Introduction

Effective test-taking is more of an art and a practiced skill than a guarantee of success. Students preparing for the state license exam should take exam preparation very seriously. Since there are no guarantees to passing, it behooves students to optimize their chances of a successful outcome. Simply put, this is accomplished by purposeful, intensive study and question-taking practice. The harder you study and prepare, the better your odds become of passing.

There are a few beneficial pointers that can be made to improve your overall test-preparation effort. These are contained in the following compilation of tips assimilated by professional educators and test-prep experts. Please take the time to peruse these observations as they will serve to better your overall chances of passing. And in any case, we wish you the best of success!!

Make and use flashcards

Understanding tested real estate terminology is a large part of passing your exam. As you prepare for the license examination, study. Don't just memorize specific definitions. Memorize contexts of content as well. Understand, for example, that a question about a deed is a question about <u>conveying property</u> in some way, shape or form; a question about eminent domain falls into the "terminology environment" of <u>rights in property</u>. A question about the cost approach relates to the challenges of <u>identifying value</u>. The more you know about "the environment" of each word, in addition to the term's specific definition, the more likely you will be able to use that information to lead you to the correct exam response.

Take notes

As you read and study, take notes. Often, just the act of writing information down helps cement it in your mind. Visualizing how your notes about a particular topic appeared on the page is helpful for students who appreciate visual cues.

Immerse yourself

Form or join a study group, review topics with friends and colleagues, chat with real estate experts, and read real estate blogs. In other words, immerse yourself in the world of real estate. To obtain a deeper understanding of a term or concept, Google it (using whatever search engine you employ with your computer or phone). This will shed light on varying perspectives or iterations of a term's meaning.

Prepare a "date and key quantity" sheet

As a memory device, students are well-advised to create a "date and key quantity sheet" to be able to efficiently refer back to in future study sessions. This particular summary sheet includes facts and data that are very commonly tested, including deadlines, dates, and quantities.

Some examples:

- 1978 – cutoff date for lead paint disclosure
- Base times height divided by two: area of a triangle
- CE requirement in hours
- Deadline (in a given state) for conveying a trust deposit to the broker
- Protected classes (in a given state)
- # acres in a section
- LTV calculation
- loan payment given a rate and loan amount
- criteria for a valid contract
- criteria for distinguishing real vs. personal property
- Recovery Fund – maximum fine per licensee per incident
- adverse possession prescription period (in your state)

Plan study time

Set a goal for yourself. Avoid the trap of just "studying until you're ready." Instead, determine the date you want to apply to take your exam and set aside enough time to finish your test preparations by that date. Try to limit how long each of your study / cram sessions will be. Study periods should not be too much in excess of one hour – after which time students begin to lose concentration and attention span.

Finally, select your study environment so as to avoid distractions and interruptions!

Reading is not studying

It may seem odd, but *reading* is not *studying*. Studying is an active process. Creating and reviewing your flashcards is studying. Develop study guides. Teach someone about difficult or complex topics. Relate what you are learning to your own experiences or the real estate topics you hear about in conversations or on the news. Create your own memory devices such as mnemonics, rhyming, acronyms, or images. These can be invaluable ways to remember cut and dry facts and figures.

Dissect exam questions

Take and review as many practice exams as you can find. Take and re-take quizzes in your textbook and any exam prep resource that you can find. Write down the topics you tend to miss questions on, then re-study those topics. When reviewing a missed question, be sure to understand the correct response and why the incorrect answers were not right.

Review the exam provider's handbook

A wealth of knowledge exists in the exam provider's test preparation resources. Review these materials thoroughly! You will learn the general topic areas covered and the relative weighting of a given subject. For example, appraisal methods will be tested more vigorously than an intricate metes and bounds description.

Exam prep materials generally present the key content of a topic and how many questions will appear on your exam, particularly if the resource is state-specific. The testing service candidate

handbook will further describe how your exam is scored. This knowledge will help you to understand how to answer questions you may not be sure about. In other words, you should know whether or not you are penalized for wrong answers.

It's almost time! Your exam is tomorrow. What do you do?

Candidate handbooks will provide full instructions about the exam day itself—what you can and can't take with you, how long you have to complete the exam, and how long you have to wait before you get your results, and so forth.

Immediately prior to the exam, you should limit how much to cram. At some point, nothing new should be introduced into your mind. In short, you either know it or you don't. Make a quick final pass-through, then leave it alone.

Okay, it's exam time. How do I avoid being a nervous wreck?

To alleviate stress, you can do a couple of things:

- Drive by the testing center so you know where it is and how long it will take to get there. On test day, allow extra time for traffic snarls, etc.
- Be sure you have an acceptable calculator (information will appear in the exam provider's handbook). Note that some providers don't allow you to bring a calculator in. Instead, you'll use one they provide or one embedded on the computer you'll use to take the exam.
- Assemble everything you need to take with you. Include test registration documents, required identification, a calculator, and a sweater or light jacket. Put everything in a bag or your car.
- Eat a well-rounded meal the evening before your exam and get a good night's sleep.
- Most exam providers give you a few minutes before you begin the exam to acquaint yourself with how the system works. You can answer a few practice questions, use the calculator, etc. Use this time not only to familiarize yourself with the environment but also to take a few deep breaths and get comfortable. You can do this!
- Budget your time. Know how many questions you must answer (more information from the provider's handbook).
- <u>Read every question carefully</u>. Be sure you understand what it's asking, in particular if the question is in the negative ("which of the following is NOT....," or "which of the following is NOT TRUE....". Then read EVERY possible response before you respond. Exam providers generally want you to select the BEST answer, not the only possible answer.

Answering questions

In most circumstances, you should answer every question. You will certainly receive a score deduction if you don't answer a question, but if you guess, you could guess right. So you come out ahead by answering every question.

This issue raises the question: "how much time should I spend on a question?" This becomes easy math. Know how much time you have for a given section and how many questions you must answer in that section. Then divide the number of questions into your time allocation to get your per-question time allowance. Do not stray too much from that estimate as you complete the section!

If you aren't sure of the answer to a question, keep these tips in mind:

- Are there responses that you know are incorrect? Eliminate them. If you eliminate two responses, you've increased your odds of correctly answering the question to 50/50!
- Dissect the remaining possible responses. Are there key words that indicate a correct or incorrect answer?
    - Terms like "always," "never," and "only" MAY indicate an incorrect response because seldom are things as definitive as these terms suggest.
    - Terms such as "usually," "generally," "typically," "most," and "some" are more likely to appear in the correct response.
- If you see a response that includes something you've never heard of, don't choose it! If you didn't see that information in your preparations, it's unlikely to be the correct response.
- Be particularly cautious about organization names. "The Department of Housing and Urban Development" sounds suspiciously like "The Division of Housing and Development."

After the exam

Depending on the exam provider and state, you may know right away if you passed. You may also receive a report from the testing center that details topic area scores.

If you're not successful on your first attempt, don't panic...and understand that you're not alone. Real exams can be notoriously difficult. As soon as you leave the testing center, write some notes to yourself about questions you recall struggling with or topics that you may need to review.

Then, dig in again. Use the textbook, your notes, and the information you remember from the exam and keep studying. Your career is far more important than not passing the test!

Appendix: Useful Websites

Alabama Real Estate Candidate Handbook

This contains crucial information regarding the Pearson Vue Alabama Real Estate Exam. Make sure to download and read this participant booklet to fully understand the entire test taking process.
https://home.pearsonvue.com/getattachment/e7c202f3-fcaa-4fe5-96cd-9d44d45bd8b4/Alabama%20Real%20Estate%20Candidate%20Handbook.aspx

Alabama Real Estate Commission
1201 Carmichael Way
Montgomery, AL 36106
334-242-5544
https://arec.alabama.gov/arec/

Pearson Vue Testing Service
5601 Green Valley Drive
Bloomington, MN 55437
952-681-3000
https://home.pearsonvue.com/Home.aspx

Alabama Association of Realtors
522 Washington Avenue
Montgomery, AL 36104
334-262-3808
http://www.alabamarealtors.com/

Birmingham Association of Realtors
3501 Independence Dr
Birmingham, AL 35209
205-871-1911
http://www.birminghamrealtors.com/

If you liked Alabama Real Estate License Exam Prep, check out the other titles of Performance Programs Company!

Cramming for your real estate exam? You need Alabama Real Estate License Exam Prep!

Where can you buy Alabama Real Estate License Exam Prep?
Alabama Real Estate License Exam Prep (AL-RELEP) is available as a printed book or e-book through nearly all online retailers.

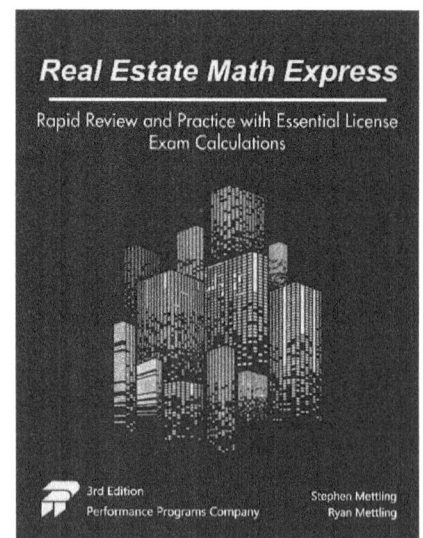

Looking for a real estate principles textbook? Get what all the students love -- Principles of Real Estate Practice in Alabama!

Principles of Real Estate Practice in Alabama is invaluable reference material for Alabama real estate professionals. Its 600-pages contain the essentials of real estate law, principles, and practices taught in real estate schools and colleges across Alabama.

Where can you buy Principles of Real Estate Practice in Alabama?
Principles Real Estate Practice in Alabama is available as a printed book or e-book through nearly all online retailers.

Struggling with real estate math? The solution to that equation is Real Estate Math Express!

Real Estate Math Express is a concise, easy-to-study test preparation guide to help real estate students improve their real estate math scores to pass the state licensing test. The primary feature of Real Estate Math Express is that it contains all necessary formulas and practice questions in 100+ pages.

Where can you buy Real Estate Math Express?
Real Estate Math Express is available as a printed book or e-book through nearly all online retailers.

Publisher Contact
Ryan Mettling
Performance Programs Company
6810 190th Street East, Bradenton, FL 34211
ryan@performanceprogramscompany.com
www.performanceprogramscompany.com

298

www.ingramcontent.com/pod-product-compliance
Lightning Source LLC
Chambersburg PA
CBHW080516220326
41599CB00032B/6105